"There is meaning in eve
— Dietrich Bonhoeffer

MW01493668

I was the kind of person t.
fear of what someone might think. That is a paralyzing thought. If
you are paralyzed from the "what are people going to think"
dilemma I hope this book will encourage you.

If you are a person who thinks that you have nothing to say, or that
you aren't as smart, or you don't have anything to offer, I hope my
book encourages you to go ahead and think out loud, tell your story,
because you do have something to offer.

If you are a person that has always wanted to put your thoughts in
writing but thought you didn't have the time, you didn't have the
know- how, I hope this book encourages you to just plain go for it.

My desire is that this book will encourage you to dream, to have
vision, and have the courage to put your eyes straight ahead and As
you go, live life to the fullest.

"The greatest of all mistakes is to do nothing because you think you
can only do a little."
- Zig Ziglar

"As I go" is about just that, as I am living my life, As I go, as I learn,
grow, fall, fail, move along, stand still, collapse, dream, learn, screw
up, run, skip, blow it, make a fool of myself, trust in God, not trust in
God, believe, doubt, jump for joy, you know, living life and as I go
there is much to think about, write about, blog about and of course to
share.

As I go is about living my life in ministry, as a devoted follower of
Christ, as a husband, as a father, as a coach of ministry people, you
know as we go there is much to observe, much to gain, and much to
give.

So this little book can be read to spur you on daily, to inspire you to
remember that as you go, you are where you are no doubt, but with
meaning. As I go, hopefully is something you are doing with all of
you heart, all of your passions, all of you.

As I go is dedicated to all the students and parents that I have been
blessed to serve. As I go is dedicated to all those that mentored me
throughout my life. As I go is dedicated to all of those that didn't try
to fix me, but gladly loved me.

A little Background Music

I grew up in the western suburbs of Chicago. I grew up in a "Christian" home and was raised in a Baptist church. It was during my younger years that I was taught much about God, the Bible and all the "do's" and "don'ts" of the day. Although I didn't understand everything, I knew that I wanted to have a relationship with God.

Oh, I heard about the "free" gift of "grace" and all, but I still felt like I had to win God's approval, and I knew that I fell very short. So I kept doing all the "right" things, but never really felt or understood the connection. After going to a large high school in Chicago, and attending a great student ministry where Dann Spader showed us the way in reaching students, I went to Moody Bible Institute like all of us in the youth group did. Once again I was into the practice of the "externals" but I didn't know about the internal things. There I failed, and I began to realize that the issues of my heart were not being dealt with.

I went on to work for several years as a union electrician. It was during this time that I began to really understand how "off the mark" how lonely and empty I was inside. I began to desire a relationship with God again, but didn't really know what that meant. I just knew that I was very empty, and with a deep despair. A friend of mine asked me to come and visit him so I hopped on my motorcycle for a visit. After a week with my friend and his family, I began to seek after God. I knew that it was to time to at least pray to Him. On the ride back from my friends, a cable broke on my bike. When I pulled over to fix it, I just knelt down to pray and asked God to forgive me for all the junk I had done, and still wanted to do. I told God that If "Jesus was real, and if He was who he said He was, then I would believe in Him." At least I would believe that He would have to change me from the inside. I believe that is the day I came to know Christ in a very personal way.

I began to see Him do new things inside, which changed the way I lived. Several months later as I was searching for the "what" to do with this new relationship with Christ. Another friend and mentor, asked me to come to Colorado and he would disciple me. I packed up a duffle bag, hopped on my motorcycle and headed to Colorado from my home in Chicago. I haven't been home since, except to visit.

There, God began to move me toward ministry. I entered Colorado Christian College, and began a life of ministry. Since then, I have always had a heart for reaching people with the truth of the Gospel. I believe in and practice being intentional, and being relational in the sharing of the Gospel, knowing that the Gospel is for all to hear and for all to believe.

Today, over twenty years since the move to Colorado, marrying Marcie, having two awesome boys, serving in three churches as youth pastor, one as the senior pastor, I am more passionate about reaching people, more passionate about equipping the local church for ministry living, and more desirous of what and how God will use me and my family for and in His Kingdom. My time as a senior pastor has helped in a significant way to see the local church as the vehicle, the tool in which God is using to reach a lost culture. My faith in this time has had its bruising and enriching. I believe that after these past 20 years of ministry the best is yet to come. My desire is to make the next 25-35 years of serving and ministering even more significant! 2 Timothy 1.12b/ Psalm 40.

I have dedicated my adult life to serving and ministering to others within local churches, the business world, schools, youth camps, colleges, civic organizations and many other venues. I fill pulpits and podiums throughout the Midwest as a guest speaker. I have been a student ministries pastor and a senior pastor. I have led bible studies and classes for youth and people of all ages. God has given me the gift and desire to reach and serve others by living as an authentic follower of Christ.

A great read- Bonhoeffer by Eric Metaxas

"I discovered later, and I'm still discovering right up to this moment, that it is only by living completely in this world that one learns to have faith. By this-worldliness I mean living unreservedly in life's duties, problems, successes and failures. In so doing we throw ourselves completely into the arms of God, taking seriously, not our own sufferings, but those of God in the world. That, I think, is faith."
~Bonhoeffer

I read the book <u>Bonhoeffer: Pastor, Martyr, Prophet, Spy</u> by Eric Metaxas. I finished a few months ago and continue to review parts of it in my heart and mind—all the while with a gratefulness that I have not experienced in some time. I find myself going back to the book on occasion for a little encouragement as well as conviction for some of the values that seem to be missing today.

Is it because I'm tired of the "new" kind of book out there about others journey's that continue to complain about the local church and how it failed them? Is it because I myself needed an inspiring book of faith, life and devotion to the Lord? Is it because for me I have often felt this past year that in truth—I often feel overwhelmed or doubtful or lacking faith or just plain tired and yet still in love with the Lord?

Maybe the truth is that I continue to struggle against "new" yet very old kind of church stuff—and as a pastor that I have deep concerns for that issue. Maybe because I'm tired of watching students self-destruct and blame others for their destruction? Maybe I'm tired of listening to people who "love" the Lord but are going absolutely crazy in the way they treat and talk about others? Maybe, just maybe, I know in my heart that all of the above isn't right and it bothers me—and sometimes I don't want it to—I want to have thick skin and the ability to blow them off--- but maybe God won't let me? I don't know—

Why hassle with that junk? Why worry about that stuff? That is for another day—although it almost seems that every day I deal with somebody who continues to live out the "old stuff" in front of me— the gossip, the distrust, the talking behind backs, the complaining, the blah blah blah.

The real issue of the quote above is so simple and yet so deep. Bonhoeffer is dealing with the fact that he is involved in something that ultimately would cost him his life. He could have avoided the whole ordeal. After all, he went to the U.S.A. at the height of the Hitler killing days.

But Bonhoeffer unlike many today who avoid the world—moreover hate the world and the unlovable people in it—no, Bonhoeffer believed and so do I that *"by living completely in this world that one learns to have faith. By this-worldliness I mean living unreservedly in life's duties, problems, successes and failures. In so doing we throw ourselves completely into the arms of God, taking seriously, not our own sufferings, but those of God in the world. That, I think, is faith."*

Yes—the Bible speaks of worldliness as a "bad" thing. (to some) So we build "youth groups" and go inward as churches in order to avoid the world, when in truth, we are prayed for by our Lord that we would live in the world but not be of the world. The issue is to live in the world period. Being of the world, well I was. But that was when I didn't give a rip about Christ—and I knew it. The flip side? Living in a worldly way, and acting as if one is not. Denying it, playing the games, being like the world in relationships, attitudes, and all the stuff that living worldly entails. All the while, call the world sick and nasty and living once a week in the closed setting. Then going out the rest of the week with disdain toward the world yet living just like it.

Bonhoeffer is saying—live by faith in the world because that is all you got. Faith. Faith in Christ for forgiveness, for life, for joy for everything. Bonhoeffer is saying, and I agree, live in the world and throw yourself into the arms of God, because you only have one life to live. So live it as you suffer, as you take seriously the work that God wants to do through me and you.

Yes—we are called to live lives of faith in a world that doesn't need Christians living behind walls, with little or nothing to trust Him for—but actually trusting Him for everything as we live in this world.

God help me to live daily in this world

And to live by faith
To love
To do the right things as I do the duties you have asked me to do.

Life

The Thinker.

I love that statue.
I love what he represents.
Contemplation.
A solitary man deep in thought.
Thinking!

Do you ever find yourself thinking about life? Thinking about deep things? Thinking about things that bring meaning to your life? Thinking about things that are great, positive, good, creative, just plain ole thinking about the goings on of your life?

The reason my last two blogs have been about characters of the Scriptures, Daniel and Jeremiah is because I have found myself thinking about matters that have to do with being a man: being a follower of Christ, being a leader, being a Biblical Christian, being a pastor and looking for the answers in the lives and through the lives of men of the Scriptures.

I personally have battled in my mind, thinking about such things as:
What is important?
What are the high values in my life?
What do I care most about?
What do I see as issues in student's lives that I can help?
What is going on in this world that I can participate in and make a difference?
How can I live out the life of Christ?
How can I communicate the truth better?
How can I make a difference in this world?

With all that running through my mind-- there is more, much more. But here is the great thing about all this thinking... God is working in me as I actually think, write, contemplate, consider, pray, and wait. Although I must confess that there are a few things that I have had to stop thinking about. For I realize the answer will not be found.

The answer is actually found in the hearts of people-- it really isn't about me. I know when I'm not doing well, when I'm being unkind, being "not" like Christ-- that my behavior is directly related to "the where" I am spiritually. It's a heart issue. Oh sure, I may be tired, I may be run down, not feelin well, but I know full well that my behavior is not right, period. So I know the truth about me, therefore I can surmise with some certainty how people even think or act towards other people is formed in their heart. I can't control them. I can only control MY thoughts when I am not thinking right. I know when my heart isn't right. I know how easy it is for me to get off track. I have found this simple truth: to keep a short account with the Lord. To confess my sin quickly and move on to new and better things.

"For although they knew God, they neither glorified Him as God nor gave thanks to Him, but their *thinking* became futile and their foolish hearts were darkened." Romans 1.21

You see,
"Jesus knew what they were *thinking* and asked, "Why are you *thinking* these things in your hearts?" Luke 5.22

Jesus knew this important truth. Of course He did, He is God...Nevertheless, the thoughts of man are things of man's hearts. It's true isn't it? That our hearts determine our thoughts. When our hearts are right, our thoughts track with right things. So, thinking is huge. Thinking matters.

I am encouraged in my life by how I have been thinking-- how bout you? Oh, I've had a rough couple of days thinking about some things that were bothering me. I have thought some tough things about being a youth pastor, some tough things about what others may or not be thinking about me. So, I thought about it, vented a little bit, and gave my heart to the Lord for some renewal.

Thinking is good. Thinking points to the heart. Thinking points out the deep things of our inner most place, our mind which is connected to our heart!

"Brothers and sisters, stop *thinking* like children. In regard to evil be infants, but in your *thinking* be adults." 1 Cor. 14.20

Yes, I love the statue of the Thinker! Thinking Matters! Thinking is a great discipline. Thinking points out some very deep things that are part of the HEART!   Looking forward to some time off... Thinking on the Beach, soaking up the sun!

"Work ethic, first; structure, second; and skill, third"

I watched an incredible comeback in a hockey game between the Sharks and the Red Wings. The Red Wings, down 2 goals, come back to beat the Sharks 4 to 3. While I watched this comeback, I was pulling for the Sharks. I marveled at how hard the Wings worked and worked and worked. Then after the win, a Red Wing was asked how they did it. The answer from a player was a direct quote from their coach..."work ethic, first; structure second, and skill, third." Exactly, right?

Yes. It's true. Work hard, always work harder than your opponent. Don't rely on skill first, rely on a work ethic-- go to work and outwork your opponent. Then work hard on the system, that is, the structure, that is in place to help the team outwork the opponent... and finally let your skill work for you.

Isn't that the way it really is? Now I have worked with students and my own children for over 20 years-- and in my humble opinion-- too many are relying on skill before hard work and without a system (structure) in place what so ever... and this is a huge problem. If a student could or would understand and begin to practice hard work at whatever it is they want to accomplish-- grades, job, relationships, whatever-- they would find that working hard brings much in the end.

The above can be said about student ministry also. You see, as the youth pastor, youth workers work hard at ministry, it's not just working hard at working hard. It's working hard with the system in which he/she created in place, right? Without a system, youth ministry can be hard work spinning plates, or just continuing to just keep doing the same stuff without substance or direction.

Putting skill before everything tends to end up causing youth workers, or youth pastors winging everything and ultimately the end is near. Just trusting in skill for the youth pastor/youth worker can cause one to believe that "they can do anything, or who needs planning, or a system, I can get by on my skill and that is dangerous.

It is the same for students today. I wonder if is there is a system or structure in place in a student's own life to develop character, integrity, goals, virtue the things that a student can work, a personal system if you will. I believe the student today may not know the what to or how to work hard at a structure of study habits, character development, choices that are for the future. I see many students today just getting through a day by doing at best the minimal, just coasting through, and really anything that comes along can take them in any direction. I see some just relying on God given gifts to just get bye-- no need to work hard, just do the easy way with the skills that a student knows they possess and that is all.

The question-- how do I help? How do I try and help this generation to see... some of the structure that has been dissed, put down, trampled on is actually not garbage. That caring for people, that caring for the future, that being honest, that having character is actually a great structure and that working hard and whatever they do-- bushing a broom, working on a paper, cleaning windows, doing homework...doing "it" with a hard work ethic has huge value.

My generation had other fathers stepping in, coaches, teachers, youth pastors, pastors, adult friends of family, or uncles that felt they had a say in a student's life. Plus, we as students, at least I did, knew that these other people in my life had something to offer. That they genuinely cared for me, that they really did have my best interest in mind as they taught me about things of character, integrity, work habits, even how to swing a bat or shoot a puck.

I really do see with my own eyes every day how many students today are trusting in just their smile to get through life. The sad part is that our whole world is struggling. The job market is at an all time low, the economy is up for grabs, so how will this nextgen move forward through life?

"work ethic, first; structure, second; and skill, third"

This generation must learn to work hard, develop a solid structure, (habits, the ability to say no to nonsense, distractions) a sound structure where a person can excel, and then hone and develop their God given skills. I really do think the big ticket for students today is the lack of "structure" in their lives. If, if this nextgen will look into their lack of structure and begin working at developing good habits, taking the time for quietness, turn off the text messages and learn to focus, they can and will be on their way to finding success toward their future. And if adults around them will let go of the notion that their structure is outdated, or too old or narrow, or that they don't have much to offer; and will take the time to reach out even if there is push back, maybe some students will begin to form a structure by which they can accomplish much, by working hard at foundational things that are no longer missing and then develop the skills that they have been given.

Luke 6.46-49
46 "Why do you call me, 'Lord, Lord,' and do not do what I say? 47 As for everyone who comes to me and hears my words and puts them into practice, I will show you what they are like. 48 They are like a man building a house, who dug down deep and laid the foundation on rock. When a flood came, the torrent struck that house but could not shake it, because it was well built. 49 But the one who hears my words and does not put them into practice is like a man who built a house on the ground without a foundation. The moment the torrent struck that house, it collapsed and its destruction was complete."

Significant?

You are significant period.

Do you believe you are significant?
Do you believe that you, your life is significant in this world?
Do you believe that your life is significant to God?

OR

Do you feel like the words from Bob Seger's song-- "Feel like a Number"?

"I take my card and I stand in line
To make a buck I work overtime
Dear Sir letters keep coming in the mail
I work my back till it's racked with pain
The boss can't even recall my name
I show up late and I'm docked
It never fails
I feel like just another
Spoke in a great big wheel
Like a tiny blade of grass
In a great big field
To workers I'm just another drone
To Ma Bell I'm just another phone
I'm just another statistic on a sheet
To teachers I'm just another child
To IRS I'm just another file
I'm just another consensus on the street

I feel like a number"

In order to be significant—
Must you behave a certain way?
Must you talk a certain way?
Live a certain way?
Have all the cool stuff?
Be together 24/7?
Be perfect?

Or are you significant period! ?

The adjective significant means:
Having or expressing a meaning; meaningful, important.
Meaningful, important. Is that you?

[12]"What do you think? If a man owns a hundred sheep, and one of them wanders away, will he not leave the ninety-nine on the hills and go to look for the one that wandered off? [13]And if he finds it, I tell you the truth, he is happier about that one sheep than about the ninety-nine that did not wander off. [14]In the same way your Father in heaven is not willing that any of these little ones should be lost.

And the Point Jesus was making?

You are significant to God!

Question?
Why does God love you?
Anything you did?
Anything you didn't do?

Anything at all?
Hmmmmmmmm

[4]But because of his great love for us, God, who is rich in mercy, [5]made us alive with Christ even when we were dead in transgressions—it is by grace you have been saved. [6]And God raised us up with Christ and seated us with him in the heavenly realms in Christ Jesus, [7]in order that in the coming ages he might show the incomparable riches of his grace, expressed in his kindness to us in Christ Jesus. [8]For it is by grace you have been saved, through faith—and this not from yourselves, it is the gift of God— [9]not by works, so that no one can boast.

God made a choice to love us!

Not because we are so good
Not because we have it all
Not because we did something to deserve it
Not because of anything— Except

We are created in His image
God has a plan for our lives
God knows everything about us
And He still made a choice to Love us

and that makes us significant!

Fair?

Fair. What is fair?

I didn't grow up with the idea that fair means that everything is equal.

I didn't grow up with the idea that fair means that everybody gets rewarded equally.

I didn't grow up playing baseball or football or hockey without a scoreboard.

I was taught that fair means that you do things without cheating. That winning was not the objective—but playing with all I had, giving 100% and a win was not guaranteed. At best, that win or lose, my team could compete because we gave our best.

I started working when I was in 7th grade doing a daily paper route. I worked the paper route till I went to high school. I played in band, I swam, I did a little homework, but I was active and responsible. I was taught that I was the one responsible to get it done or not get it done.

I worked in a grocery store from the time I was 16 through my first 2 years of college. Same store, with promotions from bagging to night crew. Nobody did it for me. I was in 2 unions over my lifetime, I worked for money, saved my money and blew my money.

There have always been people that have made more than me. There have always been people driving better cars, getting bigger paychecks, doing "better" than I. Was that fair? Really?

I can't believe that right now in this crazy world we live in that there is this idea that fair means everybody gets what everybody else gets. Or that because others are well off—they should be penalized for their hard work to even the playing field.

Oh—I have a heart. I was out of work. I had to go and find jobs. I worked crazy jobs. I worked crazy hours. But never, ever did I feel or think that everybody should be on the same page.

Why?

Simple, I don't believe for one second: That God has the view of fairness like we do.

First of all—God didn't have to do anything period.

People have rebelled. Including me

People choose to sin. Including me

Jesus came to earth, died on a cross. That is not fair.

Jesus rose from the dead. By faith people can choose to allow Him to forgive them and change their brokenness.

Not all people will respond. Is that fair?

Is it fair that people will suffer?

Is it fair that life is tough?

Is it fair that not everything turns out like we want it?

If fair is the ultimate life goal it will not happen.

Unless—unless people decide that they should determine that everyone should be on the same page. If that is the case—is that a God thing?

There is much conversation out there right now about this idea called fair. It started years ago with jealousy, class warfare, people demanding to be treated fairly.

I have some real concerns for the generations to come—

King David spent 10 years running, hiding in caves as the king.

Joseph spent years in captivity due to his brothers' jealousy.

Fair?

Romans Chapter 9 speaks from God's view about fair.

10 Not only that, but Rebekah's children were conceived at the same time by our father Isaac. 11 Yet, before the twins were born or had done anything good or bad—in order that God's purpose in election might stand: 12 not by works but by him who calls—she was told, "The older will serve the younger." 13 Just as it is written: "Jacob I loved, but Esau I hated."

14 What then shall we say? Is God unjust? Not at all! 15 For he says to Moses,

"I will have mercy on whom I have mercy,
and I will have compassion on whom I have compassion."

16 It does not, therefore, depend on human desire or effort, but on God's mercy. 17 For Scripture says to Pharaoh: "I raised you up for this very purpose, that I might display my power in you and that my name might be proclaimed in all the earth." 18 Therefore God has mercy on whom he wants to have mercy, and he hardens whom he wants to harden.

God can do many things—those things are not always fair (according to our humanness)

The fact that the Gentiles (including me) were given the opportunity to become children of God through His adoption is not fair to those that are already by faith, God's children. Thankfully "they" don't have a say.

So what about it? What matters?

What really matters? How important is your Faith?
(Notes from last talk at Dayton Christian High School)

Couple of questions?

1. If there was no age limit on being able to drink—would you?
2. If pot were legal would you smoke it?
3. If you got your girlfriend pregnant would you consider an abortion? After all, it is legal?
4. Is losing your virginity the worst thing you could do?
5. Is "Christianity" about rules or faith? Both?
6. On a scale of 1-10 how important to you is your faith?
7. On a scale of 1-10 rules? How important?
8. Do you care about a relationship with the living God?

What really matters?

Romans 14.22 Blessed is the man who does not condemn himself by what he approves, but the man who has doubts is condemned if he eats because his is eating is not from faith; and everything that does not come from faith is sin."

How important is your faith? Remember the question? How important is your FAITH? You see you are being duped to believe that faith is not important—it's no big deal. It is the most important thing. To most people the question of legal or illegal trumps faith. Christianity is not so much cognitive as it is unseen- belief, faith.
**If you care about anything today, care about your faith, or your lack thereof.
At some point you gotta move away from what others tell you is right and wrong— what is legal and illegal, what is a rule at your home or school and what is important,. Boundaries, how sin affects you , your tainted heart-- and desire a relationship with God that goes beyond all the stuff that will fail.

That moves into the realm of daily living by faith. No? What happens when you leave home? No more mommy and daddy to tell you what to do. What happens when you leave and go to study for your dreams of making money, having top of the line cars, houses –

living in a dorm and you are 21? What happens when no one is looking anyhow? Isn't that who you are really?

How bout it? Really—does smoking a joint really change life? (I have seen years of use destroy people). .Does it really get you through the hard things of life? Does having sex make you a man? Does getting drunk make you someone special, normal, or just another person that got drunk?

See here is the crux of this issue called spiritual—
Accept the one whose faith is weak, without quarreling over disputable matters. **2** One person's faith allows them to eat anything, but another, whose faith is weak, eats only vegetables. **3** The one who eats everything must not treat with contempt the one who does not, and the one who does not eat everything must not judge the one who does, for God has accepted them. **4** Who are you to judge someone else's servant? To their own master, servants stand or fall. And they will stand, for the Lord is able to make them stand. One person considers one day more sacred than another; another considers every day alike. Each of them should be fully convinced in their own mind.
Romans 14.1-5
There is a problem of disputable matters- meaning there really are things in the realm of the Christian faith that are disputable

Let me make sure we have an understanding

1. I am a 50 + year old man.
2. I am going on my 20th year of sobriety.
3. I have been married for over 25 years.
4. I am a full blown sinner.
5. I believe in Christ Jesus as the only savior.
6. I have been justified by faith.
7. I don't follow your rules and I'm not obligated, period.
8. I don't follow my parents rules—my dad is dead and my mom is 93 years old.

Make sure you understand today that I don't follow the Levitical law, I never did, I never will.

I follow rules at my job, I follow rules every day when I drive. I get up every day and go to work. I read my Bible because I enjoy it and sometimes I miss my time alone with God. I love God because He first loved me. I have found Him to be my everything in this sick, fallen, broken world.

I don't believe everything I hear. I don't put my faith in humans. I don't like socialism. I don't believe in bailing everyone out. I do believe in helping, being kind, doing right to people. I don't appreciate fake people, I don't enjoy being around people that expect me to live differently then they selves live. I don't appreciate Christians who speak poorly of the local church, and badly about those who lead the church.

I am in process like everyone else. I will die someday and enjoy heaven. Not because I ever earned it, or because I'm a good person. Not because I had it all together, or because I did this or didn't do this. But because by faith I believe in Christ Jesus as my Savior period.

I can't add to that or take away from that, period. Quite frankly, if you have been a believer of Christ for over a few years you should be getting this stuff by now, really.
The bottom line is that none of the above is that important or that spiritual for that matter. (my lil opinions and attitudes and feelings and the rules I keep aren't that big of a deal nor are yours.)

Well here is spiritual—

Romans 14.17 For the kingdom of God is not a matter of eating and drinking, but of righteousness, peace and joy in the Holy Spirit, Context—Verse 12, 13,14 Therefore let us stop passing judgment on one another. Instead, make up your mind not to put any stumbling block or obstacle in the way of a brother or sister. I am convinced, being fully persuaded in the Lord Jesus, that nothing is unclean in itself. But if anyone regards something as unclean, then for that person it is unclean.
Verse 14 is key!

Finally— So, whatever you believe about these things keep between yourself and God. Blessed is the one who does not condemn himself by what he approves. But whoever has doubts is condemned if they eat, because their eating is not from faith; and everything that does not come from faith is sin. Romans 14.22,23

Spiritual matters? Your faith matters the most period.
Hebrew 11.6

Not of faith is Sin—
Get it straight—
the issues
Of what is legal and what is not?
The issue of this or that?
Disputable matters?
Is the above really that important? Not according to the Scriptures (which by the way everyone loves to claim as their basis for what they do or don't do.) Really?

- Your faith matters

- You are going to face huge difficulties in this life

Where will your faith lead you?
Think about it? Why is the "Testing of our faith" so important?

Consider it pure joy, my brothers and sisters, whenever you face trials of many kinds, because you know that the testing of your faith produces perseverance. Let perseverance finish its work so that you may be mature and complete, not lacking anything. |
James 1.2-4

Faith matters!

The "Gimme's"

The Gimme's = Entitlement

Entitlement. What does that mean?

World English Dictionary; Verb
1. to give a (person) the right to do or have something
2. to give a name or a title to
3. to confer a rank or title or honor upon

What is it that which you or I am entitled?
Well, for starters, we are entitled to live.
We are entitled to our own little opinion.
We are entitled to work and to work hard, or be lazy.

I am entitled to do as I wish. Right?

I can love.

I can give.

I can do anything. Really?

I can sit at home and blame people for my failures.

I can... I can... I can...

I can stake my claim on something that I didn't earn or deserve.
I can sin, and sin big if I want to-- and the consequences I can pass on to others.
I can also claim that I should get what everyone has-- I want it, therefore I should have the right to get it, have it, own it....take it and call it mine. I'm entitled period.

Is all of the above true? I know, there was a time that I did live like the above. The idea that I am <u>entitled </u>to everything and anything in my estimation is not only hurting students, but allowing them to go down a path that is hurting not only their future, but their generation.

This idea that I should get what everybody else has... is now upon all of us. In student ministry this ideal, this thought, this way of life is rampant. I have a sense that there are many, youth pastors/youth workers and some parents (not all) facing the epidemic of selfishness called entitlement. If so, now what? Is there a way to deal with this word, this issue, this problem?

I think there is. I think that we, those of us that are in leadership must speak the truth about entitlement. We must talk about this truth, that following Christ, being part of His life, that entitlement as a follower of Christ is not a part of what is called following period.

First: A follower of Christ is in for a very tough life indeed. The life of Paul and Peter and the rest of the 1rst century, if not the past 2000 year followers proves the point. Jesus warns His disciple of their journey—persecution, difficulties, and suffering most likely will be part of what it means to follow the Christ.

Second: At best a follower of Christ gives up the idea that their life is their own period. Right?
I know, it is a process, it is a pursuit. Following Christ means that one is to take on His life, His heart, His view, His sacrifice, His love, His compassion, His everything. Jesus showed He was not into entitlement, the Kenosis passage (Phil.2) proves the point.

Third: Entitlement is a lifestyle that demands that a person should get whatever they want and that kind of lifestyle is in complete opposition of what it means to follow Christ. Do you know any students who demand life to be what they want it to be? Warn them, be honest with them. Point them back to the One to whom they gave over their heart and life. I know many youth pastors today who are working hard at showing students the other side, those in poverty, those in need. I am not sure that just showing them, or taking them out of their easy life is the only way. For when they get back, it seems they go right back to demanding, and living their life the way they want to live it.

We do need to get back to some basic Biblical truth, Biblical teaching.
Grace is given—it is not an entitlement.
Love is a gift—it is a choice of someone else towards another—love
is not a freebie.
I stand by this-- "People owe you nothing, they give because they
want to give." ~Rocky (Rocky 1)
Salvation is not an entitlement—it is a gift from God.

I dare say—that until we, the Youth Pastors, the youth workers,
parents, leaders, speak up about what "following" really means,
many, many followers of Christ, let alone the lost world will continue
to cry and demand what they think is theirs. When in truth— even
the gift of eternal life is not an entitlement—it is a gift.

I see daily what is happening in the lives of students who believe that
they are entitled to everything. Their hearts are cold toward the
good gifts of God as they continue to cry, whine, and pout for what
they demand from others.

Take some time this summer to work on ways to help those with
"ears to hear" the opportunity to wrestle, to grapple with moving
forward as they desire to follow Christ. You will be helping the Next
Generation move past the notion that they are entitled. We youth
people- youth pastors, parents, leaders, must take responsibility and
help others in student ministry to get past the notion that we can't
help this problem. We can.

If we as leaders believe that we are leading the Next Generation
toward furthering God's movement through the local church, in the
culture, in the world, we must make this matter a top priority. The
world economy is a disaster, the job situation is at an all time low,
the cost of living is increasing, and our world is in serious trouble.
The time has come when we as leaders, youth pastors/youth
workers, parents, must stand together to help students become
followers of Christ who get past the unhealthy entitlement life style.

if it can happen to me... possibilities abound for you

The Scripture emphasizes that much can come from little if the little is truly consecrated to God. There are no little people and no big people in the true spiritual sense, but only consecrated and unconsecrated people. The problem for each of us is applying this truth to ourselves." (Francis A. Schaeffer, No Little People, Ch. 1)

This little quote has meant so much to me over the years. Actually the whole book <u>No Little People</u> has been a mainstay for me. Why? Because of who I am. I know who I am without Christ. I know who I am with Christ—and that has made all the difference.

But the quote begs this question- what does it mean to be consecrated?

Consecrated: "to devote or dedicate to some purpose: a life consecrated to..."

Am I consecrated? Am I dedicated? To what or to whom am I dedicated? I am dedicated to my wife, I am dedicated to my kids, I am dedicated to ministry. But that dedication started with my dedication to my God period.

When did that happen? It happened when I made a choice to trust the Lord with my life without any expectation that my life would be anything but His. Really? Yes, it is true. I know that when I gave my life to the Lord, I just wanted to be His and His alone. I didn't have money in mind. I didn't have fame in mind. I didn't have a future of all "great stuff' happening. I was just committed to pursuing Him with my all.

What has happened over these years is very simple in my mind. He took my commitment, my dedicated, consecrated heart and used me in the lives of other people. But that hasn't come without a price. He has worked on me, chastened me, broken me, led me, hurt me, molded me and it hasn't stopped. For that I am grateful. I am so glad I am not my own but His alone. My heart, my life is full because of Him—and even if heaven were not promised, I would without a shadow of doubt give Him my life over and over. I love this old hymn, I find it to be more and more a reality--

"I am His and He is Mine" Words by George W. Robinson, 1876.

Music: Everlasting Love, James Mountain 1876. Mountain wrote the tune for these lyrics so the hymn could be included in the first edition of his <u>Hymns of Consecration and Faith</u>

Loved with everlasting love, led by grace that love to know;
Gracious Spirit from above, Thou hast taught me it is so!
O this full and perfect peace! O this transport all divine!
In a love which cannot cease, I am His, and He is mine.
In a love which cannot cease, I am His, and He is mine.

Heav'n above is softer blue, Earth around is sweeter green!
Something lives in every hue Christless eyes have never seen;
Birds with gladder songs o'erflow, flowers with deeper beauties shine,
Since I know, as now I know, I am His, and He is mine.
Since I know, as now I know, I am His, and He is mine.

Things that once were wild alarms cannot now disturb my rest;
Closed in everlasting arms, pillowed on the loving breast.
O to lie forever here, doubt and care and self resign,
While He whispers in my ear, I am His, and He is mine.
While He whispers in my ear, I am His, and He is mine.

His forever, only His; Who the Lord and me shall part?
Ah, with what a rest of bliss Christ can fill the loving heart!
Heav'n and earth may fade and flee, firstborn light in gloom decline;
But while God and I shall be, I am His, and He is mine.
But while God and I shall be, I am His, and He is mine.

I have found that being consecrated is by faith. Faith placed in the true and Living God. Oh, I know who I am...I am His and He is mine. Remember where this little blog today started? *"There are no little people and no big people in the true spiritual sense, but only consecrated and unconsecrated people. The problem for each of us is applying this truth to ourselves."* Yes God has done amazing things in my life. Yes, God has done more than I could have ever imagined. If God could take me, how much can He do in your life as you dedicate your life to Him?

Thank you God,for touching me. Thank you Lord for calling me to You. Thank you Lord, for your Son who freely gave His life for me. I know how much you love me, and I know how much I love You back. Sometimes I don't do it right, sometimes I fail, sometimes I desperately seek other stuff for significance, but over these years You and You alone have remained consecrated to me. I love you Lord, the rest of my life is Yours.

Vanity

"Whatcha got ain't nothin new. This country's hard on people, you can't stop what's coming, it ain't all waiting on you. That's vanity." ~No Country for Old Men

The quote above is from the movie "No country for old men" as a father and a son talk about life as police officers, the changing world in which they worked and lived. It was the father, an old timer who had lived life as a police officer, listening to his son talking about the hardships of being an officer when the old timer says "Whatcha got ain't nothin new. This country's hard on people, you can't stop what's coming, it ain't all waiting on you. That's vanity."

This little quote has stuck with me for the past few days. Maybe, because over the course of my life I have often thought that what I wanted, what I needed, what I demanded, was that life be all about me. That I should be able to stop what's coming, that it is all waiting on me.

I remember struggling through some hard changes, some new endeavors, the angst I felt, the anger I had when things didn't turn out my way. When God didn't do life my way, when my wife didn't do what I expected, when my sons didn't live like I expected, when my boss didn't respect my wishes, when peers didn't act the way I thought they should, when life wasn't what I expected it to be...that is vanity.

"It's not all about you" is used quite often these days when dealing with students, friends and loved ones. Because it's true. Life is not all about me. Life is not all about my views. Life is not all about having it my way. Life is not about being right, being #1, being the center of attention, being in the limelight, being the big deal.

I know it's tough to get this just as a person, let alone as a pastor or even more as a follower of Christ. Life really isn't about me. I'm not the center of the universe, and life certainly doesn't revolve around me. That is vanity.

Moreover, when dealing with students, when dealing with people on a daily basis this little quote rings true for many who are demanding, angry and critical of everyone and everything. There is a sense that everything should be their way, that everyone should stop, fall in line and do life like they demand it, and when we don't there will be a price to pay.

Life isn't all about me or you. Life is tough. It is no wonder that Jesus says in Matt. 10.39 "Whoever finds their life will lose it, and whoever loses their life for my sake will find it." Isn't it true that as we lose our little life desires, wants and expectations and follow after the Christ-- all that stuff we so demand and expect goes away.

Oh it may be painful, it may cut at the core of our vain view of self. But that is where we find the peace so many are searching for, not in ourselves or in our desires, but in following the Christ-- his servant attitude, His humility, His kindness, His love for people, His emptying, His care, His total obedience.

Yes, the movie "No country for old men" is not for everyone, but this little quote "This country's hard on people, you can't stop what's coming, it ain't all waiting on you. That's vanity." rings true for everyone.

It's not about me or you-- "That's vanity"

The Myth of Perfect

Perfect: entirely without any flaws, defects, or shortcomings

I have not found the perfect job. I have not found the perfect church. I have not found the perfect place. I have not found the perfect friend. I have not found the perfect steak (yet). I have not found the perfect person. I have not found the perfect country (haven't been to all). I have not found the perfect state (although Hawaii is close). I have not found a perfect anything. I have an imperfect marriage. I have an imperfect cat. I have an imperfect house. I live in an imperfect country with imperfect people running it. Imperfection is all around.

I quit the perfect hunt long ago. Well, sometimes I do catch myself struggling with myself and others on this whole subject. Sometimes I let it get the best of me, which points me right back to this truth:

I am a sinful, broken person. I have done really sinful things. I have thought sinful things, I have said sinful things, and I am sinful, and it's nobody's fault but mine period. I grew up in an imperfect home with imperfect parents. I went to an imperfect church, and I received an imperfect education. I have had imperfect jobs all my life. I have had imperfect friends, I have an imperfect wife, I have imperfect sons, oh my there is imperfection all around. Did I say I was imperfect? Yes, I am imperfect, my exterior all the way to my core. Imperfect.

I know imperfect people. I work with imperfect people. I serve imperfect people and I am imperfect perfectly. I am imperfect. Got it? Good. You are also imperfect. You don't have it all together. You fail as much as I do. Maybe you haven't failed at the things I have failed at. My failures are huge. I have imperfect people remind of that all the time. We all are imperfect. Right?

Quite frankly, I get worn out from the want for perfection. There is nothing perfect in this lost and broken world. Isn't it time to give it up already?

I lead the NextGen ministry. Do I want a perfect ministry? Do I want perfect students? Do I want perfect parents? Do I want a perfect staff? Do I want a perfect church? Do I want perfect? No! I don't want to make student perfect? Really? Like I can do that? Do I want a perfect event? Do I want anything perfect? No!

Perfection is a myth, a lie, a fable. There is nothing perfect. Perfection is not now, it will not be as long as you, me, and everyone else is still walking around in these fallen broken, dying bodies. Forget about it. It is never going to happen period.

There was a day when people, my parents and others did try and make me perfect. There was a day when I tried to make myself perfect. There was a day when I tried to make others perfect. Those days are gone. So what is NextGen ministry? Why do I do ministry? Good question. It's not to make students, or parents perfect. It's not to make anyone perfect. It's to lead students to the One who can change their broken heart. It's to lead students to the One who can forgive their imperfections. It is to lead students to the One who can change their inner angst, who can deal with their hurts, who can actually make their sinful broken, nasty, sin filled lives new. I do this to then help students grow in their relationship to the One-- you know Jesus, who is perfect. Who is the only One who will not fail. Jesus is perfection in every sense. Jesus is the only one who was and is the perfect slain Lamb so that we can believe in Him and thus be changed.

Perfection? It's a myth. We that by faith have the Christ to forgive us, to enter into a relationship with Him, are given the Holy Spirit that leads us, guides us, teaches us. He takes us through a lifetime of breaking us, molding us, bringing us through a journey called life At the end, when we meet the One who is perfection, we will wear His perfect robe of righteousness that we didn't earn, we didn't deserve, that we couldn't play or pay for. It is only through this life of imperfection that we finally will be perfected when we meet Him because we trusted in Him for our soul, our life, our heart.

Last little ditty-. Isn't it true that those who continue to look, hope for, seek after, pursue with all they have for perfection are some of the most brutal people to deal with? I wonder why? When people cry out for GRACE, but never give any it's no wonder they are miserable. Here is a bold faced truth. Grace is always around the corner if someone will just admit their shortcomings, their sin and their need for forgiveness. The problem is people want GRACE without any sort of confession, admission of wrong or a sense of brokenness. Although GRACE is waiting, GRACE seems so far away. Besides, should a perfectionist expect grace? They feel deep inside they are responsible to fix themselves and do it just right (and they can, right?) Of the giving grace the perfectionist cannot of course, "people don't deserve it" because in truth they feel and think they don't deserve it or maybe they really don't want it... That would be an admission of the truth, that they are not perfect and actually can't fix you, or me or themselves.

On being perfect--it will never happen here to me, to you, to anything or anyone until one admits they are not, that they need to be forgiven, healed and trust in the only One perfect-- the Son of God, Jesus Christ. That is the Truth!

"If we claim to be without sin, we deceive ourselves and the truth is not in us. [9] If we confess our sins, he is faithful and just and will forgive us our sins and purify us from all unrighteousness. [10] If we claim we have not sinned, we make him out to be a liar and his word is not in us. ~1 John 1.8,9,10

"God with us"?

"The virgin will conceive and give birth to a son, and they will call him Emmanuel which means "God with us" Matt.1.23

"God with us" How cool is that? Is God with us really? After all, the economy is whacked, students are struggling, families are hurting, the world is a mess, the world seems so distressed. So, where is God? If God is with us why doesn't it seem that way? If God is with us, why all the angst? If God is with us, why all the poor, the homeless, the pain? If God is with us, then where is the peace? Where is the joy? Where is the love? Is God really with us?

Here is my little take-- Emmanuel has come. Emmanuel "God with us" came in the form of man, a baby. God came to earth so that all mankind could have their totally depraved hearts redeemed. If life is hard, if life doesn't fit our dreams does that mean "God is not with us"? If life is a piece of cake, if life is easy, if all is well then what-- "God is with us"?

I have often reminded myself that following the Christ was not about a bed of roses. Believing in "God with us" was not about having my dreams fulfilled. Asking for forgiveness of my sin was not so that I could be a successful person. No, I believe in "God with us" because He is God period. Oh, I have had my struggles, I sin every day, I fail many times over but I know personally "God with us" and that changes everything.

It is true that the world is not getting better. Things are different. Life is tough. Work is work, money is money, things are still things and I can sometimes find myself like many others blaming "God with us" for all that is wrong. Herein lies the truth. Because I asked and ask "God with us" to forgive me, to reign in my life, to change me from within, things have changed. I'm not motivated by stuff, by accolades, by money, or anything else. I still have many things to overcome no doubt, but "God is with me" by faith. And because "God is with me" by faith it is He that is doing a work and He came to do that in all of humanity-- that is to redeem mankind to himself. To take care of all of man's sin.

"God with us" is a reality not because life is so good, or all the bills are paid, or everyone is happy, or because I have a job or because of circumstances. No "God with us" is a reality because by faith I believe that "God with us" is the actual God coming to earth as a baby and dying on a cross so that I can be totally forgiven. I can trust Him every day, I can actually have peace because He is God, I can have joy because I don't need all the stuff. I enjoy life because "God is with me."

How different would this world look if people would actually believe that "God with us" is true? That the results of His 33 years living on this earth, that the result of His death on a cross, that the result of His rising from the dead is to bring all mankind peace, joy, and forgiveness from a broken and sinful heart.

Giving good gifts

A new born King to see
Our finest gifts we bring
To lay before the King

I learned about gift giving from generous people. People who gave gifts to say "I appreciate you." "I love you." "This is a gift from my heart." "You are significant to me." "This gift is out of the generosity of my heart." "Here is a gift, just because."

I learned about generosity from people who had huge hearts. They weren't people with huge pockets per se, they were hard working people that loved to give gifts. My parents were not wealthy. I saw firsthand how my parents gave to others, and I saw much from my father who loved to give gifts to his family and to his friends.

I find it interesting that the people in my life who taught me much about giving were not people who pontificated about generosity. They didn't brag about their generosity. They didn't draw lines about generosity. Their generosity spoke for itself. They were people who gave because they loved to give period. They didn't envy people with more, they enjoyed seeing others enjoy their gift. They didn't give gifts to earn approval or buy friendship. They gave gifts because they wanted to give. I learned about giving from people who didn't have it all, but loved to give it away.

Isn't it interesting that there are some who give gifts "if they feel a person deserves it." You know, kinda like Santa, naughty or nice makes for the gift you receive. I actually know people who won't give to a loved one or someone that they would say is a close friend because they just don't feel they deserve it this year.

I learned gift giving from people who actually understood this:

That nothing we have from the Heavenly Father is earned period. He is the giver of good gifts because He loves His creation, His humanity, His likeness. God is the giver of good gifts and I don't deserve it. He is the giver of His Son even though the greatest gift of all of history would be rejected. I learned giving/generosity from people that understood this truth, that giving is a reflection of God period.

Isn't giving a gift not so much about the gift, but the sentiment behind the gift? Isn't the reason for giving a gift to say "you matter" " I appreciate you" or just plain ole "I'm glad you are my friend?" Is one more generous because of to whom they give? Is one more "spiritual" because they now only give to a "select" group that deserves it?

I am grateful for those who have chosen over the years to say by their gift to me that I mattered, I am loved, I am important. I know that I didn't deserve it, I didn't earn it, I didn't attain it. They just gave a gift. Too bad for those who actually will spend nothing on anyone because they would rather hold onto their "stuff". They speak about giving to those who deserve it more, while actually counting their money. So sad for those who know the Christ, the freely given gift, and have never connected the dots.

I learned about gift giving from humble, loving, generous people that more than likely never considered what they couldn't get because of what they would give. Yes, I learned about gift giving from very generous people over the years and in truth, they may not have had everything, had lots of cash, had lots of things, but they sure did enjoy giving it away.

Generosity, giving good gifts is a reflection of the One who gave the greatest gift to all mankind!

On Keeping it Simple

We shall never know all the good that a simple smile can do. ~ Mother Teresa

"If one's life is simple, contentment has to come. Simplicity is extremely important for happiness. Having few desires, feeling satisfied with what you have, is very vital: satisfaction with just enough food, clothing, and shelter to protect yourself from the elements. And finally, there is an intense delight in abandoning faulty states of mind and in cultivating helpful ones in meditation." Dalia Lama

Life is really simple, but we insist on making it complicated. ~Confucius
How many things are there which I do not want. ~Socrates

"While the impostor draws his identity from past achievements and the adulation of others, the true self claims identity in its belovedness. We encounter God in the ordinariness of life: not in the search for spiritual highs and extraordinary, mystical experiences but in our simple presence in life." ~Brennan Manning

"Truth is ever to be found in the simplicity, and not in the multiplicity and confusion of things." ~Isaac Newton

"There is no greatness where there is not simplicity, goodness, and truth" ~Tolstoy

"Simplicity is the ultimate sophistication." ~Apple Corp

It is an honor to be with all tonight. To the graduates, congratulations, you made it through-- To all the mothers and fathers and families represented... the future looks brighter... bless you all...

and so goes this little ditty called:

On keeping it Simple:

To the class of 2012 there is no doubt that there have been many times over the past 4 years that you have asked yourself—

Why am I doing this?
Or maybe, what is the point of this assignment?
Or why did I put so much time into this or that—
Why so much angst over this person or that person

Or maybe, at the end of a few days over these past 4 years you just plain asked—Really?
Your generation is known for being the generation right smack in the middle of "the social media" frenzy—

Ipad
Iphone
Smartphones
Facebook
Twitter

No one in the history of mankind has ever been so close to someone else miles and miles away.
We get to know every minute what someone is doing
We get to post every event, every moment if we so choose.
And we have the privilege of viewing every moment of someone's mood, attitude, happenstance, new shirt, new relationship and on and on...

Have you happened upon facebook and thought to yourself or maybe even said out loud—"you really posted that?" I didn't need to know that—

But tonight, this moment in time, this time together is a spiritual moment—the baccalaureate "a farewell address in the form of a sermon delivered to a graduating class"

and so in honor to you—I'm going to keep this little sermon simple—

There are many causes
There are many needs in this world
There are many many hurting people

There are many things broken,
There are many questions before each of you that may remain

Unanswered

I want to remind you all, that all that is wrong, all that is hard, all that is needing attention by every graduating class over the ages still needs just that – attention… is still broken, is still in need of repair, is still in need of this class to stand up and go beyond running so fast just to be:

noticed
appreciated
to one day retire
To one day be "all that"
To one day be "fulfilled"

To one day be—what ever

In keeping it simple
I asked myself in thinking of this moment, thinking of you all,

Thinking about
My 20 years + working with students—
Thinking about, remembering the hundreds of students that I have seen over the years that have passed through the halls of church, school—in and out of my life, what possibly could I offer you?

You see, I have seen your bright eyes for the future—every year

Not much has changed—
You all have great ambition
You all have much to accomplish
You all have much to enjoy
you all will face incredible days ahead
Some will be filled with much satisfaction

Many days will be the fulfillment of your greatest expectations
And some days ahead you will face

Consternation
Sorrow
Difficulties
Trials
Tribulations

Consider the next 60-80 years of your life—

Keep it simple—
Really?

Please consider this
From a man who was once your age
From a man who has had many ups and many downs
From a man who has had to dream many new dreams
As I watched some of my dreams dashed on the rocks

Of life—
From a man who lived in complications brought on by my own doing

From a man who did not heed the words of those who cared enough
to warn me – to keep it simple

From a man who has been on the journey of life
From a man who has learned that the journey of life is made simple

By a life of simple faith
From a man who is still learning to keep it simple—

I go back to the age old question—

On keeping it simple
What matters? What matters the most? What is the most important
thing?

To all of you tonight-- whatever faith you may be of
The question—is still -- how to keep it simple?
I go back to the Scriptures for a brief moment tonight-

The place where I find solace, instruction, truth—
I share this with you so that you may see the value in Faith

The simplicity of faith
The question posed to Jesus 2000 years ago according to the
Scriptures—

A group of people like you and me asked—

Teacher they said,
What is the greatest commandment in the Law?

In other words
Teacher—can you make this faith thing simple for us?

Teacher, can you hone down all the stuff and get real?

Teacher, can you tell us the most important thing?

And His response--

'Love the Lord your God with all your heart and with all your soul
and with all your mind.' This is the first and greatest
commandment. And the second is like it: 'Love your neighbor as
yourself.'

You see students,
On keeping it simple—
On living this life with simplicity
Love God with all you have—your heart, soul and mind
And if you want to make a difference in this world

If you want to do something huge
If you aspire to make a difference
if you desire to go beyond
Collecting a degree
Collecting a paycheck

Just "being"

Then...
Love people—love your neighbor as yourself
On keeping it simple students

If you remember anything

Love God

Love People

May God enrich your life as you seek to love God with all your heart, soul and mind

And as you love your neighbor as yourself.

Why?

"The most important lesson that we're supposed to be learning right now is how completely lost we are without God. If we don't learn this lesson, then our lives are going to have zero meaning."
~Brian "Head" Welch

"I'm real excited. I'm so blessed to have so much peace and joy inside. I just can't keep quiet about it."
~Brian "Head" Welch

In a press release on their Web site, Korn announced they "parted ways with [Welch], who has chosen the Lord Jesus Christ as his savior, and will be dedicating his musical pursuits to that end." It stunned the music world, leaving many scratching their heads and some dedicated fans saying, "It must be some practical joke."

It wasn't. The following Sunday, Welch spoke at a church in Bakersfield, California, to a cheering audience of 10,000. In his first public address, he said, "I'm the happiest man in the world right now."

Welch testified about how his life was on the brink of destruction when a friend gave him a Bible. "It's not about religion," he said, according to MTV News. "It's not about this church; it's not about me.

It's about the Book of Life, and everybody needs to be taught this. It's crazy. It's gonna do stuff like this -- like change a guy in a rock band."

A week later, Welch left skeptics with little doubt when he flew to Israel to be baptized in the Jordan River.

If this hasn't shocked you yet, then you probably don't know what kind of music Korn makes. Since 1994, Korn has been a driving force in the rap-metal genre as they fused hip-hop beats with heavy guitar riffs. Their lyrics, mostly based off of the traumatic childhood experiences of frontman Jonathon Davis, are dark, sexually explicit, and disturbing. Condemned by the *Chicago Tribune* as being "perverts, psychopaths, and paranoiacs", Korn was a staple on MTV in the late 90s for teens who didn't like pop music. With songs like "Freak on a Leash" and "Make Me Bad", anyone from this band would be the last person you'd expect to go to church, let alone profess Jesus Christ from the pulpit.

God works in mysterious ways, doesn't He?

Christians should be the people least surprised by this conversion. We know that in Luke 5:31-32 Jesus said, "It is not the healthy who need a doctor, but the sick. I have not come to call the righteous, but sinners" (NIV). If our Lord walked the earth today, we'd more likely find Him at a thrash metal rock concert looking for the wounded rather than sitting in a pew on Sunday morning amongst the righteous. God went to that rock concert and apparently found a hurting soul on stage.

You may be asking, is this for real? It is an important question. We can all name musicians who professed Christ, renounced their ways, and wound up making the same morally sketchy music they made before. After all, secular hip-hop artists are legendary for thanking God in acceptance speeches for songs that are violently graphic and demeaning to women.

However, there are exceptions of note. Rapper Mase was a protege of hip-hop mogul Sean 'P. Diddy' Combs. As a star act on the Bad Boy label, he was in the thick of the hip-hop lifestyle with a brand new, highly anticipated album set to be release. However, after God gave him a vision of leading people into hell, Mase abruptly retired and disappeared for five years. In that time, he pursued the call to be a minister and wrote a book. In 2004, he re-emerged on the rap scene but with a clean album and positive lyrics.

It can be done, and Welch's testimony may be one that sticks. Hard rock music does not always lend itself to a lot of riding the theological fence. Complete "about-face" decisions like Welch's are rare. The only one of recent note is Josh Brown, formerly of Full Devil Jacket. After hitting rock bottom, Brown found Christ and now fronts the Christian rock band Day of Fire. I met him last year. He has an amazing heart underneath his tattoo-covered skin. Just spending time with him was a lesson in not judging a book by its cover.

So, the question shifts from "Is it for real?" to "How can we tell?" It's difficult to judge, and according to Matthew 7:1, it may not be our place to. We wouldn't have picked half the people God made heroes in the Bible. The Lord explains His rationale perfectly in I Samuel 16:7: "Look not on his countenance, or on the height of his stature; because I have refused him: for the Lord seeth not as man seeth; for man looketh on the outward appearance, but the LORD looketh on the heart" (From Article CBN.com)

Why bring Brian to my church, to the NextGen ministry? Brian said it-- "It's not about this church; it's not about me. It's about the Book of Life, and everybody needs to be taught this. It's crazy. It's gonna do stuff like this -- like change a guy in a rock band."

Brian has a story of transformation to tell. The story of how Jesus Christ changed his life.

Years of student ministry can taint you. I see so many students that need to re hear, re see, re live if you will, the power of God in someone's life. Maybe, just maybe they will decide to have the same power, the same Jesus change their lives. Too many students these days seem apathetic, are doing life like everyone else, some are using, some are sexually active, and some just don't care.

Maybe, just maybe a night with Brian Head Welch will speak into their hearts.
It's not about the music, it's not about the man, it's about the work of God. The ministry I do, the ministry I am involved with, the ministry

I lead will go beyond it's walls, will go beyond it's fear, will go beyond it's external hang ups and lift high the transforming power of God, lift high the God's love for all of humanity and I will do everything I can and know to do to reach out to all people. That is why.

Shoes tell a story

Shoes actually tell a story...

I came home after watching my youngest son graduate from high school today. Oh, I gulped a couple of times during the ceremony. Nothing huge, just the thought that my son is finished with another chapter in his life. High school has come and gone with all the ups and downs and "what were you thinking" to "so proud of you" to "way to score the gaming winning goal on Senior Night."

I got home and saw these old wingtip shoes. They were my old Florsheim shoes that I used to wear. As a matter of fact, my father wore Florsheim shoes. I remember when I was a kid sticking eggs in my dad's Florsheim wingtips on April Fool's day. Well, he stepped in them and got egg all over his socks. I remember him being pretty upset. He wasn't so upset about having to change his socks, but he was upset that I messed with his Florsheim shoes. I still can remember the price he put on those old wingtips-- "those are 200 dollar shoes" he said, and "I use those every day for work. Don't do anything like that again." From that point on, I had a high respect for my dad's wingtip Florsheim shoes.

I remember when my dad took me out shopping for my first pair of Florsheim wingtips. Now, I don't see them as dorky, old man shoes. No, I knew the value of these bad boys. I also knew that going out shoe shopping with my dad meant that he was willing to get me the best of shoes because he knew that the longer they lasted, the better the shoe. My first wingtips were bought, and I was on my way to appreciating not a good pair of shoes, but a great pair of shoes.

So, when I got home from my son's graduation there were my wingtips. I forgot, Cooper has been wearing those shoes for every special, dress up days since his freshman year. Today, seeing those shoes brought those memories of my father Ray. I think of the many things that I do like my dad. He was a man of resolve, conviction, character, he to me was a stand up guy, and I am proud to wear his shoes.

This day, this graduation day of my son, I am proud to have my son wear my shoes. I hope he wears my shoes way past the day I'm gone. For me, seeing those shoes, knowing he wears them means so much to me. I wore my dad's and I am proud my son wears mine. I am proud of you, son. I hope that you will be what those shoes represent. A high value in the way they are made, the way the last, the integrity of their sole. Yes, shoes tell a story and I am proud of my father, proud to be a father, and proud of my son. Keep wearing my shoes, son.

Character

What does your name say about you?

"A good name is more desirable than great riches; to be esteemed is better than silver or gold." Proverbs 22.1

What does your name say about you?
Your name tells of your *character*

Character: "A peculiar quality; moral constitution, as of a person; a person exhibiting certain qualities."

When you or I think of Character, we can tend to first think about the external elements of a person's character. Of course, how a person lives is a direct reflection of what is on the inside.

Some might think that it is the mind that determines character. The Scriptures speak of the heart as being the place of *Character*

The *Hebrew* term or usage for the word HEART!

"The <u>innermost</u> or <u>hidden</u> part"

"The <u>center or cradle</u> of man's inner most part"

In the *Old Testament* the heart denotes
The seat of wisdom
Understanding
Deceit
Folly
Knowledge
Cheerfulness
Character

The *New Testament* use of the word heart denotes
Personality
The inner life
The seat of emotion
The will

The Heart-- The place where <u>desires, motives, and moral choices are made</u>.

Breaking it Down
What is the most expensive thing you own?
The house?
The car?
Jewelery?
Clothes?
Stocks?

"A good name is more desirable than great riches; to be esteemed is better than silver or gold." Proverbs 22.1

This verse is about _Character_
Who we are <u>in our hearts</u>
Who we are <u>on the inside</u>
And how we <u>live daily on the outside</u>.

That is our _Character._

So Solomon says—
What people think about us matters.
What our friends think about us is important.
What others think about you does have significance period.

And <u>what you think about you</u> is _important!!!!_

Yes! If you don't care about a <u>good name</u>

If you don't care about <u>what others think</u>

If you think <u>other things</u> are more _valuable_

Than <u>your character</u> won't matter.

Problem?

- False humility says- You shouldn't care about yourself.

- Believing that what others think doesn't matter.
  See if you feel that way the next time you ask a leader or a boss to fill out a character reference.

- "I can't help my flaws—I was born this way."
  What about all the people that do change for the better?

And in this day and age—If you and I don't care about our character
You and I are a small step away from big, big, big, problems--
consequences that will last till the grave. (I know)

Remember: *Character*-- A peculiar quality; moral constitution, as of a person; a person exhibiting certain qualities.

"A good name is more desirable than great riches; to be esteemed is better than silver or gold."   Proverbs 22.1

To Solomon, having a good name (certain qualities) is worth all the riches we could think of. Being known for your moral constitution is more valuable than great riches.

Let's apply

- We are God's children
  We represent Him
  He abides in us through the Holy Spirit
  Our lives matter to God
  We are His ambassadors
  We are His workmanship
  We are His heirs
  We are joint heirs with Christ
  We are adopted into Him
  We were formed by Him

- We matter to God—
  And how we live matters to God.

Jesus said it like this--
For *where your* treasure *is*, there *your heart* will be also. Matt. 6.21

The content of our Character?

"No man can climb out beyond the limitations of his own character"
~John Lord Morley

I agree! But, not completely.
Yes—we all have issues. We all have our cross to bear. We all have inner "things" that can cause each of us much pain. Some of the causes seem to be external—like—food—too much eating, or seeing things that drive us to buy beyond our means bringing shame, guilt, and pain. But—is the pain all about the outside? Or is it more about who we are—deep down inside?

Martin Luther King, Jr. in his famous "I have a dream" speech said "...I have a dream that my four little children will one day live in a nation where they will not be judged by the color of their skin but by the content of their character."
Do we really want to be judged on the content of our character? Or is our life more about the outside?

I confess—I have had to deal with my "lack of character" in some hard hard ways. I learned early on that lying sometimes worked— that sometimes its much easier to try and get away with something, rather than deal honestly with my failure. That is about character.

I confess—When I was a student, I had inner struggles with integrity—when it was easy for me to take money from my father's drawer so that I could buy something I felt I needed. That is about character.

Oh and there is much much more—but—am I stuck with my inner "lack of character"?

Not when it comes to the life changing miracle through a personal relationship with Christ. Isn't that all about the inside that then transforms the outside?

I know a lil bit about the wrong way of changing perceived character—I learned from some people that I could change the outside appearance—by looking like I was a good guy—but that failed too. Ultimately what is inside always finds a way to the outside.

I learned the hard lessons of Jesus' power as I have gone through life and allowed Him to deal with my character. It wasn't always pretty—it wasn't a cake walk—changing the inside--- character—is not fun.

But—a relationship with Jesus is wholly inside first—

I needed—I continue to need Him, to deal with my inside—my heart—my mind—me—I am glad today—He does the work—and I get to witness the change—and so do the people around me.

"The inward area is the first place of loss of true Christian life, of true spirituality, and the outward sinful act is the result."
~Francis Schaeffer

"...I have a dream that my four little children will one day live in a nation where they will not be judged by the color of their skin but by the content of their character."
~Martin Luther King, Jr.

Do we really want to be judged by our character? I don't think so. I think most want to be judged on how they look, what they have, and how big their egos get because they are stroked for all the wrong reasons.

The student, the person who understands their need for the transforming power of Christ in the internal area-- character-- will more and more understand that the matters of the heart, the inside, can change and with the power of the Holy Spirit will change.

Character matters—big time!

Honesty matters...Right?

"... and you will know the truth and the truth will set you free." ~Jesus

Honesty is always right. Right? Should honesty be part of what students learn as they follow Christ? Isn't honesty part of character? You know, character, integrity, honesty. Is honesty important to you? Would it be better for a student to lie so that you or I don't know the truth? You know, like if a student is let's say involved in something that isn't "good" for them, would you rather not know? Is it better for the student to deny or lie rather than tell the truth? Is that good for them? Of course not. It's never good to lie. Right?

I lead student ministry. I think that honesty is important to all students regardless of whether or not they have a relationship with Christ. I believe that honesty is a high value for the students now and for their future. That being said, I believe that those that follow Christ should hold honesty as part of their association with the name of Jesus Christ. Honesty is part of what it means to "follow" Christ.

Question: Is it o.k. to lie about where you are spiritually rather than tell the truth? Allow me to play the question out-- It looks like this. I love the Lord, I go to church, I tell you things you want to hear, I do the minimal, I have a secret life that I don't think you know about. I only go to church because you make me, I'm just getting by till I get out of the house. Maybe it's because the student just doesn't want to deal with the fallout. Maybe it's because the student really does enjoy the double life. Maybe the student really doesn't care about spiritual things. Maybe their heart has never really been transformed by the living Christ. So it is easier to just tell you or me what they think we want to hear? Maybe it's because the student doesn't think that lying is such a big deal. After all, this is just a phase. Why rock the boat? Why make it such a big deal? It sounds like this, "I accepted Jesus as my savior back in 3rd grade, I don't need church, or anyone else. I'm not doing anything wrong (at least what I'll admit) I love the Lord, I just don't like church. I don't like the other kids at youth group, they are hypocrites, I'm not like them. Is that honest? Really?

You and I know the truth. The longer the little lie goes on, the longer the lying continues. The longer the faking it, the more deceit goes on, the more deceit goes on the easier it is for a student to believe "this character flaw, (the lack of honesty) is o.k. I'm not hurting anyone, I'm just getting by."   If, let's say a student is dabbling in smoking pot, a weekend smoker if you will. The student is not found out until a few months pass by. The student will say, "I only smoked a few times" it's not that big of a deal right? Well, a few times is a few times. Is smoking pot not that big of a deal? They may say "I only do it with friends or occasionally". Is that a lie? Yes. They actually smoke every weekend. They tell the lie so that the reaction is not severe and so that they can continue to use. After all, if you or I believe that it really is just a few times by next year it will not be a problem right? Wrong. The lie that is just once in awhile is for you or I. The lie is so that they can continue. The lie is so that we will get off their back, forget it and move on.

The above is just one little example of dishonesty or a half truth , if you will. Any way you want to cut it it's only to cover ones rear end. How bout it this way? Wouldn't it be better if we allowed students to be honest about who they are and where they are spiritually? The problem is that many "Christian" students are working so hard at covering up the truth that they don't realize that both are hurting them. The behavior and the deceit blend into a lifestyle.

You see, I know -I did it. I did all the above and when I finally gave up trying to hide (I had already been found out) I could finally say "alright, obviously I don't love God or care about Jesus, you got me." I finally could live with integrity. I partied and didn't lie about it. When I was going out, I told my parents the truth. It was up to them to decide how to deal with me. My youth pastor, I no longer lied to (he already knew). Now I could finally live free. Oh I was sinning big, but I knew I was at least telling the truth. I wasn't gonna blame anyone, I wasn't gonna talk about "those people" or compare lists, or play semantics with God's word. I had had it with all those who wanted to believe that they were better than me. I at least had character. Sure, I was sinning but at least I wasn't playing games any more. I was a sinner, but not covering up or lying about it.

Interesting though, that I had already done an incredible amount of damage in my life. I learned how to deceive, to lie and play the game and as I continued to believe that I was honest, I was loving the party life, the booze, and all that goes with it. Honesty was fleeting because not quite all of me was about character. All of me was about me ,and that is sin. Sure, when people had something to say to me I couldn't blame my behavior on someone else. Like, "oh man they said that about me, that's not true." I would actually say things, "look, I was at the bar last night, what's it to you?" No more lies, no more faking it, no more playing the games.

I have treated my sons like that-- all I ever want is honesty. When they did things that were not right, I never asked them to lie to me so that the consequences would be less or to not tell me the truth because if they did I would love them less. No, I have always told my sons and also my students to tell the truth. Don't lie to me. I even had the courage to tell my sons, "you don't have to love God." You don't have to pretend, but I do expect you to tell the truth. By the way, to all my friends who read my blog. Yes, both of my sons have broken my heart with the things I know about (and I know some really bad stuff). Both of them have blown it. Both of them have been caught. Yes, it hurt. Yes it bothers me. Yes they are a chip off the old block, and yes, when they asked for forgiveness, I forgave them. Yes trust was broken and that takes time to rebuild.,

I see what is happening with some students today. The issue has become that it is better to deny, to not tell the truth because then people, important people will know the real me. They are not sure that the real me will be loved or accepted. So it is easier to hide behind the lies and the facade so that they can be loved for what they think they will only be loved for. Or maybe the truth is that partying is fun. Maybe it's because students like sex. Maybe it's because we all love to sin. Maybe, just maybe, it's because they actually do know what is right and don't care and are afraid to admit it. Maybe they want what they want period. Well, at least that is honest.

Do the scriptures tell us that God knows our hearts? Do the scriptures teach us that our hearts are impure, totally depraved without the redeeming blood of Christ? Yes. Even with the redeeming blood of Christ don't we all still struggle with sin? Romans 8. Are we doing a disservice to students by making them feel that it would be better to lie, to not tell the truth because, what? Then the truth won't set them free? That Jesus won't love them because He finally found out? That the truth that they don't care about what we care about will hurt us terribly? Lying is only hurting them.

The fact that students over the years have lied to me never hurt me. It only hurt them. They are the ones who continued to struggle with how to have integrity. They are the ones who struggle with the "why should I follow Christ?" They are the ones who ultimately end up getting pregnant or getting someone pregnant. They are the ones who ultimately use to the point of addiction. They are the ones who ultimately lose credibility. They are the ones who miss opportunity after opportunity to live free with all their admitted faults, defects and sin.

You see, as long as I'm a youth pastor, I will always try to help students to just be honest. Tell the truth even if it's not what you think others want to hear. Tell the truth even if it rocks your parent's world. Tell the truth even if it hurts. Tell the truth even if it shocks those that love them. Why? Because until we all get to the point that we are honest about who we are, we are telling the Lord that His Word isn't real or true. He doesn't really love us for who we are. He doesn't really love us sinful people. If somehow we can do something good one day and then do a little sin over here it's not that big of a deal. Right? That is not what the Scriptures teach. The scriptures teach that sin is sin and only He can forgive those sins that we think nobody knows. In truth most people do know. Truth-- If one person knows 3 people know and then lots of people know.

Look now, if anyone thinks I'm passing judgment-- I'm not. The truth is that I have paid dearly for my lies. I have done it, I lied to keep my issues alive and well. I lied to keep people off my back. I lied because I didn't want the truth to be known. I paid for my lying and I'm glad I paid. I'm glad I got caught. I'm glad that I was found out. ,Therefore, wouldn't you think that this stuff matters to me? I hear the way that people talk about others-, questioning whatever... I know that gossip and lying fall in the same category, and I know what the lack of honesty did to me. Don't you think it matters to the Lord? Don't you think I should care about students enough to keep these issues as important? Or should I rant about music, or dating, talk about the Bible that students don't even read, talk about issues that students don't care about?

I believe that the ministry that I do is first and foremost about the truth. I can say that for every student that is continuing to lie to themselves and to their parents it is not until they come to an honest place that they will begin to decide to follow Christ for the right reasons-- that they need Him in their lives for everything. Until students get honest the road of hard knocks will continue to get harder and harder and the knocks will bring much pain. Maybe pregnancy, maybe addiction, maybe extreme pain, maybe even death.

Funny, how most students like my own 2 sons find me to be a very gracious dad, pastor, person, human when they are honest and truthful. Funny, how with the Lord that is what He desires. "A broken and contrite heart." How does that happen? By honest introspection and confession. Give me 10 students no matter what the sin, who are honest, who are truthful, who are broken and contrite, even if the sin is some little thing and I'll show you a ministry that is doing things for the Kingdom of God.

Honesty matters. *"... and you will know the truth and the truth will set you free."* ~Jesus

Contentment

Proverbs 4.7 says "Wisdom is Supreme; therefore get wisdom."

James 1.5 says "If any of you lacks wisdom, he should ask God, who gives generously to all ."

The book of Proverbs

Every once in a while, I pick up the Word for some reading in the great book of Proverbs.

A read in Proverbs helps to—

1. Keep life in <u>perspective</u>
2. Learn Biblical principles <u>again</u>
3. See the <u>relevance of Scripture</u>
4. Make some <u>headway in our personal walk with God</u>.
5. Living wise from the <u>inside-out</u>

Example

Proverbs 20.27

"The human spirit is the lamp of the LORD
that sheds light on one's inmost being."
The Lamp of the Lord

- The <u>conscience</u> given to all humanity
- The <u>Holy Spirit reveals</u>, shines light <u>on the inside</u>

Thus, being wise means we can
Live with Clarity!

As <u>we listen to the Holy Spirit</u> as <u>He reveals what's on the inside</u>.

Living in the Now

Proverbs 17.1

"Better a dry crust with peace and quiet
than a house full of feasting, with strife."

What in the world?

A couple of questions--
What would make your life better?
What do you need to have happiness?
What is your next pursuit?

And

If all is attained, is
Life better?
Happiness lasting?
More to pursue?

Ahh, Contentment!!!!!

Is it reachable?
Is it attainable?
Is it just a dream?

Lessons from Solomon (found these historical lil facts in my study
Bible)
Solomon inherited a unified prosperous kingdom—His reign was
known as Israel's golden age.

950 B.C. Solomon's Temple finished-- The Ark was brought to rest.
To the Children of Israel-- where God's name dwelt.

The Temple—inside complete Gold
Solomon saw to it that
His royal palace was built—stone wood and gold
The House of the Forest of Lebanon—the council chambers
The Hall of Judgment—Solomon sat on a throne of ivory and gold
For his foreign wives—homes and shrines
Monuments of Solomon's grandeur –leading to Israel's bankruptcy

Solomon raised taxes
Payment to Hiram for the cedars rafted to Joppa
125,000 bushels of wheat
1,200,000 gallons of oil
twenty coastal towns in Galilee

Solomon understood—
"Better a dry crust with peace and quiet than a house full of feasting and strife."

Contentment comes—

- Not by things
- Not by lots of parties
- Not by money
- Not by more

Ray Pritchard writes—"Contentment is realizing that you are better off the way you are right now. If you are dreaming of more money and bigger material possessions, contentment is realizing how much God has blessed you and how much you have right now."

The Apostle Paul wrote—Phil. 4.11

"I have learned, in what ever state I am, to be content."

Contentment? Being satisfied with <u>God's provisions</u>.

A. W. Pink says contentment is the opposite of murmuring, which is the Spirit of rebellion—the clay saying to the potter, why have you made me like this?

Timothy wrote—"Godliness with contentment is great gain." (1 Tim. 6.6)
Living in the Now

What we have in Christ.

A well known Christian speaker was going to see the president,
A friend asked this Christian speaker how he would feel meeting the president.
The speaker said, What will the president think when He visits with an heir of the King?

And that's what we have today. Contentment?

Just a small list

- God, who is rich in mercy, made us alive in Christ
- God raised us up with Christ
- Seated us with Him in heavenly realms
- We have the gift of Salvation
- We are God's workmanship
- Brought near to God through the Blood of Christ
- He is our Peace
- Fellow citizens with God's people
- Members of God's household
- In Him and through faith we can approach God
- With freedom and confidence
- Sons of the Living God
- Clothed with Christ
- Abraham's seed
- Heirs according to the promises
- A new creation
- Reconciled to God through Christ
- Christ's Ambassadors
- We are to God the aroma of Christ
- God leads us in triumphal procession
- We are a letter from Christ
- Justified
- God has poured out His love to us

And all this is now

What more is there to want?

On Being Mean

Mean: adj. characterized by petty selfishness or malice; causing trouble or bother.

Bully: n. a blustering browbeating person; *especially;* one habitually cruel to others who are weaker

I have been around students for a long, long time. I was once a student, I have 2 students of my own, I have been around students for a long time going all the way back to 1970 when I was in junior high. So, I have seen all sorts of students.

I'll admit right up front before I go any further: I personally don't enjoy the mean students that continue to bash, hurt others intentionally, lash out, verbally beat up, cut down, talk behind others, say mean things and all that goes with being mean.

Nobody does. Right? Who likes to be around mean people? Who likes to be around those who love to put others down, talk behind others backs. Does anyone really like to be around mean people? The definition of mean is "petty selfishness or malice; causing trouble or bother." What is even harder to deal with is this: Students that supposedly know Jesus Christ and treat their peers and actually those that care about them with malice. What is that? Why is that? Really?

I wish I could put all the mean students (whoclaim to know Christ) in a room and have Jesus the Christ walk in just to say hello. I wonder what they would do if He started to interact with them. Like he did with the adulterous women, or with the pharisees... you know they would call Him mean. How dare He point out their sin. How dare He speak to me about my stuff. How dare He point out my short comings. How dare He deal with me. Isn't that the truth? Isn't that the way mean people would react? Always deflecting, always feeling sorry for themselves, always willing to call those caring, mean?

I have seen this for years. I see these silly bumper stickers that say "mean people suck". I often wonder who really is the mean person? The person who cries about others while at the same time causing grief because they have been found out? Or those who love to pout about how bad their life is because of those who just aren't going to listen anymore to their mean, selfish attitudes anymore. How bout it? You know the mean person who calls others mean because they can't stand others who might have it together, that just might live by a code of morality, ethics, care and concern. Those mean people who actually will call sin sin-- those people are so mean.

Frankly, as a youth pastor it really is hard to deal with mean students and mean people. The truth is that the truth to a mean person is mean no matter what. Even if said in the most loving, kind, caring way to a mean person the message is mean and the person delivering the message is mean. Caring for a mean student and to their parents has to be the way they want it or they consider it mean. Caring and loving the mean, unlovable student is very difficult indeed, for the fallout of caring and loving them brings with it all those that they have "tricked" into thinking that they are right or good, or at best being mistreated. The fallout of talking into their lives brings with it all their personal baggage of why they are so mean. You know, their personal hang ups, their dashed dreams, the way they have been treated, the way their parents have spoken badly of others for years, their personal hurts, their personal deep down hatred for the things that have let them down.

What to do? Again, this is only from experience here-- I have noticed quoting scriptures isn't going to do much. Speaking honest and directly isn't going to do it (they consider that being mean, go figure) Being kind isn't going to do it, they love to mock kind people. Being just the youth pastor means nothing to them and to their parents so that isn't going to do it. Bring Jesus right to them and that isn't going to do it. As a matter of fact, they don't want anything to do with Jesus. So?

So, the time comes sadly that just letting them go is about all one can do. Go and learn from others in the real world that your meanness isn't going to be tolerated by all people. Go out and learn from those that don't want to be around you period. Go and learn from those that actually will be direct without love and tell you how they really feel about you, you may even get punch in the nose. Maybe even something much worse.

Maybe, just maybe the Holy Spirit that is in them if He is will speak into their brokenness. Maybe the Jesus that they have avoided for years will speak those kind words of His "I love you, and want to help you" will be heard. Maybe, just maybe they will stop looking at everyone's imperfections, including theirs for once and wake up and realize the only perfect person is Christ Himself. Maybe the Lord will finally break through their broken, mean heart.

Being mean isn't vogue, cool, the thing to do. Being mean is actually a sign of one's stunted growth, childish "I want my way kind of attitude". Oh my, is that too mean to say? Sometimes love and truth hurts but only till one realizes that they can benefit from those who actually care enough to speak into their mean spirited hearts. Being mean is toxic no matter what you may think. For every mean student I'll show you 5 more students who have been contaminated because of their mean, selfish tude. Mean is not good. Mean is sinful. Like the saying "speed kills" so does being mean.

and be content

Keep your lives free from the love of money and be content with what you have, because God has said, "Never will I leave you; never will I forsake you."
Hebrews 13:5

Ever had a day where it just seems to fall flat? How bout a day where you are just flat? I'm into that—just plain flat. I'm just not myself. I just don't have it together. Funny—when I'm flat it seems—my perception—not too many people want to be around me. Maybe I don't wear my emotions very well. I really try to have it together—but I may just be too transparent—or maybe—I'm just not settled inside—but I do try to keep it real.

All that to say that in the midst of all the above—I am learning to trust in the Lord. Really—trusting in the Lord about—circumstances—is that being content? Trusting in the Lord about direction—is that about being content? Trusting in the Lord to take care of the details that I am absolutely clueless about—is that about being content? Interesting that for the first time while reading Hebrews 13.5 reference I noticed something—that God recognizes full well the correlation between "the good life" being content and trusting in Him.

I am convinced that I—in the midst of being flat, not having it together that He, the Lord wants very much to enter in—to be my all, to be near, to be what I need—and want . True? Yes—actually for all people that "follow the Christ". He wants so much to be what takes care of me, what I need, what is essential.

He says—"Keep your lives free from the love of money and be content" Living in a world that lives by capitalism, maintains life through money, maintains a standard based on income is the rub. Then, being content with what you have goes completely against the world we live in—because I am continually bombarded with new, better, cooler and on and on.... Oh, I was flat today—but not anymore—He and I are more than O.K. —and I will seek Him all the more.

Heavenly Father—help me to trust you with the little things, the big things, with life. Thank you for always being there—even when I'm flat.

The Sting of Anger

Anger: n. a strong feeling of annoyance, displeasure, or hostility

Forgiveness: n. the action or process of forgiving or being forgiven.

"Anger is "an emotional state that varies in intensity from mild irritation to intense fury and rage," according to Charles Spielberger, PhD, a psychologist who specializes in the study of anger. Like other emotions, it is accompanied by physiological and biological changes. When you get angry, your heart rate and blood pressure go up, as do the levels of your energy hormones, adrenaline, and noradrenaline.

Anger can be caused by both external and internal events. You could be angry at a specific person (Such as a coworker or supervisor) or event (a traffic jam, a canceled flight), or your anger could be caused by worrying or brooding about your personal problems. Memories of traumatic or enraging events can also trigger angry feelings."
~American Psychological Association

Sometimes I wonder-- why am I so angry? What is it deep down inside of me that stirs so deep? What is the hurt that is causing my anger? What is it that drives me crazy with anger? Ever ask those questions to yourself after a blow up? I have.

I'll admit on my blog that yes, I sometimes get angry. I get angry at circumstances, I get angry with people, I mostly get angry at myself.

I have been personally attacked. I have heard what people say about me without ever talking to me about their critical view. Example. "I don't like Don, because of this or that about him." O.k., but is that legit? The truth is that I'm just not accepted. That bothers me, that sometimes angers me. That angers me because it is "about me", you know? They just don't like me. The problem is that I have been down this road. Being liked means that I will have to "change" for them. I get angry because that is not fair. That seems so childish. You know, "I'll like you, even love you, if you live the way I want you to live and be." No thanks. So my anger comes from a knowledge of what that kind of tude towards me and others does and says. It says "I determine" who is loveable according to my standards and views. I have lived under the scrutiny of others for years-- thus, I get angry when it comes back around.

I can get angry when I'm put down for something that I may not be so "good" at or my inability to overcome something that others seem to do so much better and easier. It seems to me that I'm just not good enough. That can sometimes anger me. Like, you know, the whole "belittling" or "pettiness" that others love to perpetrate. It looks and feels like I'm back in High School and anther student wants me to feel inferior because I got a C on a test and they got an A, and for some reason they think that is so superior than my hard work I put in for a C. It's petty, its purposeful and that drives me nuts. My wise father used to say "Never compare yourself to anyone. There is nobody else like you." He was right. Except, that is not how the world, people or Christians play.

But the real anger thing is simply this: I get the most angry when I wanted this and I got that. When my dream or goal has been blocked or dashed. When I want to be and I failed. When I thought this and got something completely different. When I went for it and failed. When I tried and tried and tried and got zero. That is what I have been the most angry about. Then, then the anger of my own failure comes into play. Then the blame game starts, then looking at faults of those that let me down come into play then the blame on something bigger than me comes into play and then... the long road of despair, and more anger and more despair and more blame and yada yada yada.

Here's the good news. The fight to be right is pretty much gone. The fight to be heard is pretty much gone. The fight to be the best, to have the best is all but gone. The fight to be liked and loved is going away. The fight is pretty much out of me and that is a good thing. I'm pretty much over trying to be approved by those that don't like me. I'll never do it the way they want and that's o.k. The desire to be heard is pretty much over, because in truth I know who listens to me and I am learning to TRUST Him as I tell Him my hurts and fears.

Yes, anger comes along every once in awhile. Yes, the old tapes of not being good enough get played when I do this thing called ministry. I know I'm not good enough. And, yes I get angry when I think to myself, why does this bother me? I am better than this. I have tough skin, ministry brings critical people. I sometimes get angry with myself, and then take it out on others.

We all know some pretty angry people. They are angry at the church, although the church never did anything to them, but people did. They still blame the church, but its imperfect people that did it. Oh the church is people right? Then talk to the people that jacked you up. If it's circumstance from people, Jesus said it in His way to pray, "Forgive us our sins, as we forgive those who sin against us." Forgiveness is a real thing. I have learned to forgive those that have jacked with me because I know that Jesus forgives me. I therefore will forgive others. That is not easy, but it is doable. Forgiveness matters. Forgiveness is the way to move forward.

Oh, I could go nuts with all the stuff people have said and done to me. Absolutely nuts, but I'm learning to forgive those who have talked behind my back. Those who have said mean things about me. Those who judge me. For you see, I'm not going to let my anger rule me. I'm not going to let the petty garbage from other people hurt me. No, that is their issue. Mine is to forgive and move on.

One of the hardest things I have seen over the years is the inability of others to seek forgiveness from Jesus, receive the forgiveness and not forgive themselves. Forgiveness is the beginning of taming the anger within. While the people of God, the followers of Christ love to spout off about forgiveness, love to be forgiven, forgiving oneself is the next step to health.

My father used to say it like this, "How long are you going to wallow in the mud? I forgive you, forgive yourself now. Get up and move on." He is right. Too many times I have not forgiven myself, the old tapes come back to haunt me, I blame others because I am not able to forgive myself for an honest mistake, or a difference of opinion, or I did fail, or I blew it, or because I just feel like I don't deserve it. I'm getting past it. I'm forgiven.

Psalm 32. 1,2
Blessed is the one
whose transgressions are forgiven,
whose sins are covered.
Blessed is the one
whose sin the LORD does not count against them
and in whose spirit is no deceit.

I am stirred by forgiveness. I am stirred by words of songs of forgiveness. I am stirred deep down inside for everything I have been forgiven of and from. So this day I choose to forgive myself and those that have been mean and cruel towards me. I will start this day with an attitude of forgiveness. I may fail, I may not do it right, I may let some people down on the way but I'm not perfect, I am willing to admit my wrongs, I am willing to rely on the forgiveness of the only one that can completely forgive.

[4] Surely he took up our pain
and bore our suffering,
yet we considered him punished by God,
stricken by him, and afflicted.
[5] But he was pierced for our transgressions,
he was crushed for our iniquities;
the punishment that brought us peace was on him,
and by his wounds we are healed.
[6] We all, like sheep, have gone astray,
each of us has turned to our own way;
and the LORD has laid on him
the iniquity of us all.
Isaiah 53.4-6

I believe! Because of Him I have been forgiven!

Envy? What is that?

Envy: a feeling of discontent or covetousness with regard to another's advantages, success, possessions

Covetous: inordinately or wrongly desirous of wealth or possessions; greedy.

I don't know about you, but I'm really tired of people complaining about what others "have" and what they don't have. I'm tired of hearing from those that actually want it all regardless of how those that have got it all got it. In truth that is called ENVY. Why doesn't anyone stand up and say it? That others are actually envious of what others have and I want what they have regardless of how they got what they have. I want it. I want it now, I deserve it, I should have it, and if I can't have it, then those that do have shouldn't have it. That is not fair, that is not what I want. That is not what I expected. I expected to have everything that everyone else has. Furthermore, if I can't have it then the playing field isn't fair, that "fairness" means all are equal, life is equal, work is equal and on and on.

> The bald faced truth is that envy is killing people from the inside out. That envy actually IS the issue, that what others have is really not the issue. Sadly even "Christians" have gotten into this whole issue only not by dealing with the right issues, but by siding with those that are envious rather than dealing with what everyone knows envy really is. True? What is envy? What is covetousness? What is it?

When I was a kid way back, I wanted a new Schwinn Continental bike. I worked all summer at cutting lawns, painting my house and I was 15 years old. My parents wouldn't buy it for me although other friends were given their bikes. I sulked for a little bit. That wasn't fair. I wanted the bike and I was determined to get it. So, I worked for it and ultimately bought it. Wouldn't you know that someone else wanted my powder blue Schwinn Continental ten speed and stole mine. Wow, right? Envy. Envy drives people to do, to believe, to become what envy really is. What is envy? What is covetousness?

Seriously. Why do those that actually believe in the Scriptures and its value and definition of envy refuse to engage in the truth? That envy is something. That envy has its root from something. That envy drives people to cry out for things, for stuff that is not theirs and may never be theirs. What is that called?

Envy is going to be the ruin of many people in the days to come. It won't be because they don't have it all. It won't be because they have less. It won't be because they want something they need. It will be because envy is something.

Thomas Aquinas "it is a sin directly against one's neighbor, since one man cannot over-abound in external riches, without another man lacking them... it is a sin against God, just as all mortal sins, inasmuch as man contemns things eternal for the sake of temporal things."

Paul said it like this, "Put to death, therefore, whatever belongs to your earthly nature: sexual immorality, impurity, lust, evil desires and greed, which is idolatry." Col. 3.5

Interesting the covetousness is 1 of the 10 commandments. Shouldn't everyone have what everyone else has? Shouldn't we that follow Christ show, live out this principle? You know, life is fair and if it is not fair its our job to make it fair. Is that what we are supposed to do? How bout the we as followers of Christ should stand up and say "hey, we want what everyone else has so the government should even the playing field?" Shouldn't we be the first people in to be all about giving everyone what they want or at least fighting for that? Isn't that our job as followers of Christ? You know to make envy something as a high value? Is that our deal? After all, we all that follow Christ know that He gives us everything we want. He is the great Santa Clause and if we are good then we get our hearts desires. If we want it, we should have it. We love Jesus and He owes us fairness, everything we want, and a good life. Right?

You know, I'll never make 6 figures and that's o.k. I most likely will never have a 6 figure car, a half a million dollar house, a fully stocked this or that, the ability to retire, the money my parents had, the money others have, the stuff the have's have and that is fine with me. Since when did it become the right thing to want what others have? Since when did it become o.k. to judge others for what they have?

What is envy? What is covetousness? What in the world is it? I suggest we know what it is. Right? Until followers of Christ get this right, I'm afraid we have become so P.C. that we can't even call envy what it is anymore

On Honor

The Medal of Honor is the highest military decoration awarded by the United States government. It is bestowed by the President, in the name of Congress, upon members of the United States Armed Forces who distinguish themselves through "conspicuous gallantry and intrepidity at the risk of his or her life above and beyond the call of duty while engaged in an action against an enemy of the United States."Due to the nature of its criteria, it is often awarded posthumously (more than half have been since 1941).

Citation: BOLDEN, PAUL L.

He voluntarily attacked a formidable enemy strong point in Petit-Coo, Belgium, on 23 December, 1944, when his company was pinned down by extremely heavy automatic and small-arms fire coming from a house 200 yards to the front. Mortar and tank artillery shells pounded the unit, when S/Sgt. Bolden and a comrade, on their own initiative, moved forward into a hail of bullets to eliminate the ever-increasing fire from the German position. Crawling ahead to close with what they knew was a powerfully armed, vastly superior force, the pair reached the house and took up assault positions, S/Sgt. Bolden under a window, his comrade across the street where he could deliver covering fire. In rapid succession, S/Sgt. Bolden hurled a fragmentation grenade and a white phosphorous grenade into the building; and then, fully realizing that he faced tremendous odds, rushed to the door, threw it open and fired into 35 SS troopers who were trying to reorganize themselves after the havoc wrought by the grenades. Twenty Germans died under fire of his submachinegun before he was struck in the shoulder, chest, and stomach by part of a burst which killed his comrade across the street. He withdrew from the house, waiting for the surviving Germans to come out and surrender. When none appeared in the doorway, he summoned his ebbing strength, overcame the extreme pain he suffered and boldly walked back into the house, firing as he went. He had killed the remaining 15 enemy soldiers when his ammunition ran out. S/Sgt. Bolden's heroic advance against great odds, his fearless assault, and his magnificent display of courage in reentering the building where he had been severely wounded cleared the path for his company and insured the success of its mission.

- Honor: n. personal integrity; allegiance to moral principles-- fame or glory

- Honor: v. to hold in respect or esteem -- to show <u>courteous behavior</u> towards to worship--- to confer a distinction upon

Let's say it is you that is on a mission...

You are holed up – gun fire all around.

Your friends are with you—

And a grenade lands in your area...

Just before it goes off—one of your friends dives on it—takes the complete blast

His body parts and blood land all over you—yet your life is saved because of what he did.

How would you honor his behavior?

Would you hold him in high esteem?

Would you hold your friend in high respect?

Check this out
2 He grew up before him like a tender shoot,
and like a root out of dry ground.
He had no beauty or majesty to attract us to him,
nothing in his appearance that we should desire him.
3 He was despised and rejected by mankind,
a man of suffering, and familiar with pain.
Like one from whom people hide their faces
he was despised, and we held him in low esteem.

4 Surely he took up our pain
and bore our suffering,
yet we considered him punished by God,
stricken by him, and afflicted.

5 But he was pierced for our transgressions,
he was crushed for our iniquities;
the punishment that brought us peace was on him,
and by his wounds we are healed.
6 We all, like sheep, have gone astray,
each of us has turned to our own way;
and the LORD has laid on him
the iniquity of us all.

7 He was oppressed and afflicted,
yet he did not open his mouth;
he was led like a lamb to the slaughter,
and as a sheep before its shearers is silent,
so he did not open his mouth.
8 By oppression and judgment he was taken away.
Yet who of his generation protested?
For he was cut off from the land of the living;
for the transgression of my people he was punished.
9 He was assigned a grave with the wicked,
and with the rich in his death,
though he had done no violence,
nor was any deceit in his mouth.

10 Yet it was the LORD's will to crush him and cause him to suffer,
and though the LORD makes his life an offering for sin ~Isaiah 53

Is this the man that saved you?

Is this the man that by His death forgives you completely?

Is this the man you call lord and savior?

Is this the man you love and admire?

Is this the man who calls you his friend?

Is this the man that bore your sin?

Is this the man that gave you a new heart?

Or is this the man

That makes your life miserable?

Is this the man you blame for not giving you the life you think you want?

Is this the man that says to you – you can't have fun?

Is this the man that says to you have self control and you don't like it?

Is this the man you pretend to love?

Is this the man that you despise?

No?

How do you honor this man?

How do you show your love for this man?

How does the fact that He saved you change anything?

How does the fact that this man died on a cross to save you—change the way you live?

After all-- and by his wounds we are healed.
6 We all, like sheep, have gone astray,
each of us has turned to our own way;
and the LORD has laid on him
the iniquity of us all.

Honor: v. to hold in respect or esteem -- to show courteous behavior towards to worship--- to confer a distinction upon

You see honoring the one who saved you is a great thing.

Maybe people really don't believe they were saved from anything.

After all, if we do all the fixing ourselves—who the heck needs somebody to save our hearts and souls—we can do it ourselves

I know some people feel that way—

Here is the Christ who dies on a cross for the sin of mankind

Here is the Christ who takes 40 lashes on His back so that we can be healed

But we don't really need healing—right?

After all, we don't have problems with our hearts?

We aren't sick

Other people are sick

You know those sick who are into porn

Those sinful people who are into sex

Those twisted people who smoke dope everyday

Who love to drink and puke and just do stupid things

That man Jesus took all that for those types of people

But not us... our hearts are not that jacked up—at least we don't do those sick and twisted things-at least.....

not so that people can see it

We go to church
We aren't into partying on weekends—Really?
We don't use drugs. Hmmmm (not often)
We aren't having sex before marriage. (at least not that anyone knows about)

As far as honoring the one who did all that for me?

The person Jesus—the one who died on a cross—how do we honor Him?

Well?

While Jesus was walking this earth

There was a group of people that had no idea who Jesus was—

Jesus claims to be God in the Flesh, the Messiah

This group of people had nothing to do with Him

Matter of fact, they didn't think they needed a Savior for their broken live

The in their minds knew that they could save themselves

Jesus says

You hypocrites! Isaiah was right when he prophesied about you:

8 "'These people honor me with their lips,
but their hearts are far from me.
9 They worship me in vain;
their teachings are merely human rules.

Look my friends—

First of all you have to come to terms with this

This man—the son of God

Did he really take the grenade for you?

Did He really die on a cross for you?

If that is true

How do you honor Him?

All of mankind is broken

There are none righteous

People cannot save themselves

Peoples hearts are sick

People need the Savior

You need the savior

You me everyone in this world

Has tried to fix themselves

Rules won't do it

Rules are here to protect you

But not make you righteous

Rules are here all around to help you—following them may be part of honoring the one who died for you. But that does not bring righteousness.

Go a step further

You don't want to be like the Pharisees who practiced their

Set of rules and then talk and sing about a savior you don't believe in.

You don't want to play the game for someone you could care less about

You don't want to be like those who don't give a damn about the man that hung

On the cross

Who bore their sin

Who took on pain and suffering

If you think you can do it yourself

That is just flat out garbage and a lie from the pit of hell (humanism is alive and well)

But if you know the one who jumped on the grenade

If you believe that He bore your sickness and sin

If you believe that it is He that loves you

Then honor him with the way you live

Honor him with the way you love people

Honor him in the way you care about people

Honor him in the way you keep pure

Honor Him with your LIFE

Making a choice either way builds integrity.

I do Student Ministry. I have done it a long time. Yes, there have been many, many changes over the years. I remember when Bill Gothard was the man-- that was crazy (and not the man I listened to) I remember when the Band Kiss meant Kids in Satan Service-- pa lease. I remember when a youth group was about Sunday School, church attendance, ice cream socials and on and on. Oh, one more thing...

For those interested!   "for those who have ears to hear, let them hear."
Of course—meaning, you have got to be willing to apply my word
It doesn't happen by osmosis
And Jesus isn't going to pound it into you

When Jesus says this to His listeners He is giving them the choice to either listen and trust. Or not listen and they would be responsible for blowing Him off. Jesus didn't try and control people, He gave them a choice to listen or not listen.
1 Thing that hasn't changed over the years is this simple little truth.How we listen to Christ. How we love Christ. How we obey and live out our relationship with Christ is lived way past an hour or 2 on a Sunday or at an event.
How we listen or don't listen to the words of Christ are lived..

On the street
In the home
At work
With our friends
With our culture
With our neighbors
With our world

"For those that have ears to hear" is all about..
The Heart
Character
Conscience
Honesty
The opportunity that Jesus provides without twisting an arm. Now that is Godly, that is wisdom.

The Living Bible states Proverbs 10.9 like this: "A good man has firm footing, but a crook will slip and fall."
The King James states it this way:
"He that walks upright walks surely; but he that perverts his ways shall be known."
The NIV says this:
"The man of integrity walks securely, but he who takes crooked paths will be found out."

Integrity or <u>straightforwardness</u> or <u>strength</u> or <u>honesty</u> or <u>whole, complete</u>.

The word integrity carries with it a whole lot of meaning.
The integrity of a bridge depends on the <u>integrity of the beams</u>
The integrity of a building depends on a <u>sound foundation</u>.
The integrity of a person depends on their <u>volition, their will, the choices they make everyday</u>.
Integrity comes when one decides—<u>I will listen, I will obey, I will put into practice, it is my choice and I'm choosing to hear, to listen and to apply</u>.

I will do what I think. I will say what I think. I will be who I am.
In its simplest form—
What you see is what you get. There are no loose ends that threaten their reputation.

Think about it like this: It's as simple as being what you say you are.|

Let's apply:

- <u>The Lord searches our hearts. Psalm 139</u>
- <u>The Spirit knows all things Romans 8.27</u>
- <u>The Lord knows the thoughts of man Psalm 94.11</u>

I know many students who are not straight about their relationship with God. They should be able to be part of a ministry that does it like Jesus. If you want to "hear" join us. If you don't want to, that is o.k., still join us. You may someday want to listen. In the meantime, you can be honest here.

I say, teach students to understand--

If you want to walk with Jesus Christ
<u>Be straight with Him.</u>

If you want to have integrity with people
<u>Be straight with all people</u>

I am convinced that every student, from any walk of life, Christian home, Christian parents (by the way, those types of home do not guarantee healthy relationships), every student should be given the chance to hear and decide, and to hear and decide. To have opportunities to struggle, to wrestle with, to seek, to be honest enough to decide... I want to hear from Christ or I don't. Either way in the long haul of life at best they get to choose and that builds integrity. It might not be what we want, but hopefully they will find Jesus to be more than a forced Sunday School lesson or a forced 1 hour event once a week.

I believe that the hard hearted student, the most difficult students to deal with are those who have never been given the chance to decide to hear, to make the choice to either follow Christ because they made the choice or not.
Effective ministry says it like this:
"For those that have ears to hear, let them hear." In the meantime, you are welcome hear to decide.

Devotion

The Great Pursuer

1 "I revealed myself to those who did not ask for me;
I was found by those who did not seek me.
To a nation that did not call on my name,
I said, 'Here am I, here am I.'

2 All day long I have held out my hands
to an obstinate people,
who walk in ways not good,
pursuing their own imaginations-

3 a people who continually provoke me
to my very face,
offering sacrifices in gardens
and burning incense on altars of brick;
Is.65.1-3

Hmmmmmm-- does our God really pursue? Does God really reveal
himself? Who are the people that did not ask for Him? Can people
really find Him if they do not seek Him? Is that still true today?

Yes! But, if I listen to the 'ones" who know so much about God, what
hey have said-- "it's about the way we pursue Him that He reveals
himself. They say there are certain things you have to do to seek
Him. Really?

But that is not what He says--

I revealed myself to those who did not ask for me;
I was found by those who did not seek me.
To a nation that did not call on my name,
I said, 'Here am I, here am I.'

All day long I have held out my hands
to an obstinate people,
who walk in ways not good

I find this portion to be very interesting-- even more filled with hope-- for in this life, this world, this universe-- He is continuing to say-- Here am I, here am I"...to all peoples, to all those that don't know, that don't care, that are seeking everything else-- there is hope.

Thank you God for caring
When people don't.
Thank you God for stretching out your hand to me continually
Thank you God for finding me.
Continue to go after the students that are so far away.
Continue to Pursue Oh God, those that aren't even looking for you

Faith and the Potter's House

What does faith look like?

Or

If faith had a body, what would it do? Anything?
Just look good?
A statue?
A medallion around your neck?
A medal with a blue ribbon?

 What does your faith look like?
Active?
Seeking?
Steadfast?
Teachable?

What does our Faith look like?
Complaining?
Seeking?
Expanding?
Fleshed out?
Skeptical?
Burned out?
Just for Salvation?

Jeremiah 18.1-10
1 This is the word that came to Jeremiah from the LORD: 2 "Go down
to the potter's house, and there I will give you my message." 3 So I
went *down to the potter's house, and I saw him working at the wheel.
4 But the pot he was shaping from the clay was marred in his hands; so
the potter formed it into another pot, shaping it as seemed best to him.*

5 Then the word of the LORD came to me. 6 He said, "Can I not do
with you, Israel, as this potter does?" declares the LORD. "Like clay in
the hand of the potter, so are you in my hand, Israel. 7 If at any time I
announce that a nation or kingdom is to be uprooted, torn down and
destroyed, 8 and if that nation I warned repents of its evil, then I will
relent and not inflict on it the disaster I had planned. 9 And if at
another time I announce that a nation or kingdom is to be built up
and planted, 10 and if it does evil in my sight and does not obey me,
then I will reconsider the good I had intended to do for it.

The people of God = The clay
The Potter = God
Verse 4 "shaping it as seemed best to him."
The people of God, being shaped?

Does your journey of faith allow for this?
You know being shaped by God?
How does this feel?
What is that like?
Does your journey of faith produce a teachable heart?
Are you sure?
Lots of God's people are stuck.
"the way I was raised"
"we have always done it like this"
"unless God speaks to me…"
"I'll obey… when it's the way I want it."
Are those comments from people being molded,
Or already molded as far as they want to be?
Or just plain stuck as the mud?
Or just plain old stubborn beyond God?

Verse 4
The original pot was marred, so—
The potter molds a new one.

Verse 5-6
To the People of God, the house of Israel—
"Like clay in the hand of the potter"

Verse 7-10
The potter is about molding
The clay is about responding
The potter is about building even in the tearing down
The potter is about planting and building
The clay is about responding
Lets keenly look at specifics

Verse 9-10
Who builds and who plants nations?
Who builds and who builds Churches?

The answer

Verse 10
There are conditions!
Really?

Evil could wreck the building, the ministry,
What evil?

Disobedience!

What does disobedience look like?
According to this passage
-the lack of being moldable
-teachability
-personal agendas

In reality—the lack of Faith, that God's plan to build and plant and grow

Is exactly that-- His plan.

Seeking God Produces a Thankful Heart

What is that which brings you great Joy?
What are the things in which you take great pride?
What do you celebrate?

Chronicles 16.8-11

Give praise to the LORD, proclaim his name;
make known among the nations what he has done.
Sing to him, sing praise to him;
tell of all his wonderful acts.
Glory in his holy name;
let the hearts of those who seek the LORD rejoice.
Look to the LORD and his strength;
seek his face always

Glory in His holy name;
What are the things in which you take great pride?

Take Pride in God!

Let the hearts of those who seek the Lord rejoice!
Internally – Our hearts, as we run after or pursue God— we
Celebrate Him!

Seek God and Celebrate!

Look to the Lord and his strength;

Seek the Lord, study the Lord, further look; *check Him out and His power!*

Seek his face always!

Pursue His presence—at all times

Thanksgiving comes from Seeking
Look to the LORD and his strength;
seek his face always!

Isn't it true? That when you and I seek the Lord, we find Him to be all He says He is? That we find Him to be faithful. That we find Him to be strong. That we find Him able to take care of all of our needs. All of our hurts. That we do find Him to be strong and that fills us and we become thankful.

I have found over and over that as I seek the Lord, as I pursue Him, my heart becomes thankful period.

What's on the top of your list?

In the early morning hours of February 1st, 2003 the Space Shuttle Columbia disintegrated over Texas during re-entry into the earth's atmosphere. There were seven crew members aboard, the captain was Rick Husband.

I want to tell you a little bit about the Captain of the Columbia's last mission—Rick Husband.

This story is from a Columbia technician that knew Rick Husband. He said that after the astronauts suit up they walk down a hallway and then open a door to "face the press!" Rick stopped the crew before they opened the door and said he wanted to pray for them. Later the technicians talked about this and one said that in all his years he had never heard of a captain praying for and with his crew.

Rick Husband's wife told this story--The spouses of the crew each get to pick a song for them to wake up to one of the mornings they're in space. Rick's wife selected "God of Wonders" by Steve Green. Steve played a tape for us of Rick communicating with Mission Control after the song was played. The conversation went something like this: Mission Control - "Good morning. That song was for Rick. It was 'God of Wonders' by Steve Green." Rick - "Good morning. Thank you. We can really appreciate the lyrics of that song up here. We look out the window and see that God truly is a God of wonders!"

And-- Rick Husband himself wrote in his daily journal while in space about how overwhelming it was to see God's vast creation from space. He said he had never cried while exercising before, but peddling on the bike and looking out the window at God's incredible creation brought tears to his eyes.

Oh and one more thing about this captain, this follower of Christ, this man who was tragically killed on Feb 1st, 2003

His friend Steve Green said that Rick's son was around 5 years old and his daughter 10. and that Rick made 34 devotionals, by video, before he left on the Columbia. There were 17 for his daughter and 17 for his son, one for each day he was to be gone. So each day his daughter and son had their own "devotion with Dad" by video.

And Dad never came back to his earthly home—but—because of the way he lived his life— everyone knew what he believed—what he lived for—what made him tick—

His comrades
People outside of his circle of friends
His family
His children
Everyone he came in contact with knew what was on the top of his list--

Read—Luke 10.25-37
The question? Verse 25 "What must I do to get eternal life?"
Jesus answers with 2 questions Verse 26
"What is written in the law?"

"How do you read it?"

- <u>Priorities</u> Verse 27 <u>Beliefs = Behavior</u>

Loving God completely
Heart, soul, strength, and mind
Loving Neighbor as self

The 2 loves are a priority—one follows the other

- <u>Doing</u> Verse 28 <u>"... and you will live"</u>

Christian Problem:
Why is it that we (Christians) move toward the first and neglect the second?|
It's easier
It's what we've been taught
It makes us feel spiritual
Too time consuming
Others do it better

Francis Schaeffer says it like this
"Jesus' first commandment is to love the Lord your God with all your heart and soul and mind. And the second commandment is to love your neighbor as your self. The emphasis in our generation is on

subjective religious truth, and this is our great enemy. But it is also true that in the midst of fighting this enemy it is possible to back off the other side of the cliff, to think of these things only as dogmas, only creeds, only as bare propositions, and to forget that they have a personal aspect as well.

The end of the matter is not—it is not the bare dogma---even proper theological dogma; it is the propositional, true knowledge that has the result of our loving the Lord with all our heart and our neighbors as ourselves in our present moment by moment lives.

So then, what is on the top of your list today?
Everyday we have the opportunity to
Love God with all of our heart and soul and mind.
And to love our neighbor as ourselves.

Or course you know what happens next, right? Jesus shares the story of the Good Samaritan. The parable of the Good Samaritan is an example of a person living out loving God and loving his neighbor. How hard is it really to make the effort to love our neighbor? If we can't make this effort, what effort will we make?
Typical response
I had my devotions
I went to church
I pray
I fill myself with "How to love God"
I want so much to be like Jesus
I give when I can
I don't have time
I don't know any hurting people
Who is my neighbor?
Truthfully—I don't want to
So, when we acknowledged that Jesus is true, alive and in us
But, we make a choice to not heed His message, what is that called?
<u>Disobedience?</u>
<u>Free will?</u>
<u>Our rights?</u>
<u>Sin?</u>
What will we do to right this wrong?
Jesus said—"Go and do likewise" Well, when?
Well, what's on the top of your list?

Loving God, with all your
Heart
Soul
Strength
Mind

And loving humanity?
Look my friends—me must admit—to ourselves first—
That loving God with all our hearts--- looks like something---
and many, many believe that what it looks like is relative—
I love God and that is personal
I love God and I keep it to myself
I love God and I prove it by going to church—
I love God period—and what that looks like is
The way I was taught—
The way I am …. And nobody is going to tell me what that looks like

Except this—
That Jesus says it looks like the good Samaritan and not like the
Priest—
That passed him by
Not like the Levite that passed him by—both religious, pious people
that could say—I love God period.
Jesus rips the external code of their day and our day---
Loving God takes on the feet, the Hands, the mind of God—
As we love Him—it looks like something—it looks like people that
Show mercy
That Give
That care—
This is a story of priorities a—story of what is called being enmeshed
in wrong thinking and wrong living—There is a time in all of our
lives as followers that we can break the enmeshed power of thinking
like the many—Jesus said and you will know the truth and the truth
will set you free.

Have you ever noticed a follower of Christ—that you said—I
certainly hope my walk with God is not like that persons—it seems
so rote, so fake, so just going through the motions—there is no joy,
no sense of life, no sense of meaning to the religious activity.

Have you ever noticed a Christ follower that you said—how do they do it—how do they love like that? How do they give like that? How do they seem so like—so like a real Christ follower?

Well—at some point in time that person said—I'm going to follow after Christ like He wants me too—I'm going to leave the pack, and learn to love God a new. I'm going to Love God and let it shine through me— even it goes against the many, even if it goes against the way my parents do it, even if it goes against the way I was taught—

Loving God—and loving my neighbor looks like something—are you willing to put that at the top of your list? Are you willing to surrender everything to God this morning and become a lover of God and a lover of people?

Resolve

Are there things worth digging in for? You know, fighting for?
Are there things worth digging in against? You know fighting
against?
Is your faith part of the above?
How does the above manifest in your life?

Or is it – go with the flow, don't make any waves, keep the peace?

Daniel 1.1-7
1 In the third year of the reign of Jehoiakim king of Judah,
Nebuchadnezzar king of Babylon came to Jerusalem and besieged it.
2 And the Lord delivered Jehoiakim king of Judah into his hand,
along with some of the articles from the temple of God. These he
carried off to the temple of his god in Babylonia and put in the
treasure house of his god.

3 Then the king ordered Ashpenaz, chief of his court officials, to
bring into the king's service some of the Israelites from the royal
family and the nobility— 4 young men without any physical defect,
handsome, showing aptitude for every kind of learning, well
informed, quick to understand, and qualified to serve in the king's
palace. He was to teach them the language and literature of the
Babylonians. 5 The king assigned them a daily amount of food and
wine from the king's table. They were to be trained for three years,
and after that they were to enter the king's service.

6 Among those who were chosen were some from Judah: Daniel,
Hananiah, Mishael and Azariah. 7 The chief official gave them new
names: to Daniel, the name Belteshazzar; to Hananiah, Shadrach; to
Mishael, Meshach; and to Azariah, Abednego.

Jerusalem captured
Young men of Israel are to be trained in Babylonian culture
For the King's service

A Lesson on *Resolve*

Daniel 1.8-10
But Daniel resolved not to defile himself with the royal food and

wine, and he asked the chief official for permission not to defile himself this way. 9 Now God had caused the official to show favor and compassion to Daniel, 10 but the official told Daniel, "I am afraid of my lord the king, who has assigned your food and drink. Why should he see you looking worse than the other young men your age? The king would then have my head because of you."

Already in the King's service
A new King for Daniel?
Which will he choose?

Daniel has come to the 2 roads-- which will he choose?
The pay off or pay out?

Daniel 1.20
In every matter of wisdom and understanding about which the king questioned them, he found them ten times better than all the magicians and enchanters in his whole kingdom.

Digging in, when does it stop?
Can't there just be a little break?

Over 20 years of student ministry, and examples in my own life... when I resolve, make a choice to go with what I believe, what I know is right and stay with it, the 2 paths become just one.

Next up

Daniel 3.1-6
1 King Nebuchadnezzar made an image of gold, sixty cubits high and six cubits wide, and set it up on the plain of Dura in the province of Babylon. 2 He then summoned the satraps, prefects, governors, advisers, treasurers, judges, magistrates and all the other provincial officials to come to the dedication of the image he had set up. 3 So the satraps, prefects, governors, advisers, treasurers, judges, magistrates and all the other provincial officials assembled for the dedication of the image that King Nebuchadnezzar had set up, and they stood before it.

4 Then the herald loudly proclaimed, "Nations and peoples of every language, this is what you are commanded to do: 5 As soon as you

hear the sound of the horn, flute, zither, lyre, harp, pipe and all kinds of music, you must fall down and worship the image of gold that King Nebuchadnezzar has set up. 6 Whoever does not fall down and worship will immediately be thrown into a blazing furnace."

Daniel has to:
Not only serve the King
Bow down to the King

2 Paths again
What will Daniel Do and his friends do?

Question
Would it be that bad to fudge a little?
You know, keep everybody happy. Especially the king?

Daniel 3.8-15
8 At this time some astrologers came forward and denounced the Jews. 9 They said to King Nebuchadnezzar, "May the king live forever! 10 Your Majesty has issued a decree that everyone who hears the sound of the horn, flute, zither, lyre, harp, pipe and all kinds of music must fall down and worship the image of gold, 11 and that whoever does not fall down and worship will be thrown into a blazing furnace. 12 But there are some Jews whom you have set over the affairs of the province of Babylon—Shadrach, Meshach and Abednego—who pay no attention to you, Your Majesty. They neither serve your gods nor worship the image of gold you have set up."

13 Furious with rage, Nebuchadnezzar summoned Shadrach, Meshach and Abednego. So these men were brought before the king, 14 and Nebuchadnezzar said to them, "Is it true, Shadrach, Meshach and Abednego, that you do not serve my gods or worship the image of gold I have set up? 15 Now when you hear the sound of the horn, flute, zither, lyre, harp, pipe and all kinds of music, if you are ready to fall down and worship the image I made, very good. But if you do not worship it, you will be thrown immediately into a blazing furnace. Then what god will be able to rescue you from my hand?"

The Answer?

Daniel 3.16-18

"We will not bow down period."
because Our God is able to save us—
But, even if He (the real King) does not—
"We have *resolve.*"

Application:
There are things worth digging in for. Are there any being neglected in your life? Your children, your marriage, your walk with God?

People will always be unhappy with our resolve, when will that be o.k. for you?

A life of faith is not the same as opinions, family background, experience and other "spiritual" mumbo jumbo. In other words—faith in God is just that. His character, His word, His truth, His way. There are a lot of things being said about God that aren't worth dying for. There are things about God that are worth everything. Resolve does matter.

A life of Faith trusts God even if the outcome could be painful.

Note: Antonyms from the word-- Backbone: ineptness, powerlessness, spinelessness, weakness.

Love is STRONG.

Place me like a seal over your heart,
like a seal on your arm;
for love is as strong as death,
its jealousy unyielding as the grave.
It burns like blazing fire,
like a mighty flame.
Many waters cannot quench love;
rivers cannot sweep it away.
~Song of Solomon 8.6,7

How strong is Love? Really? Does love go away?   I don't have a
Hebrew Lexicon in front of me, nor do I have a commentary, so I'm
just taking these 2 verses at face value.

Love is a word that is thrown around all over the place. I love you, I
love this, I love that... we love to love. Right? Love makes the world
go around. Love makes life better. Love is a many splendid thing
right? (Sorry, that is an old soap opera title) Nevertheless most of us
if not 99% of us love and enjoy love, love to be loved and love to give
love right?

I have thought about these 2 verses over the past few weeks. I have
thought about the context of this passage, love for another, a strong
powerful love for someone as in this passage. A love that "is as
strong as death" a love that "burns like a might flame" a love so on
fire that "many waters" cannot quench it. Now that is a powerful
statement. A powerful picture, indeed, a powerful love that is almost
inconceivable. Right?

After all haven't we all "been in love"? Used the word Love,
expressed the word love, felt this kind of love?

The longer I live this life, I'm starting to get a fuller (not complete)
but a fuller idea of this strong, powerful, unquenchable kind of love.
Really? Well, yes. I was once told by either my dad or a very
important person that I believed in-- not to throw those 3 words
around to just anybody. "I love you" is a powerful statement and I
did listen to those words. I didn't throw those 3 words around
because I somehow innately knew that those 3 words represented

something much greater than I. That those 3 words were not just a statement for 2 people that were getting closer, or were "possibilities". No, I think I understood in some form that God was love, that God loves so much that He was willing to show the statement "I love you" to the fullest. God does love, and His love is a blazing fire that cannot be quenched. Meaning that love lasts, and lasts and goes on as fire that will never be put out.

You know, I feel that. I actually understand that kind of love a little bit more these days. How long does love last? I know I have had my fleeting moments of love and then on to the next thing to be passionate about, or the next cause to embrace with love, or the next person that needs to know they are loved and on and on. But this love in Song of Solomon is a picture of God's unfailing and immovable love towards us and that it can be a reality to love.

When I look back at love in my life, I actually understand this kind of strong love. While yes these verses are about 2 people, and yes this book Song of Solomon is about 2 people, and yes this love is strong and powerful and this kind of love does not go away because while this love from this passage of Scripture could be taken as romantic or for only 2 people, these verses to me actually point to the definition of love. Love is strong, unquenchable through, good, bad, hard times, through mistakes, through failure, through time.... really? I know first hand that many waters cannot quench it, that love may burn sometimes very dim, but it cannot be put out, that love does not go away regardless of life's tough, unrelenting ticking. I know first hand this kind of love because it does not go away-- ever. Now that is love. Now read the words from David Crowder and consider the love defined in Song of Solomon--

He is jealous for me,
Loves like a hurricane, I am a tree,
Bending beneath the weight of his wind and mercy.
When all of a sudden,
I am unaware of these afflictions eclipsed by glory,
And I Realize just how beautiful You are,
And how great Your affections are for me.

And oh, how He loves us so,
Oh how He loves us,
How He loves us all

Yeah, He loves us,
Whoa! how He loves us,
Whoa! how He loves us,
Whoa! how He loves.
Yeah, He loves us

We are His portion and He is our prize,
Drawn to redemption by the grace in His eyes,
If grace is an ocean, we're all sinking.
So Heaven meets earth like a sloppy, wet kiss,
And my heart turns violently inside of my chest,
I don't have time to maintain these regrets,
When I think about, the way…
He Loves
~David Crowder

What can stop that kind of affection that kind of love? What can put
out that kind of Love?
That kind of love lasts forever!   I love it!

He Lives! Really? What difference does it make?

"He is not here; he has risen, just as he said. Come and see the place where he lay." ~Matthew 28.6

"To them God has chosen to make known among the Gentiles the glorious riches of this mystery, which is Christ in you, the hope of glory. ~Colossians 1.27

"And if Christ has not been raised, our preaching is useless and so is your faith." 1 Corinthians 15.14

Easter. He is risen. Right? So? What does that mean? What is the value of the Risen Savior? What does it mean? What's the big deal? I have celebrated Easter since I can remember. I was given new suits for the 2 hours at church. I went to huge family dinners. What is the big deal?

Christ alive. What does it mean? There was a time in my life that it was all about the "knowledge" at least I knew in my head the basics-- you know, Virgin Birth, death on a cross, risen on the third day. So? I also know today plenty of students, plenty of people that know the whole shabang. Celebrate Easter-- dress up, go to church, and then go eat. What difference does it make?

Personally it means: "...the glorious riches of this mystery, which is Christ in you, the hope of glory." ~Colossians 1.27 Christ lives in me. By faith I received the whole shabang. You see, I believe with my heart that Jesus the Christ the Savior of the world took upon Himself all of my sin. He was murdered and He rose from the dead. My sin forgiven and forever gone. By faith I receive His robe of righteousness and nothing I can do will add to it or take away from it.

By faith He is in my heart, He is Alive in me, therefore my life is His to do what He so chooses. He guides me, He leads me, He speaks to me. I desire His things, I want His ways. Does it mean I always live like that 100% of the time? No. Truth is-- without Him in my life, I would love all the external things, the list, the outward approval, I would appreciate sin, I would move toward everything my flesh loves to indulge. If Christ were dead I would not get near religion, or those that practice a dead religion with all the silly rule that go along with it. I would not listen to those that would want me to believe in a dead leader, nor would I care. I would not care about anything but me and me alone. Kinda like those that "know" the story, that have said they "know" the story, but whether He is Alive or dead makes no difference.

How bout you? Does the Alive Christ live in you?

I know there are many judgers, haters out there-- in the church, and outside the church. They want the Alive Christ to look like they think He should look. They love the list, they love to be the Holy Spirit, they love to point out what they think about this or that or how they think I should live, look like and ultimately "be like"-- but Christ is in me, Christ is Alive, Christ is leading, Christ breaks down the "stuff".

I am thankful for the Risen, Alive Savior.

How does one really live as Christ is Alive? By Faith period. "For it is by grace you have been saved, through faith—and this is not from yourselves, it is the gift of God— 9 not by works, so that no one can boast." Ephesians 2.8,9

I see so many stuck. So many that believe in other "stuff" oh Christ is Alive, and Christ has forgiven them-- but somehow the works, the idea that you or I can add or subtract from His raising from the dead is what its all about. That is nonsense period. Time to let the Risen Christ, the Alive Christ live in you or can you do it better? So what that He is alive, what difference does it make?

"And if Christ has not been raised, our preaching is useless and so is your faith." 1 Corinthians 15.14

Christ is Risen indeed!

Ministry

Next Gen Leader—What matters most to me?

I have one of the most awesome, incredible, rewarding, and difficult jobs in the world—sometimes! So, What are the things I think about? What are the things that matter to me—leading the Next Gen ministry?

After 20 years or so of Student ministry—High School mainly and a Church plant pastor--- what matters to me? What do I see? What do I feel? What am I hearing? A few things come to my lil ole mind and heart. What is this Generation going to do? To do about Jesus? To do about knowledge? To do with the local church?

For starters—How many students that are sold out followers of Christ in this generation care about the local church? How many hear from their parents that the local church is not important—oh not by their words per se, but by the way they treat leaders, attendance, giving and the like. I see students today—with not much support of the local church by their parents— which trickles down to the student which in turn is lived out as a take or leave it (a no big deal attitude) the church should be this or that, I'm not getting fed, I'm going to get my stuff somewhere else, I don't need the church or I'll go find a place that suits me and my needs, and when the new joint fails—I'll go find another one.

Is that the way it is? To a degree—yes it is. I know, I work with the students that complain, opt out, are apathetic, come to things that are only "their thing" and so on. I believe that this behavior is learned and enabled by parents that finally decided, "Hey, church is not such a big deal, I can be involved in my little clique of people I like, I'll just do the minimum." After all, the local church isn't that big of a deal.

I am a parent—both my boys have said—"I hate this, I don't want to go, I don't like the youth guy, I'm not interested." So—I could have said—"you are going to go and like it." Or "o.k., go else where" or forget it." But I didn't. —I just said—we as a family are going—and I want you to give it a try—church is important, and being part of the youth ministry is important, and I'm asking you to give it a try."

They would ask—for how long? And I would respond—just give it a try and we will talk about it.

Why? Why give it a try? Because—the local church matters to God. The Ecclesia is important. The local church is God's tool for the world to see, touch, and for "followers" of Christ to Love one another. Paul even states that "a man should love their wife as Christ loves the church. Pretty important kind of love, don't you think?

So—What matters to me? That the Next Gen will follow the Living Christ because they made the choice to follow Him. That the Next Gen will follow Him no matter what happens. That the Next Gen will love the local church. That the Next Gen will embrace the local church, that the Next Gen will be loyal to God's purposes through the local church—

Sad to say—that many, many parents—are not teaching the above— in reality—the ministry I work in at best is with students only 3-6 hours a week—where is the real influence?   Home—parents do matter—attitude is caught not taught—love for the local church is modeled— and finally many things said contradict just attending— you can't serve 2 masters—and students in return model what they see and hear—many, many unconnected students— is it not enough programs? Is it not enough bible teaching, is it not enough whatever? I contend that when the church no longer becomes the place to get, but the place to give, to serve, to engage, to call home, a healthy love for the church begins to grow.

Some could read this and say "Hey, what about knowing Christ?" Of course that is the most important thing. I'm not talking about any student.   I am talking about those that know Him, follow Him, trust Him. These students are the first that hopefully will love the local church, will give to the cause of the local church, will speak highly of the local church, will care about the local church, will be part of the local church for the rest of their lives.

What am I most concerned about?   The Next Generation embracing the local church with the heart of the one who loves it so much that He is returning for it. I believe that this generation can do huge things for God through the local church.

Live like a Champion today

Play (LIVE) like a champion today!

Proverbs 22.29

"Do you see a man skilled in his work? He will serve before kings; he will not serve before obscure men."

The issue for us!

People who are skilled are MADE, not born.

Leaders work hard at their passions.
People that love their God, pursue vigorously His likeness.
No one comes into the world as a person of excellence. It takes work.

To become such a person takes time, effort, diligence, and most of all desire.

Some things to ponder.

What do you desire most?

- What are you passionate about?
- What do you want to be known for?
- How much are you willing to put into your desires, and passions?

What are the top three things you want to do well?

Parent?
Walk with Christ?
Good marriage?
Successful business?
What are you willing to risk?

"A skilled" person will hone the answer to that question and work at results.

This is a trustworthy statement: The people who rise to the top and stay there are those who pay the price in long hours of study, preparation and practice.

"The quality of a person's life is in direct proportion to their commitment to excellence, regardless of their chosen field of endeavor." ~Vince Lombardi

Solomon is speaking about a life of <u>excellence.</u>
The story of the excellent harp player
1rst Samuel 16.17-22
This young man was know for:
How well he played
Brave
A warrior
He speaks well
Good looking
The Lord is with Him

Many would say that last ingredient is what made David great.

Not so—What made David great?
He worked hard at his skills
He cared about the right things
Excellence mattered.

David was prepared for his time.
God honored his hard work.

Excellence matters
Our Church
Our families
Our walk
Our lives

But how?

Legalism verses boundaries.
My take-- legalism is the idea that rules and regulations bring righteousness.
Setting boundaries and goals brings excellence.

Set goals in your life.
Set boundaries to accomplish these goals.

Remember—setting boundaries and goals does not bring righteousness. It brings quality to your life.

A couple of helps—It's easy
Do life with passion
Get rid of Apathy
Go to work on time
Have dinner together
Have down time
Make time for Christ
Pray
Read
Run your house—don't let the children
Take care of your stuff
Most of all—follow your passion and make it excellent.

Why?

You are preparing for serving the King.
Live like a champion today!

Friends and the change of direction

"One who has unreliable friends soon comes to ruin, but there is a friend who sticks closer than a brother." ~Proverbs 18:24

I know, it has been a while since I blogged. This time of year is so so busy. Fall kick off stuff, new things underway, seems like 24 hours in a day just isn't enough.

So, I'm talking with a student today and he shares with me some of the "issues" he is facing. Like loneliness as he watches his friends self destruct. Should he continue to be close to them? What does he do? No doubt I see this dilemma all the time. Really I do. I just went out to BGSU to visit my son and he stated the same issue. It's tough when the people all around you are going down a different path than you.

Sometimes, students may feel that they shouldn't do anything. After all their "friends" may think they are being judged. Not true though. Not true at all. The truth is that the student that has chosen not to do or be what his "friends" are doing or being is absolutely correct in avoiding the stuff that he doesn't want to be around. It's a choice he must make, just as "friends" make the choice to do what they want to do. Isn't is true that this generation is overly concerned with "what people will think" that they will leave, or put aside their personal choice for the approval of others.

Here in lies the hard stuff as the NextGen pastor. I see students everyday that are leaving the "stuff" they were taught as important for the attitudes, the junk, the substance, the parties and so on. In truth there is not much I can do if at home there is denial from parents, or maybe even a sense from a parent "I don't know what do?" going on without seeking help. Partnering with parents is huge but I don't find enough takers in this area. I think most parents know that all is not going well, but stepping in may just be too hard for most.

Back to the student I was talking with-- He is really struggling with his friends-- actually he is saddened, his heart is breaking because his friends are heading in the wrong direction. He just doesn't know what to do because

1. The fear of being judged for walking away.
2. The question of what he should do?
3. The problem with his own questions of himself and his relationship of God being in question

First off, I have no problem helping this student recognize that walking away is o.k. If, his "friends" are causing him to stumble, it is right to put distance between he and his friends. That is not judgmental even if P.C. Christians call that harsh or mean or whatever. It is important for him at this time in his life to develop new friendships and a steadfastness in who he is becoming.

As this student struggles with his own faith because he is watching many of his "church" friends head down a destructive path, he is seeing first hand and beginning to understand that following Christ is not about having or being happy, circumstances turning out "right" and everything always together. He is learning that following Christ is just that, following Christ as this young man walks through life hits the bumps, the pits, the up and downs. While his friends bail on what was once an important part of their life (if it really was theirs-- could be the truth is that it was merely for mom or dad or...)

Nevertheless, this young man is seeing life as tough, choices he must make not everyone will like or accept. He is also learning that the love for friends comes with a price. Love does do the hard things. Love does stand for right things. Love does care about others and that doesn't always feel good. Love does determine priorities and if loving God takes a back seat to friends that don't care, then sometimes one must motor on, be there when "friends" get honest. But love does not enable "friends" to self destruct by being P.C. Or the fear of losing that friendship.

The truth for this student and for me is that it really does break our hearts to watch student after student, friend after friend, chose to forsake great stuff for what we all know full well is a lifestyle that is selfish, destructive and painful for all.

It is a hard time of life for students as they decide who to follow, who to love, how to be a friend, and all that goes with being a friend. Life is tough at times, but this I do know-- that this young man does have a true friend as he continues to call out to Him, tell Him, talk to Him and follow Him.

"One who has unreliable friends soon comes to ruin, but there is a friend who sticks closer than a brother." ~Proverbs 18:24

de·ter·mi·na·tion

1. the <u>act</u> of coming to a decision or of fixing or settling a purpose.

I have been thinking a lot about this word determination. I am not sure that determination is used much these days. Let me explain.

This word determination is an important word. Especially when talking about NextGen, parenting, living life, overcoming, discipleship/following Christ. I remember when I was a high school student. I was involved in many things and in the many things there were things I was determined to accomplish and in others not so much. I was a swimmer and I was determined to do the best I could. I did. I know I did, I spent many mornings in the pool, many after schools in the pool, lifting weights and so on. When I was in my 40's I was determined to bench press 400 lbs and I went past my goal. When I was in school I was determined to graduate from High School and I did.

That stuff seems now just a blip on the radar screen.

Of course I lead a ministry called NextGen. I work directly with a staff of 5 people, I lead the High School ministry, I speak to students every week, I interact with students from all over the place. Some are students that have grown up in the church. Some students come from homes without a church background. Some students have much head knowledge, some students don't know much about the Bible, or Christ, or the church, or theology. Some students want to love the Lord with all their hearts and some students only want the benefits of trusting Christ for eternity. Some students want to love the Lord and fit in, some students want to follow Christ with everything they have.

The point?

I was thinking about my own High School days and my lack of determination when it came to following Christ. I actually believed-- that following Christ was more about kinda like being a sponge-- you know, going to church, hanging out at the student ministry, having church friends, going to events and so on. I didn't really get that being determined was part of following Christ. It wasn't until I started to understand the difficulties of life, the difficulties of living this thing called following Christ, the difficulties of being like Him while being pulled from every direction, from everything from what girl to date, to how far I can go, to how bad is pot really, to why not do what everyone else is doing to why follow Christ anyhow? And I grew up knowing a whole bunch.

And so, NextGen ministry has many like me. Many that believe that following Christ is about desire yes, without much determination. If I can follow Christ by faith, by His Grace, He accepts me as I am, then why work at this relationship? Right? After all, I desire to love Him, I desire to follow Him isn't that enough?

I am in my 18th year of sobriety. I remember the day I started. I was determined to quit. I was determined to live without it. Yes, I had a desire but desire was the first thing. Then it was time to get determined. It was time to daily seek God for His help, it was time to face the cravings, my want to self-medicate, my want to drink again. And I will say this... I was determined and that price was high and I am still determined not to go there ever again.

Determination matters. When students want to follow Christ, determination plays a huge part in how that following will go. Really? Yes. If a student says, I want to get a 4.0 and is a student that knows it will take lots of work, they by sheer determination can reach their goal. When a couple walks the isle and says their vows that marriage can make it with much determination. I know, I have been married for 25 years and it ain't easy. Determination has played a huge role in my marriage. When I went back to school to study youth ministry at age 27 I was determined to graduate and I had been asked not to go back to one school, I had floundered around studying all my life, I didn't even know how to study. When I went back to school I was married taking 25 hours in a semester and I was determined to do well. Low and behold I finished with a 3.8 out of sheer determination period.

I am watching many students really struggling with their relationship with Christ these days-- just like I did. Have they decided to give it all they got? Have they said I will drop everything to follow Christ? Have they said I will do it no matter what? I will follow Him with every last drop of my will? That is the question.

I see it in my own 2 sons. I see it in adults around me. Following Christ isn't easy. There are none perfect. But desire is not the only thing one needs (Just read Romans chapter 8) No, determination is an ingredient that is missing for many. Yes, we all are determined to make money. We all want good things, we all will work extra hours for a raise. We all are determined to chase the dream. But are we determined to follow Christ with everything we have, we are, we can give?

Determination is an important word when it comes to following Christ. I know that I am not the poster boy for determination all the time. I know full well that my I like everyone else understands that my flesh is weak. But, without determination, without fixing our sights on a target we won't hit anything.
Yes, the challenge today is to assists students in their determination or lack thereof to follow the Christ in every situation, every dream, every goal, everything that this life will bring.

Proverbs 4.25
Let your eyes look straight ahead; fix your gaze directly before you.

Then he called the crowd to him along with his disciples and said: "Whoever wants to be my disciple must deny themselves and take up their cross and follow me.   Mark 8.34

I can think of many ways the determination looks and feels, and its outcome. One of the reasons I do NextGen ministry is:

5 In your relationships with one another, have the same mindset as Christ Jesus:

6 Who, being in very nature God,
did not consider equality with God something to be used to his own advantage;
7 rather, he made himself nothing

by taking the very nature of a servant,
being made in human likeness.
8 And being found in appearance as a man,
he humbled himself
by becoming obedient to death—
even death on a cross! ~Philippians 2

Christ was determined and without determination not much really can get accomplished.

Sadly, I have watched many many students struggling with this life called following Christ lately. No doubt desire is good but it can only go so far. With much determination to a life given to following Christ much newness, much vigor, much joy, much can be accomplished.

"Every wall is a door. Whatever course you decide upon, there is always someone to tell you that you are wrong. There are always difficulties arising which tempt you to believe that your critics are right. To map out a course of action and follow it to the end requires courage."
Ralph Wald Emerson

Last little note. With God, with faith in the Living Christ much can be accomplished no question, I know many that stop there. Try this-- wake up everyday and ask God to help you to do, to be all that He wants you to be and then press on through every situation as He is with you. Determine to live for Him daily and go for it.

I see Zombies

The Zombie craze is all around right? There are television shows about zombies, of course movies, the Zombie craze is all around for sure. I remember the first Zombie movie I ever watched. The year was 1967 the first Night of the Living Dead came out. I watched that movie around 1970 with my sister in black and white of course and I will admit as an 11 year old I was freaked out. I didn't like Zombie movies back then and I'm not that big of a fan of them now.

Interesting on this Halloween day that I am thinking about Zombies. Right? Seriously. You should be asking what is my deal? Right? Zombie movies. Zombies? Truth is, I know many Zombies. I see Zombies everyday. I talk to Zombies, I try and help Zombies. I was once a Zombie.

You know? A Zombie. A person that is dead, walking around in a dead body looking for others to prey on. A Zombie. Know any? A Zombie. They walk around with no joy in their life. They have no smile, no laugh, no passion (except when their football team is winning) They even come to church for an event called worship. I know lots of Zombies. Zombies are all around.

You know the Bible speaks of Zombies. Check it out.

"As for you, you were dead in your transgressions and sins, in which you used to live when you followed the ways of this world and of the ruler of the kingdom of the air, the spirit who is now at work in those who are disobedient. All of us also lived among them at one time, gratifying the cravings of our flesh following its desires and thoughts." Ephesians 2.1-3

Yes, I was a Zombie. I was dead in sin, walking around, running around, following my personal need to feed my flesh. Now don't you find that statement by Paul interesting today? Zombies are all around. Dead, but feeding the flesh. Hmmmmmmmmmmm Yes, I was once a true Zombie.Do you know any Zombies?

How bout the Zombie maybe a son or a daughter that is pursuing all the stuff that feeds the flesh? How bout you? Is all the stuff out there what you crave? Do your thoughts, my thoughts the things we pursue bring life? What are the things that feed you? What are the things that give you a little life in the Zombie state? I was once a Zombie. My parents were like, "Hey you coming to church?" I would be like, no way. Why would I go to something that is not exciting? Why would I care about something that gives my nothing. Oh, I'm alone in this? Really? I see Zombies all around. They are just like I was and nothing was going to snap them out of the Zombie state. Nothing.

So, what does a youth pastor do? I mean really? Students with no real joy, just looking for the next thing to give them a little life. Students and parents that just attend. People that only know an hour or 2 a week called church. They attend, but where is the life? You see, I love the Zombies. I care about the Zombies. I know how much greater life can be when one is truly alive. I want to reach all Zombies.

Paul answers the Zombie problem in Ephesians 2.4-10
"But because of his great love for us, God, who is rich in mercy, made us alive with Christ even when we were dead in transgressions—it is by grace you have been saved. And God raised us up with Christ and seated us with him in the heavenly realms in Christ Jesus, in order that in the coming ages he might show the incomparable riches of his grace, expressed in his kindness to us in Christ Jesus. For it is by grace you have been saved, through faith—and this is not from yourselves, it is the gift of God— not by works, so that no one can boast. For we are God's handiwork, created in Christ Jesus to do good works, which God prepared in advance for us to do."

How does a Zombie come to Life? We are made alive with Christ because of Grace through believing in the Son of God that died on the cross, took all our Zombie tendencies (our desires for the flesh) as we were walking around dead.
So why all the Zombies? Am I being judgmental? Not at all. Just stating an observation. For if a person that was once a Zombie but now is made alive with Christ wouldn't that look like someone alive? Unless of course the Zombie still believes that somehow they must do.

That they must continue to work for their life. After a certain point the Zombie remains a Zombie because there is not Alive Christ in them. The Alive Christ is something unattainable. The Alive Christ is for someone else. For those that need forgiveness. For those that have done awful things. The Alive Christ was a prayer a long time ago. Grace to the Zombie is a myth. They will keep working for life. The Alive Christ is no where to be found in the way they live life. No? That is not the case?

Ever wonder why it is so hard for those that have received the free gift of grace to at least be kind. At least care, at least want to share this New Alive with Christ thing with others? After all, the outcome of Grace, receiving this free gift by faith produces something. Right? Ephesians 4.10 says it like this:
"For we are God's handiwork, created in Christ Jesus to do good works, which God prepared in advance for us to do."

Are you a Zombie or is the Alive Christ in you? The Walking Dead going through the motions, or is the Alive Christ in you?

Ministry is hard work.

"...through painful toil you will eat food from it
all the days of your life.
It will produce thorns and thistles for you,
and you will eat the plants of the field.
By the sweat of your brow
you will eat your food..."
Genesis 3.17-19

1 Thessalonians 1.2-3 2 "We always thank God for all of you and
continually mention you in our prayers. We remember before our
God and Father your work produced by faith, your labor prompted
by love, and your endurance inspired by hope in our Lord Jesus
Christ."

I am moved at these words of Paul. Sometimes in the long haul of
Student Ministry the word "work" can sometimes be misunderstood,
written off, even looked down upon. Sometimes the word "work" can
be marginalized as if working and ministry shouldn't go together.
After all, we (youth ministry people) build relationships. We don't
pursue #'s. We don't do things like other churches. We don't work;
work is what the corporate world does. We do ministry and that to
some these days in not the same as work. At least, if I'm honest... I
have even said that. When my ministry was flat. When it seemed my
bag of tricks was gone. When it seemed that the Sr. Pastor wanted
more from me. When I may have felt that the board was looking at
me funny. When I was burnt out. When I had had enough of spinning
all the plates...I found myself speaking badly about work/ministry.

You see, I have been at this thing called ministry now for almost half
my life. I know that when I was a young buck doing Student Ministry
I was all about ministry. Yes, sometimes I was driven by #'s.
Sometimes I was driven by approval. Sometimes I was driven to be
liked, to be smart, to be the guy that knew more, or was this or that
or even better. I didn't think that it was work driving me. Work was
what the world did. I was doing ministry. For me working hard at the
wrong things made ministry a lousy endeavor, and the easy way out
was to blame working hard on my situation.

At some point I think we all come to the place where we get our issues brought to light and then if one so chooses can work at getting things in the area of work and motives straightened out. Being driven and working hard in my estimation is not the same. Ultimately the benefit of all who partake in the adjustment go on a little painful but in the end a relief as new important adjustments take place. Most likely a new vision, a new work ethic can be established and the jumping out of the sheets to go to work/ministry become a reality.

I left student ministry after a long stint at 1 church for almost 10 years. I thought my time was done. I was ready to go be part of a place where I was the boss, the senior guy. I believed that it was my time to preach, to do ministry with adults. So, I went to a 4 year old church plant. Short story, after 3 years I left the church plant. I had preached at least 100 sermons and more. I had developed a building program. The church wasn't growing, the church was standing still and I just plain gave up. So I went out to find a job. Oh, I looked at all the church employment placement places, I wrote letters, sent out resumes, and not many were calling for me. God had a plan and I had no idea what it was, nevertheless I landed a job in corporate sales. Landing the job was brutal.

When I met with the CFO/CEO he looked at my resume and said "So, you have been in ministry for 15 years? "Why do you want to sell?" And I humbly said, "I need a job." I need to WORK there is that word- - work. I needed a job. I needed to work. I was hired and this CEO was my boss. So what did I do? I worked my tail off. I wanted him to see that we pastor's work hard no matter what. Interesting that in this day and age I often hear some youth pastors talking badly about hard work. After all some have said, "ministry and work aren't the same." Or are they?

I believe that ministry is the hardest of work. It's hard because there are students that need to be reached. It's hard because there are expectations of building a ministry and not just maintaining. It's hard work because there are fights to fight. There are people to deal with. There is a flow of work to pursue. There are budgets to make. There are strategies to put in place and then work toward. There is much to do.

To those that put down corporate church work. The 3 years I was in the real corporate world I can say that I am glad-- I am thankful, I am a different person for working with people that pursued the task at hand everyday. I am a different person because I loved the challenge of prospecting. I loved working to produce. I loved helping my customers. I loved hearing from new customers that came over to my product because I went the extra mile. I pursued, I pushed, I planned, I strategized, and I prayed everyday that I would make a difference in the office and to the people with which I worked. I made my job my ministry. When my boss said "I should be putting in 60-75 hours" I went for it. If I could do it for the this guy, I certainly can do it for the Lord. At least that is how I felt about it. I had to learn the hard way once again-- ministry is as unto the Lord and it is lots of hard work. I wasn't driven by money or things or the corporate ladder.

This new job was about working hard for the benefit of my family, the benefit of those around me, the benefit of a CEO that didn't believe that people in ministry worked hard and for the benefit of those that have distinguished between ministry and work. I was in corporate world but my goals, my purpose, my desires were about things that to me were of high value and I was willing to go the distance.

I do believe that parents and students should be practicing a relationship with Christ that is more than church attendance or even doing things. I do believe I must hemorrhage in order for students to bleed. (Leading by example) I do believe in doing things with purpose. I do believe in building relationships with students. I do believe that I need to spend time with my team. I do believe that there aren't enough hours in a day to accomplish things that I am called to do period. So herein lies the rub. I do believe that pursuing Godly things in ministry is right period. I do believe that reaching students is a high value that student ministry should be about. Some would call it #'s. I don't. The easiest thing in student ministry to do is maintain a happy youth group. Really? Really.

So here I am at 52 with people that may think... what is he doing in student ministry again? Well... I am finishing raising 2 boys from high school and sending them off to college. I look at High School parents much different now that I have been in the trenches. How I deal with parents now is way different then the way I dealt with parents back in the day. I was a parent during some tough times for my guys; some parents need some tough words given to them about the things going on with their students. Tough words are hard work. Tough words for those afraid of hard work often opt out. "It's too hard. It's too tough. I like safe and easy."

Students, parents, churches need you to go all in. If not, maybe it is time to go all out. Students and parents are in need of leaders that lead by going all out for the right things. Speaking against the P.C. world. Showing students and families that the local church is loved by Jesus Christ. That the local church with all it's blemishes is the place where you work not because you get a pay check, but because you believe in it and love it. That the local church as corporate as it may be is where you get paid to give your all. I look back at over 20 years of student ministry and I can say that I work harder today then I ever did before. 2 reasons:

1. There is not much effort placed in just maintaining a youth ministry. The world today is absolutely crazier then it was 20 years ago... and I believe I – we have the answer-- the power for transforming lives is found in the Gospel. Making ministry outward focused is about believing that the Gospel is still the vehicle in which God transforms students-- all people... so keep the mission clear.
2. I believe that hard work is the essence for ministry. Ministry is work and work is ministry. Just like spirituality does not happen by just sticking students in a Bible Study or "Sunday School" class. Students today need a ministry working hard to reach them, to guide them, to help them, to be honest with them to be even what parents are not-- that is hard work. What they don't need in my estimation is a glorified YMCA. Spinning plates to appease people is work for sure, but is it the right work you want to spend your time doing. Stop spinning plates and get back to working lean. Don't be afraid of hard work.

After all-- the people of Thessalonica were remembered for-- "*We remember before our God and Father your work produced by faith, your labor prompted by love, and your endurance inspired by hope in our Lord Jesus Christ.*"

Things to do:

- Build a team around you that want to work hard at their giftedness for you and your vision. (they believe in you and the ministry)
- Don't bring warm bodies on any more. You need go getters.
- Ask for vision, seek God for vision and then go and get it.
- Chase it, live it, breath it, don't give up.
- Take your days off and take them off.
- Get your Faith on. Trust God with His vision and go.
- When you face a difficult time-- don't blame people, or the church or your boss. Take some time to get re energized and get back at it.
- Break down the stuff you do just to do and don't do it anymore. Simplify to get the Maximum out of your hard work.

Just some words of wisdom from an old youth guy that is still going for it! I believe that working hard as unto the Lord is a great, great endeavor. If you ever want to talk or chat or need a friend...feel free to contact me.

Making the Hard calls

The Hard calls of Ministry

Being a parent has meant and still means making hard calls.

When I was a student, my parents had to make hard calls. I know for a fact that I kept things from parents so they wouldn't make the hard calls. I also know that when I was a student and I personally struggled with "following Christ" doing things I shouldn't be doing the last thing I wanted to do was have someone point out to me the things I really already knew I shouldn't be doing.

Interesting that I do ministry. Interesting that I have 2 sons. Interesting that I have been around the block many, many times with the above matter. I have told my sons many, many times that they could always be honest with me. I have pointed out to them the things I thought, believed they were doing that were not good for them, not right, not pleasing to God. 9 times out of 10 I was either told not to worry, that they had it under control, that it was not what I thought, and that everything was o.k. 9 times out of the 10 what they told me was closer to what I had warned them about and even exactly what I told them would happen.

Now, I know many could say, "Hey, way to throw your sons under the bus." The point I am making is simply that I have seen, I have been part of the hiding, the blaming, the bald face truth that behavior says everything about where we stand in our relationship to Christ. I will not in this blog play self-righteous, I am the chief of sinners I know full well. I have lied, I have covered up, I have not wanted to get caught in my stuff.

I work with students every day that struggle with all of the above stuff. I do ministry. I live ministry. So, what should a youth pastor do when students are living double lives? I know as a parent what I have done. I have called them out. Not to embarrass them, not to belittle them, not to hurt them. The truth is that making the hard call of calling a person out about certain behaviors is solely for the benefit of them period.

I know first hand what it means to live a lie, get caught and blame the messenger or the one that "found out" on the hardship of the truth. I know first hand what it is like to be the messenger of truth, to make the hard call for the benefit of the student and then to be the one that is criticized for doing the "right" thing. Trying to help a person to walk in the light is a very difficult task.

You see, I know first hand what it means to have the light shined right on my sin. I know first hand the freedom that it brings to walk away from the garbage, to run away from stuff that I was found out about. I know first hand what it means to get free from the sin that I hid from. I know first hand what is like to finally admit my double life. Guess what, it wasn't about the messenger, it was about me.

All that to say how disappointing it is to be a parent and watch a double life being lived out and the constant denial. I have told my sons, just tell the truth. If you don't want to follow Christ fine. Don't lie about it. Don't play the game. You are still responsible to tell the truth whether you follow Christ or not period. But don't ever lie about loving God and then live a life of hatred towards Him.

Same goes with students today. I see so much garbage going on and the flat out denial is hurting students in so many ways. I know it first hand in my own life, therefore I would never enable students to continue down the path of playing the game, lying about the truth, and treating God like He was to blame for the lack of fun they were trying to have doing things they know full well they shouldn't be doing period. Drinking under age is wrong period.

Should I just over look that? Count that as what every one does? Sure thing right? I mean, why not just say the same about sex, pot and all the other stuff. The problem is this: If one claims to be in the light, but they re walking in darkness, what is the truth? Really? Wouldn't it be right to tell a loved one that what they are doing is exactly what John says it is? Lying. And wouldn't it be better to help students understand that they can live truthfully by just admitting, "I live like I don't want a relationship with Christ." Or "I live my life like God is the last thing that matters." That is the truth. At some point in time, love means that the truth will set someone free. The bottom line the hard calls matter more than the pain the person will have because of the truth. The hard calls matter more because they are there to help the person, the student, the child to get honest, to get real, to get to the point where they can see that they are found out. That they can make choices that will benefit them, in their relationship to Christ, in their relationship with others, with their relationship with people in general.

End of story here. If a student, a friend, a son want to live large, sin big, or whatever. I say fine. Just don't lie about it. Don't make a mockery of God, don't live a double life, don't talk the talk and not give a care about what is real. What I am saying is that there is a disservice to my sons, to students to others when there is knowledge of blatant stuff going on and if I, or friends, or anyone in the know turns their eye to the truth. So many things can go wrong. Pregnancy. Drunk driving accident. An overdose. So many things can go wrong. If the people in the light refuse to care then what? How long should I allow my sons to live a double life? I have called them out. They know where I stand. How long should I let students live a double life? Should I say anything? Should I do anything?

As a youth pastor, I should. As a follower of Christ, I should because the issue is not about being the "righteous one" or about embarrassing them, or hurting them. The end result is for helping them to become honest period. What they do with Christ may be to finally see His forgiveness as a reality. That when a student is honest, life becomes much better, richer, freer.

The sign reads "Rough Road".   The road becomes rough when people in the know refuse to warn, to tell the truth, to care. I know first hand the benefit of someone caring enough to call me out when I was living a lie.   As a father, as a pastor, as an adult that has experience all of it, I must do the right thing.

Hard calls are tough, but hard calls are right period.

Danger in making the Hard Calls

Speaking of Hard Calls--

In my early years of Student Ministry I made a little bit of a hard call. It wasn't huge, it wasn't too harsh... let me tell you the story and you decide.

There was this student that attended the church where I was the youth pastor. I noticed that every Sunday this student would go to "big church" but never come to my High School class. I also noticed that this same student never came to the Wednesday night deal we had going on. The Wednesday night thing was growing, there were some new things happening, there were students participating, it "seemed" to be a good thing. I wondered. How come this student just doesn't want to join in? So, one day I just asked? "How come you don't come to any of the High School things we have going on?" This student replied something like "I don't really like it, it's not important, I would rather go to church." (I don't remember exactly the conversation it was a long time ago.) But I do remember that I got the sense that this student was just appeasing her parents, so I wasn't going to go any farther. That was between the student and the rents.

Then a few weeks later on a Saturday night as I was riding my motorcycle I noticed this student at a drive through beer joint loading beer into the car. The next day was Sunday and sure enough this student was at church. So, I decided to say to the student something like this, "so you don't like the High School stuff because you'd rather be throwing back beer instead." This student said nothing, just kinda smiled and moved on.

The next day was Monday and as I closed up my office at the end of the day, (I was the last person in the building) I got a knock on my door. I said, "come in" and the person at the door was the above students mother. She came in, and I asked "what can I do for you?" She said that I owed her an apology for calling her student an alcoholic. I said, "I never said that" and she then called me a liar, pulled out a gun and said, "@%&* You, You are a liar" as she pointed the gun at me, "all you pastors are liars and I'm gonna blow your #@$%ing head off." And I said, "go on and pull the trigger cause where I am going I'll never see your face again." Well that totally ticker her off, she popped the clip out, threw the gun at me, poured a boat load of bullets from her purse on my desk and headed out the door. For REAL!

Nice story ehy? Was that a hard call? Did I do something wrong? Really?

You see, that is just one of many times I have gently confronted a student about some behavior issues. I say gently, because to those that really know me, that really desire to know me understand that me saying something is for the benefit of the person and not me. Sadly, 7-8 times out of 10 parents have not been good at their response to my desire to get to the honest truth of where their student is regarding integrity, character, and spiritually. When parents play the game, why should their student stop playing the game? Oh the joys of student ministry. Obviously I haven't given up even after a mother pulls a gun out. That story of the mom and gun happened over 2o years ago.

If I was trying to embarrass this student there were plenty of other things I could have done. If I was trying to damage this student, there are other things I could have done. I was simply trying to get this student to say what they really felt, what they really believed, what they really cared about. Basically to just get honest. I was watching one way of life, while this student is believing that living 2 lives was not seen.

Hard calls are tough indeed. That incident did bother me a little bit. Over the years, I believe that the best Youth Pastors I know are those that tell the truth, regardless of the fall out. Regardless of being liked by a few, or being liked by parents that don't want to face the truth of where their student is living. I believe that I have to do the right things, speak right things regardless of the pain for me and for the student or their parents. The pain is just the beginning of the possibilities of a life that lives in the joy of forgiveness in Christ, the peace that can reside in their hearts for being totally honest, for a life that is walking after Christ with Character and integrity under all circumstances.

Lastly, for those that are P.C. screwy, Jesus was not safe to those that didn't want to move forward. Jesus called out the Pharisees, Jesus let the adulterous women know He knew, Jesus called out the Lepers that never said thank you, Jesus was and still is in the business of honest, straightforward speaking in order to benefit the hearer with ears to hear.

If you are a parent and you have been bamboozled or your students fits or fights win the day-- fight on and keep talking truth. If you are a youth pastor/worker keep doing and saying what is right. Never give in to the P.C. garbage. If you are a student and you want to grow, then accept those that care enough to tell you the truth! Psalm 40

Let's Pretend

Let's pretend for this blog that you are the youth pastor of a Senior High ministry. You youth pastor for a large church of 3-4000 people and you have 100 students that regularly attend your weekly event. The church you work at has a possible of 5-8 high schools represented at your weekly event. The demographics of the surrounding area are that there are at least 12 to 15,000 high school students throughout the surrounding area. Not known is how many are attending church or have a relationship with Christ.

Still pretending that you are the youth pastor. Weekly you notice that there are students that attend your church but never attend the weekly meeting that has worship, fun, relevant topics, Biblical talks and you know that you are praying for, working for, planning for opportunities for students to grow in their relationship to Christ, to exercise their faith, to reach their campuses to love one another, to be challenged and to be at least, given the opportunity to have a relationship to Christ if they don't have one but they just won't put their foot in the door. Why? Your fault? What is wrong with the ministry you are providing?

Now remember that you are the youth pastor. You know of students that are partying, you know there are students that don't care about growing, at least they are there but they don't engage in worship. You know that there are students that aren't doing well in their relationship with Christ and it seems to you that they don't care.

As the youth pastor you know that yelling at them doesn't work, guilting them doesn't last. You know that small groups (Life in Life) works for growing in the Lord, but when you do small groups only 30% of the 100 students get involved.

What will you do? Will you continue to do all the same things you have been doing? Will you go after those that want to grow and say to those that don't – "later". Will you continue to teach the Word, speak the truth? Desire to help even though not many say by their actions and body language that they care. Will you continue to challenge your students to reach their campus or will you take them on a short term missions trip to jump start their heart for missions?

How long will you continue to work, work and work at trying to engage students?

You are the youth pastor. You are watching students, going through the motions about their relationship with Christ, they are selling out (like you once did) to being liked, being at least ok in the eyes of their peers, they are getting closer and closer to the fire that is roaring all around them, what will you do?

You are the youth pastor and very rarely does any of the parents that have students in your ministry engage you in conversation about their student. Very rarely these same parents ever ask you about you. What should you do? What will you do?   How do feel as you see parents weekly that rarely if ever speak to you?

You pray daily for the ministry. You meet weekly with your team for leading and Biblical direction. You have spent hours if not days seeking God for His direction. You care about every student but know that you can not even come close to relating to each one. You pray, you seek help, you continue to try to be relevant, honest, truthful, Biblical, authentic, Christ-like but you notice 1 by 1 for reasons like busyness, sports, home, study they are no longer attending. What will you do? You start to think it's you. You think, maybe they don't like the way we do things, maybe they don't like you, maybe they just don't care about the things you know are so valuable for everyday life. What will you do?

You believe that they are the church, that they can call church home, that the church has a high value to God's purposes in the world but many seem to be indifferent about God, Jesus Christ, the Scriptures, the leading of the Holy Spirit. What will you do?

Lets pretend that you are a youth pastor of a Sr. High ministry. What would you do?

Postmodern NextGen

"Of the last two friends of yours who had the modern mind one thought it wrong to eat fishes and the other thought it right to eat men" ~ G.K. Chesterton
Hmmmmmmmm   Kinda like the way it is. Right?

Post Modernism is here. It's been here. Post Modernism affects everything, everyday, in every realm of life. Really? Absolutely.
Ask yourself this little question. What is right?
Now try this one. Are there absolutes?
How bout this? What is true? How do you know?

Now ask a student this question. What speaks the loudest into your life?
Books? Teachers? Friends? Music? The Culture? Parents? Jesus Christ?

How bout this question? Who or what is the most important source for decision making in your life?   Friends? Parents? The Bible? Jesus Christ? Teachers?

So, I asked the other day "if you were the youth pastor, what would you do?" First, one better know this: Postmodernism
"A general and wide-ranging term which is applied to literature, art, philosophy, architecture, fiction, and cultural and literary criticism, among others. Postmodernism is largely a reaction to the assumed certainty of scientific, or objective, efforts to explain reality. In essence, it stems from a recognition that reality is not simply mirrored in human understanding of it, but rather, is constructed as the mind tries to understand its own particular and personal reality.

For this reason, postmodernism is highly skeptical of explanations which claim to be valid for all groups, cultures, traditions, or races, and instead focuses on the relative truths of each person. In the postmodern understanding, interpretation is everything; reality only comes into being through our interpretations of what the world means to us individually. Postmodernism relies on concrete experience over abstract principles, knowing always that the outcome of one's own experience will necessarily be fallible and relative, rather than certain and universal.

Postmodernism is "post" because it is denies the existence of any ultimate principles, and it lacks the optimism of there being a scientific, philosophical, or religious truth which will explain everything for everybody - a characteristic of the so-called "modern" mind." ~Faith and Reason

Ask a student that has a relationship with Christ where they get the truth? Do they read the Bible? Do they know what it says? Do they care about what it says? Ask a church going student the same questions. You may find they answer the same way? Oh first, you may get the standard answer they are supposed to give you. But, after some time the answer becomes up in the air. Truth is found not in the text, but in the understanding or lack thereof.

I can honestly say that as a youth pastor that has been doing this thing for over 20 years postmodern thinking and living has been around a long time. When I first started I used to press students to seek out the truth. Go find out why parents believe this or that. Go find out why Jesus says this. Read the Scriptures to find the truth. Believe me when I say, many adults back then thought, "Hey my kid knows this stuff they grew up in Sunday School. Just teach them." Of course, parents then didn't understand that they and their students were already not on the same page. That a student way back then was already way past believing something because I said so, let alone the Scriptures said so.

Today the same issues are at right in front of all of us that interact with students. What is truth? Where do you find it? Who is Jesus Christ? Why follow Him? What is life? Why are you here? What is your purpose in this world?

That is the essence of the struggle for all of us today. Isn't it? Why follow Jesus if it's only about eternity. It's my life, I'll do what I want. Ask me about issues like abortion or sex or whatever and you will find students, adults, all over the place. After all, there is nothing certain. Really? If you are in the philosophical ideal of postmodernism its up to you to decide or interpret, or believe.

Now then, how to deal with it?

I believe it starts first by hearing it. By listening to students in what they are saying and how they are living. Students say much by their actions and by their words. Listen, dialogue, talk, wrestle with them about ideas, the Scriptures, their feelings, the drama in their lives. Listen and find opps to point back to these questions: What do you think Jesus thinks about this matter? Or what do you think the Scriptures say about this? You may find them telling you that they don't know, they don't care, they are no longer sure. Now you will know what you are actually dealing with.

Postmodernism living is here, it is what our students are up against daily. The most difficult part of the job of student ministry is continuing to work at breaking through by being honest, being authentic, always pointing students to the Scriptures, to the living Christ, seeking the power of the Holy Spirit to break through and that takes a long time. It's no longer about sitting students in a classroom and teaching what we know as the truth. They aren't convinced that there is truth, that there is relevance in the Scriptures, or that the Christ is actually meaningful. That is postmodernism. We have to back this thing up and start over.

Please pray with me for a break through-- it can start with one student, but pray that God can break through.

"Modern intelligence won't accept anything on authority. But it will accept anything without authority." ~ G.K. Chesterton

"Postmodernism is difficult to define, because to define it would violate the postmodernist's premise that no definite terms, boundaries, or absolute truths exist. The term "postmodernism" will remain vague, since those who claim to be postmodernists have varying beliefs and opinions on issues."
~All about Philosophy

Front and Center

Front and Center! The Basics. The Essential ingredient. Important.
High Priority.

NextGen, student ministry, the High Value? Some might say "that's
easy, it's all about Jesus." Or some might say, "It's all about
education." Or some might say, "It's all about keeping students
safe." Or some could say "....." Well, so what is it? Over the past 20
years o so, I would say that student ministry is all the above adding
that there are some fundamental things that must continue to stay
on the top of the list. So, what is it?

It is fundamental—help students learn to think. Help students learn
how to integrate their faith in Christ—into the "real" world, their
world. Make opportunities to allow, to coach, to help, to train
students how to integrate their faith in Christ as their Savior- into
the everyday life issues. There is an important ingredient to all of
the above and that is parents matter. Student ministry is a help to
parents. Student ministry is not done in a vacuum. Student ministry
is not done alone. Student ministry, the NextGen ministry is done
best as parents do their role as model, as parent, as faithful, as
honest, as transparent, as seeking, as caring, as loving as they can be
and more. I believe now more than I ever did before that parents
need to help their students think, apply, build upon their
relationship with Christ. Parents need right now to help their
students to see value in integrating Biblical truth into daily living.

Oh this is so easy to say, but hard to do. I have been doing it since I
started youth ministry over 20 years ago. Why? Because I was
burned as a kid—burned by those that said—just believe, just do this
or that and all will be well. Going to church, having devotions,
praying, doing, doing doing without any reason other than because
somebody said it, is not good enough period. Really?

Oh, going to church, having quiet time, praying is what I do because
it's my job right? Because it's what I'm supposed to do. Right? It's
because I am paid to love God and teach students that stuff. Right?
Not even close. I do it, I enjoy it, because I love it, because I have
integrated faith into my life. I have an understanding that I need
Jesus Christ for everyday living. I know it full well, after all, I am

forgiven from things that no one else could forgive me of. My heart has been transformed because of what Christ did and nothing less. I have been given a great salvation. This is why I pursue God. This is why I care. This why I am passionate about student ministry. This is why NextGen is so important period.

But.... and it is a big but— I don't believe in holding devotions over students heads for quote "being better" or for being part of a youth group or for rewards. That may work for little kids—but in the long run—devotions becomes just a hoop to jump through. Is that worthy of praise? For some yes—for Jesus— ummmmm? Where would a parent find what Jesus thinks about that which would bring praise from Him to their student? Find the answer and one is thus integrating truth into the life of their student.

Oh yea—I've been doing the above for years—and for many—they are very uncomfortable with that—why? Their student might come to a conclusion they might not be ready for—i.e., "I don't want to do devotions." Why? "Because it is just a magic potion or something I'm supposed to do without meaning." It's like a lucky rabbits foot that I can tug on when in trouble. It's not much, but at least I do it.

Youth ministry in this day and age must be, must be a vehicle to help student integrate their faith in Christ into everyday life—and sorry to say—not many parents have done that themselves. Faith in Christ might just be a road to heaven. Not a relationship. Faith in Christ may just be a form of morality, not a way of life. I see it all the time.

Then, then, I get the students and they are completely confused. Faith in Christ is much more than the road to heaven, right? Faith in Christ is much more then a moral code—right? Faith in Christ moves through every aspect of life—but how, who will help them integrate their faith in Christ to living it?

I take students every year on the annual raft trip. Why do we go down a rushing river? Why do we get away? To integrate their faith by....Looking at God's creation—we saw a bald eagle, a red fox, an unbelievable canyon. We do things together, in a large group we worship, we celebrate, we learn from the Word, we do community groups, we do things-- why? For each other, together with their peers so they can see who, how, why from their peers.

Seeing peers that love God and have a relationship with Christ that is way beyond attending church and the message "because that is what we do." Hearing peers talk about how being on the New River rocked their world as they trusted Christ to go through the next huge rapid. Hearing peers share their faith openly. Watching student get baptized and the guides watching and being move by their outward declaration.

There are so many ways to help students integrate their relationship with Christ into reality... and I will continue to work at it. Interesting that many "churchy" people struggle with my approach—they just want their student to think—without really thinking.... In truth—just do what you are told—and all will be right— but does that really work?

I have seen and am continuing to see—many, many students clueless about a relationship with the living Christ—what some make sacred is not at all— Far from it! Will it bother some to say that? Yes. Our students need the truth and the ways to integrate truth into everyday life.

Yes! We have been given the ability to think and take those thoughts and integrate our faith in the living Christ into life everyday, all situations, Life.

I had a conversation with a few guys that really never thought through this simple integration process. I asked "what do you believe about the Bible or about Jesus as the only Savior?" Their answer was not their own. Possibly parents or school or the church's but not theirs. How do I know? I pressed them a little bit— by asking—you believe this or that? All they could say was... "well, ummm, I don't... I'm not sure."

Wait till they get to college. Then what? They will drop other peoples belief's in a second. If their faith in Christ is not integrated into their life choices and ideal's.... it won't be worth much. I know. Been there and done that, hated it then, hate seeing it today. I know first hand the destruction of all the above.

I remember all the hassles from those in the "know" about rock and roll. I remember hearing a guy rant and rave about the "evils" of rock and roll and how "I needed to burn my albums." Because I was never taught the how to integrate Biblical truth into everyday life, I just did what I was told. That was dumb on my part... because in 3 weeks I was buying all the albums I had thrown away back. Why?

1. I didn't really believe that Jesus was that jacked up about rock and roll... is He? I think He is more jacked up from disobedience of the things that His Word teaches. As a kid I used to think, "Man, you are willing to rip into people about hair and music and anything other than what fits your likes, but the way you treat people seems to be so not right. After all, is it really about the beat? Is it really about the externals? Is it really about the stuff that tomorrow changes. Funny to me that I still to this day think and laugh about how my parents got all in a lather about the length of my hair and when I got it cut off, I actually thought to myself, that didn't change one thing about me.

2. I threw the albums away because someone told me to do it. I was under the assumption that somehow that brought righteousness. Where does righteousness come from? The answer is in the Scriptures-- Hint the book of Romans and it would help students to hear from their parents about what the scriptures teach about righteousness.

It's time to let students wrestle with idea's, truth, their faith and point them to the truth found in the Scriptures. There really are many ways to do this-- it just may mean taking the time to get real creative. This generation is facing some difficult times. We youth pastor's and youth workers have an opportunity right now to make a difference.

Student Ministry must be about helping students integrate even their small "child like" faith into everyday life. Everyday life is not pretty. Everyday life is not easy. Everyday life is full of depravity, sin, issues that are difficult to understand. Everyday life has with it the whole emotional gambit.

To parents-- model your relationship with Christ. Model, model, model.
When it is time to talk to your student about "issues" speak to students like the Lord relates to you. How does He do that? How does He relate to you? Better find out don't you think?

Jesus is not always safe. He was not afraid to call out the pharisee's and the adulterous women or His disciples when they fell asleep. So, talk to your student like He dealt with those He loved and cared about.

The Scriptures say to "lean not on your own understanding" so seek Him when it comes to dealing with your student.

Parents do matter to me. I am a parent. I haven't done everything correctly or 100% all the time. I have learned much trying to raise 2 boys. I do know this though-- I'm not the parent of the students. I can only do so much. Student ministry needs parents to use it as a "help" for their students period. Parents model everyday, every hour what their relationship to Christ looks like as they live everyday life.

Front and Center?   Parents, NextGen ministry is to help students learn to think. Help students learn how to integrate their faith in Christ—into the "real" world, their world. Make opportunities to allow, to coach, to help, to train students how to integrate their faith in Christ as their Savior- into the everyday life issues.

Integrating Faith into daily life. What matters to God?

Every once in a while I go through a little question answer time as I seek to lead, develop students in the difficult yet rewarding job Youth Pastor. I start with this kind of questioning: What is important to God? How do I help students integrate their faith into life? Remember—faith in the complete work of Christ produces righteousness— not works, not good behavior, not good grades, not any of the stuff that we all as youth workers and most parents want students to call their own—but—behavior does not bring righteousness. So—so what about helping students be better young people? Well, the how of integrating faith produces really great students—so how?

What are the things that matter to God? Isaiah 66. 2b says *"This is what I esteem: he who is humble and contrite in spirit, and trembles at my word."* Ahhhh there it is... the beginning of integrating faith into life, integrating faith into attitude, integrating faith into behavior.

Here is how it works

When a student recognizes their NEED for the Savior—due to the reality of their sin, their need for forgiveness, their need for reconciliation, their need for restoration—I call it becoming aware— the student that feels the above—not just head knowledge (which I know many, many students with tons of head knowledge) and they are arrogant, and believe that they are their own savior—they know it all, they don't do such terrible things—so, they are good... right?

Back to the Need for the Savior and the feeling of neediness and the overwhelming sense that I, they, you—are thus humbled by our sinfulness, and come to God with contrite hearts because we know, feel and sense that without the Christ our works, our lives are but filthy rags. The problem, we have really hurts students by connecting some "good" behavior with meaning that all is well, i.e., not drinking, but nobody deals with them about their lying, their back talking and back biting (like some adults) and other such sins that just aren't so bad.

Integrating faith, becomes a complete understanding that the student needs their relationship with Christ to live daily and thus the end of Is.66.2b "trembles at the Word."

The student that recognizes their complete and utter lostness finds humility in what Christ has done, has a contrite heart and spirit because the student knows that they at their core are needy, and thus go to the word as not something called devotions that a person does because somebody told them to—but because they are so thankful for what Christ has done, they put their faith in Him and Him alone and that drives one to remain humble and contrite.

You may ask, "what about my student that is o.k., never in trouble, tows the line, does the right things-- I say-- on the outside-- but what is going on inside? Inside, where the mind is at work, where the heart is deceitful, where things may be going on-- and the student is waiting for the "right time" to finally live out the inside- i.e., heading off to college where nobody knows them, where the folly of stuff is right in front of them, where they can live out the inside stuff? I see it all the time-- students waiting to chuck all the "right stuff" because it really isn't part of their inside-- just the outside.

Try to integrate the above into your life and see how that changes this idea that we are so much better than people, and that because we don't do this or that—that we are somehow good. Nowhere in Scripture is that taught—and yet, our human fallenness wants us to believe that we somehow can pull that off. Add that to students that already feel like they have to prove themselves by doing everything right and good and can't slip up-- the student today needs a ministry where truth is taught, give an opportunity to dialogue, struggle, wrestle and be honest. We all need to make that a high value.

Students need the truth today! Maybe we have become so Politically Correct that we (youth pastors) have lost the ability to talk to students about the real issue. Our fallen, broken heart. Maybe we have fallen into the trap that when students make an effort to be part of the ministry we are doing, maybe we shouldn't be so hard on them.

I say that most if not close to all the students I have seen and known over the years that it is always better to tell the truth about this matter than to speak with indifference about it. Isn't it true that many students are actually wanting somebody they trust to speak honestly about the purpose of Jesus for their lives. If we shy away from the truth who will they listen too? Who will speak into their lives?

I suggest:

Ask this question to yourself. If heaven were not promised, would you follow Christ? Would you have asked Him to be your savior? Would you continue to keep a short list of your short comings? Would you come to Him as the only one that can change your heart?

I know I would. I don't believe in any other Savior. I don't believe that I can change my heart. I know I couldn't, I can't and I need Him exactly as the one that can forgive me. How about you? Frankly I wouldn't follow Jesus if it were only about heaven. I tried that back when I was a kid, and ultimately I lived like hell for a long time until I came to the conclusion that I needed the one and only Christ.

Suggestion:

That heaven is not most important reason for coming to Christ. It is because He is the only one that can restore mankind's broken heart. He is the only one that can transform humanity. He is the only one that can fix students. Unless of course you or I believe we can fix them.

Suggestion:

That a very high value of being a youth pastor/youth worker is because we believe that the Christ that we teach about, talk about, say we live about is actually the answer to all of life. If He is not, maybe we have been bamboozled by all the junk out there that says something like this; "A relationship with Christ is not that important, just do the stuff that you are supposed to do." Then we all struggle with the next question; and what is it that the youth pastor deems I am supposed to do? Now we go down the road of "the list" that we believe matters most and thus, the belief that somehow if a student does all the "right" things, they can clean up themselves. They may then say, I can do life without the Savior. Ultimately the slope gets so steep that soon there is no longer a need for community, the local church, the Scriptures or you or I in their lives. They are doing just fine without any of it so they think.

Here in lies the last suggestion:

The Scriptures teach that "And without faith it is impossible to please God, because anyone who comes to him must believe that he exists and that he rewards those who earnestly seek him." Hebrews 11.6

What then pleases God? Faith. Faith in what? The air, a dream, a notion? No. Faith in God, that He exists, that He is real. The Faith that it takes to believe that Jesus is the Christ, that He is the only one that can right a broken heart, that He is the only one that can actually transform anyone. And so goes the slope upward. Why read the scriptures? Because by seeking Him, that pleases Him. Why go to church? Because by seeking Him through worship, that pleases Him. Why seek spiritual God at all? Because that pleases Him.

Help students today to live out their faith by providing opportunities for them to Seek Him. You will find your ministry to go beyond anything you could imagine.

My Church, My work, ministry

In 1987 when I started searching, asking God to lead me as I began looking for opportunities-- my first church to do youth ministry for, at and in for the first time. I went out full steam ahead, ready to get to work. Ready to reach the world ready to do youth ministry.

I had interned at a church for a year. I enjoyed students, families, the church in general but I'm not sure that the church would have been a church where I would have attended if I wasn't working there.

So I made this rule. I wouldn't work at a church that I would not attend. The reason why I made the rule is important. I wanted to get behind everything it stood for, that it supported, the community life, the style of worship all that a church offers. I wanted to be not just a part of it, but be the church.

I did break the rule one time because I was running. An opportunity came along and I jumped at it.

So, here I am at a thriving church. Fairhaven Church in Dayton Ohio. I was here from 1992 to 2001 and now from 2009 till present and I am so glad it is the church where I work and worship. I love this church. I appreciate what it stands for, what it's here for, why we do what we do. Here is the question? If I didn't work here would I attend with my family?

Yes! I would.

But that is not why I wanted to write this little blog. What is behind this little blog tonight is simply this: Church matters period. The local church is here in this world for a purpose. Yes, the local church is an institution. Yes, there is much man made about the church. Yes, there are blemishes in all churches. Yes, the church has some politics to it. Yes, the local church has had times of utter disaster, failure and sin. Yet, the local church has been and is now an instrument of God through out the centuries.

The instrument to reach people, to love people, to worship together, for community life to impact the world. Some people go to church for one of those reasons, 2 or 3 or all. I love the local church period. I'm not into idol worship, I am into worship of God and I appreciate the church that raises Christ high, the Scriptures high, worship high, the community high and desires to make a difference in the culture in where it resides.

So, I am grateful for the church where I attend, worship and work.

I'm thinking about one last little thing. When Dietrich Bonhoeffer was a pastor in Germany during WWII he had a choice to make. Would he succumb to the wishes of the "National Church" as it sold out for Hitler's desires to change the Scriptures taking out the Old Testament and making Jesus an Arian, to hang Swastika's in the church, change the Bible on the alter and replace it with his own book Mien Kumpf? Bonhoeffer's love for Christ, his love for the church drove him to develop the "Confessing Church" an underground church that would hold fast and strong to the reasons for church being church. Bonhoeffer loved the church.

Bonhoeffer loved Jesus Christ and His Church enough to take a stand for the right things-- the local church mattered enough for one man and the other pastors of the "Confessing Church" that they stood against the tyranny of evil that the National Church could not and would not do. Ultimately hundreds of the "Confessing Church" pastors were sent to the front lines and killed for what they believed in-- the local church and all that it stood for and against.

I love the local church. I love my church.

Now to him who is able to do immeasurably more than all we ask or imagine, according to his power that is at work within us, to him be glory in the church and in Christ Jesus throughout all generations, for ever and ever! Amen.
~Ephesians 3.20,21

From Saving Private Ryan

I just watched the scene again... private Ryan is told to "earn this." And then the cemetery scene when an elderly Ryan he asks his wife—

Old James Ryan: Tell me I have led a good life.
Ryan's Wife: What?
Old James Ryan: Tell me I'm a good man.
Ryan's Wife: You are.

The fear in Old James Ryan says it all.   Did I earn my being found and saved?

I have viewed these scenes many times—and what stands out over and over and over—

Understanding and feeling what Miller says to "earn this" and how Ryan must have felt over the years—I often hear the voices of many many people over the years speaking on earning God's approval or His love, His mercy, His grace, His salvation—when I first saw these scenes I felt the sadness of the ones that paid a price for saving private Ryan.

I felt the sadness of my own life—wanting so much to earn God's forgiveness, God's grace, God's salvation and inwardly knowing full well, I fell short, I just couldn't do it.   In truth-- I never have earned anything for and from God.

I am so grateful that the idea of earning God's grace is almost completely gone. Yes! The truth that His grace, His love, His care, His salvation is never ever earned.

I am at 52, free—oh I get stuck on approval of others sometimes— but I am no longer stuck on earning God's love period.

4But because of his great love for us, God, who is rich in mercy, 5made us alive with Christ even when we were dead in transgressions—it is by grace you have been saved. 6And God raised us up with Christ and seated us with him in the heavenly realms in Christ Jesus, 7in order that in the coming ages he might show the incomparable riches of his grace, expressed in his kindness to us in Christ Jesus. 8For it is by grace you have been saved, through faith—and this not from yourselves, it is the gift of God— 9not by works, so that no one can boast. 10For we are God's workmanship, created in Christ Jesus to do good works, which God prepared in advance for us to do. Ephesians 2.4-9

Thank you Jesus for your dying for me! Thank you for your unconditional love and kindness regardless of my actions. Thank you for loving me because you made the choice to love me.

Today I live free to love others like you love me. Help me to do that right—not to earn your love—but because I love you period. Amen

Memorial Day

"Let every nation know, whether it wishes us well or ill, that we shall pay any price, bear any burden, meet any hardship, support any friend, oppose any foe to assure the survival and the success of liberty." ~ John F. Kennedy

May 28th is my birthday. For 50 plus years now I always get a day off for my birthday. That's right, my birthday is always on memorial day weekend. I love Memorial Day. I spent today with family and friends celebrating. My facebook page was filled with greetings and Happy Birthday wishes. I feel so loved by my family and friends.

This weekend is so much bigger then my lil ole birthday. This weekend represents the kind of people that I look up to, I appreciate, I honor... the cause of freedom, the cause of fighting for what is right, the cause to stand up and defend this great country. I honor the past soldiers in this little blog. I honor the present soldiers, I honor this great country period.

I know that it is not P.C.right now to stand up for this country. I know many people have been bamboozled into talking down about this great country. I know that there are many that speak against this country. I don't! I am grateful for America. I am grateful for the life I live in this free country. I am so glad that I get to walk, breath, live life in this great country. I am grateful for all those that have defended this cause called freedom. I am grateful to all of those that fight the fight so that I can enjoy such a great life.

I will never look down at those that have shed their blood to fight for my freedom period. I will honor those that have fought this fight and are fighting today by living my life freely. In speaking my heart, by speaking the truth, by living the truth. I will honor those fighting and those that have fought by not being p.c., by standing up, by putting my hand over my heart when the National Anthem is played, by being patriotic. I will speak highly of this great country in honor of those that have gone before and are now fighting for my freedom.

"My God! How little do my countrymen know what precious blessings they are in possession of, and which no other people on earth enjoy!" ~Thomas Jefferson

I believe Thomas Jefferson is right and Memorial Day is here to remind us all of what precious blessing we are in possession of... America is blessed.

I may be considered off in this day and age, but that is fine with me-- you see, I believe in bravery. I believe in courage. I believe in fighting for what is right. I believe that there is a right and a wrong. I believe that there is evil. I believe that what I believe is worth dying for therefore I honor those that have fought the fight and are fighting today because of what they believed in.

"It is foolish and wrong to mourn the men who died. Rather we should thank God that such men lived." ~George S. Patton

I hope that one day I will be remembered as a man that stood for what was right, what I believed in, that I was as brave as past and present soldiers, that I loved my freedom and honored my country and countrymen by the way I lived. Thank you great men and women of the past and great men and women of today. Thank you. I am blessed to live in this great country. I am blessed to be an American. I am blessed to call this great land home. I will honor those that have fought for freedom because it is right and honorable. I am a grateful man.

"My country, 'tis of thee, sweet land of liberty, of thee I sing. Land where my fathers died, land of the pilgrim's pride, from every mountainside, let freedom ring."

Ode to Parenting

The countdown continues. Just a few more days with my 2 guys around the house. I have been doing a lot of thinking over the past few days. I have been thinking about parenting. Specifically my parenting with 2 boys, now young men.

I have been in student ministry for 20+ years. I have seen many, many styles, opinions, views about parenting. I have been preached at, spoken at, read books, seen some great parenting, and I have seen some disasters. I have seen those that have raised their students with all they had only to watch their students leave the house and not do so well. I have been part of many many families lives through ministry, as a pastor and as a friend. I have been with families through ups, downs, the good, the bad and the ugly.

I have seen students not raised in Christian homes turn out very well. I have seen it all. I have seen the control freak parents, I have seen the Bible pounding parents, I have seen the "non-faith" parents, I have seen the "free" type of parent, I have seen the "Gothard" parent, I have seen the home school parents, the private school parent, I have seen most of the styles of parenting and quite frankly from my observation after high school and college (I know students in their late 20's and early 30's) some have remained faithful, some have chucked the faith, some are doing well and some are not doing so well. Some have been married and divorced, some have had major pain in their lives, some continue to walk with God. Some of the students loved church, some students not so much. Some students went to "Sunday School" and liked it, some never connected, some just flat out made the choice to not engage and those that made the choice to engage?   Well, some got it, and some didn't.

I have seen the products of all the above. I have known the student that is rebellious, obnoxious, full of head knowledge, the timid, the scared stiff, the totally free, the student that could care less about God, the student committed to Christ, the apathetic student, the selfish student, the addict student, the every type of student there is and was. Really? Well, I have seen a lot, that is for sure.   (Personal note: I like John Rosemond's stuff the best.)

From all the above and now sending 2 young men off to school-- I like many parents have tried my best, trusted God, tried to give my boys Biblical truth, tried to let them make choices (good and not so good) I have pointed out, directly, with toughness, with straight shooting, with patience, with a large heart, by absorbing pain, by giving out some pain, but always with my love for them period. I have tried to parent by watching mine, by watching others, by trusting the Lord, with prayer, with Biblical truth, with all my heart.

So? So this blog is to those parents that like me that have watched others parent and said, no thank you. I'm not going to beat Jesus into them by putting them down, by perpetrating the sad idea that our students should live for what other people think, or our kids should live so that others think that we are such good parents. For those parents that feel defeated or have tried to do what others have done, or try try try, for those parents that feel put down by those that think they are God's gift to parenting, or that their students are the way they are because of their great parenting or not so great parenting, I feel with you. I know parents even today that won't even talk to me in the halls as we pass through life going to the same church-- I guess because I don't measure up, or I don't do it their way or I represent something of all the above that in truth is exactly the point-- I have seen it all and all of it is parents trying their best. It may not be what others want or expect or even what you want, but loving your student with the love of the Christ that you know will make a difference.

I have had all sorts of parents in the ministry over the years and what I have come to conclude is that parenting is a great, God given job, ministry, and life. That parenting is at best a short stint of helping their students become healthy, honest, students of character, students that make the choice to follow Christ, that their student will learn to trust in their God, that their student will learn to love God, that students will love the church, love people. But-- and a big but here-- but at the end of the day how a student decides to obey, live, do right, stand up, be above reproach, be honest, be all that God would want them to be in their journey is up to the student with the work of the Holy Spirit doing His work in them and through them.

I know that I created many of my own personal hang ups. I know that my guys have created their issues as well as what they inherited from my sinful heart. I know that I should have listened to my parents, I should have heeded the warnings, I should have.... but I didn't. I went a hard road, I learned things the hard way but I made a choice to love Jesus Christ because I knew and know how much I needed and need Him.

I hope, I pray that becomes a reality for my 2 young men.

I still believe that God is at work in my 2 guys regardless of my parenting skills or the lack thereof. I still believe that they must be the ones the make a choice to pursue the Christ with all they have. I don't see this as the end of my parenting not one bit, it is a new time, a new era. I will never stop being their dad. As I learned from my dad who taught me this great spiritual truth-- He once told me "there is nothing you could do that would make me stop loving you." And I am passing that truth on to them, but especially about the Heavenly Father to me, and 2 my 2 sons. Remember the little book mom and I would read to you at bedtime? Love you forever by Robert Munsch

To you Alex and Cooper

"I'll love you forever,
I'll like you for always,
As long as I'm living
my baby you'll be"

That will never ever change!

To every thing there is a season, and a time to every purpose under heaven:

A new era is fast approaching my life. My 2 sons head off to college in the span of 2 days this week. This new era means that my wife of 25 years are almost back to where we started-- just the 2 of us. What does that mean? It means for me that I get a do over on the first 5 years. The first years of marriage, the first years of living together, the first years of ministry together, the first years of just the 2 of us.

I have some crazy emotions going on-- I can't help but think of all the early morning hockey with both boys. I think of all the travel hockey. I am thinking about the early years with Alex and Cooper. Man o man where did time fly? I chuckled out loud as I listened to Alex shred his guitar during Uprising. I thought back at how he used to try and play guitar after being between the pipes (hockey goalie) after his team lost in O.T. How his guitar playing soothed his pain.

I was thinking about Cooper scoring the game winner on Sr. night as his teacher that he invited watched on. I was thinking about how fun raising these 2 guys has been. The many nights I went into their rooms as they slept and prayed over them, cried over them. The many times I felt disappointment, the many many times I have been so proud of them, the many times I knew full well that I blew it, the many times we together laughed at our boyish stuff and mom just didn't get it.

Oh I could blog all week about all the great memories, but some of these memories are just for me.

The thing that stands out is simply this: When I left home and headed out on my motorcycle to Colorado life did change. My relationship with my father and mother went to new heights as I began to appreciate both my parents. Things changed and I had to grow up. I had to move forward without my dad or my mom. It was a great time for me. I know it was a great time for my parents.

So, I am looking forward to being in the bleachers now. I'm looking forward to my boys becoming men without me so close. I'm looking forward to how God worked in my life back then to see God work in their lives. I believe they are His and it's time to let Him have them completely. I am looking forward to what God will do with them, through them, in them.

The time has come to trust God to continue to do the work in them which He started. So here we go!

[1] There is a time for everything,
and a season for every activity under the heavens:

[2] a time to be born and a time to die,
a time to plant and a time to uproot,
[3] a time to kill and a time to heal,
a time to tear down and a time to build,
[4] a time to weep and a time to laugh,
a time to mourn and a time to dance,
[5] a time to scatter stones and a time to gather them,
a time to embrace and a time to refrain from embracing,
[6] a time to search and a time to give up,
a time to keep and a time to throw away,
[7] a time to tear and a time to mend,
a time to be silent and a time to speak,
[8] a time to love and a time to hate,
a time for war and a time for peace.
Ecclesiastes 3.1-8

"work ethic, first; structure, second; and skill, third"

I watched an incredible comeback in a hockey game between the Sharks and the Red Wings. The Red Wings down 2 goals come back to beat the Sharks 4 to 3. While I watched this comeback-- I was pulling for the Sharks, I marveled at how hard the Wings worked and worked and worked. Then at the end of the game after the win a Red Wing was asked how did they do it? The answer was an exact quote from a player was a direct quote from their coach..."work ethic, first; structure second, and skill, third." Exactly, right?

Yes. It's true. Work hard, always work harder than your opponent. Don't rely on skill first, rely on a work ethic-- go to work and out work your opponent. Then work hard on the system, the structure that is in place to help the team out work the opponent... and finally let your skill work for you.

Isn't that the way it really is? Now I have worked with students and my own children for over 20 years-- and in my humble opinion-- too many are relying on skill before hard work and without a system (structure) in place what so ever... and this is a huge problem. If a student could, would understand and begin to practice hard work at whatever it is they want to accomplish-- grades, job, relationships, whatever-- they would find that working hard brings much in the end.

The above can be said about Student Ministry also. You see, as the youth pastor, youth workers work hard at ministry, it's not just working hard at working hard. It's working hard with the system in which he/she created in place, right? Without a system, youth ministry can be hard work spinning plates, or just continuing to just keep doing the same stuff without substance or direction.

Putting skill before everything tends to end up causing youth workers, or youth pastors winging everything and ultimately the end is near. Just trusting in skill for the youth pastor/youth worker can cause one to believe that "they can do anything, or who needs planning, or a system, I can get by on my skill and that is dangerous.

It is the same for students today. I wonder if is there is a system or structure in place in a students own life to develop character, integrity, goals, virtue the things that a student can work, a personal system if you will. I believe the student today may not know the what to or how to work hard at a structure of study habits, character development, choices that are for the future. I see many students today just getting through a day by doing at best the minimal, just coasting through, and really anything that comes along can take them in any direction. I see some just relying on God given gifts to just get bye-- no need to work hard, just do the easy way with the skills that a student knows they possess and that is all.

The question-- how do I help? How do I try and help this generation to see... some of the structure that has been dissed, put down, trampled on is actually not garbage. That caring for people, that caring for the future, that being honest, that having character is actually a great structure and that working hard and whatever they do-- bushing a broom, working on a paper, cleaning windows, doing home work...doing "it" with a hard work ethic has huge value.

My generation had other fathers stepping in, coaches, teachers, youth pastors, pastors, adult friends of family, or uncles that felt they had a say in a students life. Plus we as students at least I did, knew that these other people in my life had something to offer, that they genuinely cared for me, that they really did have my best interest in mind as they taught me about things of character, integrity, work habits, even how to swing a bat or shoot a puck.

I really do see with my own eyes every day how many many students today are trusting in just their smile to get through life. The sad part is that our whole world is struggling. The job market is at an all time low, the economy is up for grabs, so how will this nextgen move forward through life?

"work ethic, first; structure, second; and skill, third"

This generation must learn to work hard, develop a solid structure, (habits, the ability to say no to nonsense, distractions) a sound structure where a person can excel, and then hone and develop their God given skills. I really do think the big ticket for students today is the lack of "structure" in their lives. If, if this nextgen will look into their lack of structure and begin working at developing good habits, taking the time for quietness, turn off the text messages and learn to focus they can and will be on their way to finding success toward their future. And if adults around them will let go of the notion that their structure is outdated, or too old or narrow, or that they don't have much to offer and will take the time to reach out even if there is push back, maybe some students will begin to form a structure by which they can accomplish much, by working hard at foundational things that are no longer missing and then develop the skills that they have been given.

Luke 6.46-49
46 "Why do you call me, 'Lord, Lord,' and do not do what I say? 47 As for everyone who comes to me and hears my words and puts them into practice, I will show you what they are like. 48 They are like a man building a house, who dug down deep and laid the foundation on rock. When a flood came, the torrent struck that house but could not shake it, because it was well built. 49 But the one who hears my words and does not put them into practice is like a man who built a house on the ground without a foundation. The moment the torrent struck that house, it collapsed and its destruction was complete."

You want it, you got it.

Over the past 20 years of doing student ministry and being a father of 2 sons means sadly to say that I have seen my fair share of poor choices. Now, I know I have made some very bad choices and I have reaped the consequences of my bad choices. Consequences of much pain, some physical, some emotional, some financial and some scars that will never leave me.

Some actually believe that poor choices happen in a vacuum. Like, hey no blood no foul, or hey I'm only hurting myself, or hey everybody has to go through this or that rite of passage, so I'm going for it.

Some actually believe that God will work overtime to protect them. Some actually believe they are invincible, some actually believe that surviving is easy. After all, they have gotten away with being crazy for a long time so because the have gotten away with bad decisions in the past why not keep making them? Right? At some point the lying catches up. At some point something will give. At some point the consequences may not be so easy. Sadly to say, I am watching this generation making some scarey, poor choices that will ultimately going to cost much.

It boils down to this little idea: "I want to live the way I want to live period. I don't care about consequences, I don't care about the future, I want it my way now. I want to feel good, I want to have fun, I want to experience the other side, I want, I want, I want and I want it my way.

Here in lies the real rub. Where is God in all this? Some students, my sons included don't really understand that tomorrow is no guarantee. They don't know that the consequences of their choices are not all on some grid that says the end result will not be so bad. No one knows what the end result of a night out drinking will do tomorrow, or a year from now. No one actually can know the consequences of their choices. Getting away with lying will ultimately come to an end. Getting away with using drugs or underage drinking or sex outside of marriage will ultimately cost period. So where is God in all this?

1 Samuel 8

1 When Samuel grew old, he appointed his sons as Israel's leaders. 2 The name of his firstborn was Joel and the name of his second was Abijah, and they served at Beersheba. 3 But his sons did not follow his ways. They turned aside after dishonest gain and accepted bribes and perverted justice.

4 So all the elders of Israel gathered together and came to Samuel at Ramah. 5 They said to him, "You are old, and your sons do not follow your ways; now appoint a king to lead us, such as all the other nations have."

6 But when they said, "Give us a king to lead us," this displeased Samuel; so he prayed to the LORD. 7 And the LORD told him: "Listen to all that the people are saying to you; it is not you they have rejected, but they have rejected me as their king. 8 As they have done from the day I brought them up out of Egypt until this day, forsaking me and serving other gods, so they are doing to you. 9 Now listen to them; but warn them solemnly and let them know what the king who will reign over them will claim as his rights."

The Children of Israel wanted a King like everyone else right? We want what we want and we want it now. That was their cry. The prophet Samuel hears them, goes to God, God says better tell them the consequences of their desires. What they want is not in God's timing. What they want will not benefit them, but they are determined.

10 Samuel told all the words of the LORD to the people who were asking him for a king. 11 He said, "This is what the king who will reign over you will claim as his rights: He will take your sons and make them serve with his chariots and horses, and they will run in front of his chariots. 12 Some he will assign to be commanders of thousands and commanders of fifties, and others to plow his ground and reap his harvest, and still others to make weapons of war and equipment for his chariots. 13 He will take your daughters to be perfumers and cooks and bakers. 14 He will take the best of your fields and vineyards and olive groves and give them to his attendants. 15 He will take a tenth of your grain and of your vintage and give it to his officials and attendants. 16 Your male and female servants and the best of your cattle and donkeys he will take for his

own use. 17 He will take a tenth of your flocks, and you yourselves will become his slaves. 18 When that day comes, you will cry out for relief from the king you have chosen, but the LORD will not answer you in that day."

If you are a parent, or if you are in student ministry, I know you feel the above. I can't write all the times over the past 20 years how many times I have warned students, warned parents of the consequences of poor choices. I have even been in trouble with students and parents for "coming on too strong" about the consequences that were coming for their poor, bad, selfish choices.

Where is God in all this? What did He do?

19 But the people refused to listen to Samuel. "No!" they said. "We want a king over us. 20 Then we will be like all the other nations, with a king to lead us and to go out before us and fight our battles."

21 When Samuel heard all that the people said, he repeated it before the LORD. 22 The LORD answered, "Listen to them and give them a king."

God gave them what they wanted. They got their King. It was the wrong King. It wasn't the right time,it wasn't God's choice, but He went with it.

Where is God in all the poor choices? Give them what they want. It's gonna hurt, it's gonna be painful, it's not gonna be good for them, it may cost more than they have calculated, it may be well past what they have thought, but "You want it, you got it."

I personally will never stop warning students and even my own 2 sons of the consequences of their poor choices, but I will not give in to making students or my own 2 sons not responsible for the consequences of their choices. What scares me is simply this: There are some consequences that could be very costly, painful and even dire. Where is God in all this? Give them what they want. Why? Maybe, just maybe the self centered attitude will turn around and realize how doing life their way is actually not the right way at all. Hopefully many will come to their senses before it's too late.

Ode to the two sons

When Jesus approached Matthew and said, "Follow me" the text says that Matthew got up and followed Him.

I wonder how many students today actually are like Matthew? You know, following Christ. Just up and at it. Leaving the moment to follow the Christ? How bout this? I do this thing called NextGen with and for students that at some point raised a hand, walked an aisle, said yes to following Christ...but they know, I know they are not. They said yes, maybe they just wanted "heaven" maybe they wanted to follow but....

Compare and Contrast to Matt. 21.28-32

"What do you think? There was a man who had two sons. He went to the first and said, 'Son, go and work today in the vineyard.' "

"I will not,' he answered, but later he *changed* his mind and went.

"Then the father went to the other son and said the same thing. He answered, 'I will, sir,' but he did not go.

"Which of the two did what his father wanted?"

"The first," they answered.

Jesus said to them, "Truly I tell you, the tax collectors and the prostitutes are entering the kingdom of God ahead of you. 32 For John came to you to show you the way of righteousness, and you did not believe him, but the tax collectors and the prostitutes did. And even after you saw this, you did not repent and believe him.

"Which of the two did what his father wanted?"
"The first," they answered.

See-- there is hope. There is hope. I say it is better to say an honest no because at some point following will become theirs. (repent and believe him.) The student that says yes and never does, does not have much character. I see both everyday I work with students. A

No means that God can do a work and it becomes a yes because that person said yes with their heart. Mom didn't say yes for them, friends didn't say yes for them. They turned and followed because they wanted to.

Ever think about this little parable?
Ever think about how to deal with this stuff?
This is my world of NextGen
Which one are you?

The Journey

I was in my day doing the pastoring NextGen job as I was thinking about this:

Where would I be if I had I not had a "youth group" growing up? And where would I be had I not made choices to pursue the "stuff" that took me to some bad, dark places mainly by my selfish, unbelieving heart.

2 Questions both 2 reasons why I believe I am in student ministry and have been in it for over 20 years.

At the end of the 2 questions and 2 reasons is this:

I know the value of student ministry.

I know the what we all know deep down inside. That nobody causes the dark, bad places but me. I was the one that listened to the junk. I was the one that followed the "stuff". I was selfish. I was self absorbed, I was into wanting to be loved and so on.

So why the blog tonight? What is this about?

Simply this: I know that the journey of following Christ got me through. I know that faith in the living Christ, His forgiveness, His transforming power is greater than anything I could have tried or done on my own.

I watch students everyday continue to pursue the selfish path. I know the destruction they are in for. I have hurt over my own 2 sons pursuit of "stuff". I know the denial, I know the fear, I know the shame, I know all the stuff that comes with pursuing all the stuff.

I can say today as well as tomorrow, and the next day that this truth: That by trusting, by following, by being honest, by seeking by admitting the truth, by asking for forgiveness, by believing His word that He does forgive, that He will forgive, that He conquered the very things I pursued-- a new life can begin. The journey is not easy, there is a time to say I will not, there is a time to turn down the "stuff" there is a time to say no, and another time to say no, there is another time to say no, there is a time to run, there is a time to deal with the truth again, there is a time to ask for forgiveness, there is a time to stop, a time to trust, a time to seek, a time to... and so the journey goes.

I am grateful for the day I said, I'm done, please help me to trust you, to love you, to believe in you, to give you the future. I know the journey and I know that there are many students that need to at some point leave the "stuff" and pursue the Christ. That is why I do this job called NextGen ministry.

"This is this"

This is This!
I can vaguely remember when I would tell my sons to do a task or a chore... and they would respond... Why?

I remember thinking to myself, hmmmm should I tell them what my dad told me? "Cause I said so? When did that become the not right thing to say? When did the parent stop being the one that could say... "because I said so." After all, soon that child grows up to hear a boss say, "do this or do that" and that was all that was needed. Right?

I remember when my dad got a little tired of me asking why? I think he knew I was actually trying to get him to bend a little-- Like if he didn't explain the why then I didn't have to do it. So he would say

"This is this" meaning, I'm not going to explain, I'm not going to tell you anything else-- "This is this" meant this is the way it is period.

That phrase "This is this" has stuck with me, "This is this" means that I don't have to know everything in order to do the right thing. It also means that when it comes to God, to His works, His Word, His everything and anything, I don't, I can't, I won't understand everything, I won't get everything, I won't agree with everything. But that does not change God, change His Word, change what His plan is, change the definition of sin or anything else of God. "This is this" from God is very difficult on those that have to have a "why" or it must be what I think, or it must fit my life.

I was thinking about my dad today and "This is this" really did come to my mind. I thought of how those 3 little words has helped me over the years as I struggled and sometimes struggle with and in my relationship with God. I thought about the times when "This is this" was all I needed to trust my dad because I actually at some point believed he was telling me to do things for the right reasons, because he loved me, because he wanted very much for me to be successful young man, a help to others, a good guy.

The same goes when I began to believe that God didn't need to explain anything to me in order for me to Trust Him, to follow Him, to live for Him. I don't know when it was, but I began to read the Word as "This is this" and really it did become and is becoming more and more the simple way that my faith has grown. I don't know all the answers, I certainly don't know all His ways, I certainly don't do the faith thing consistently (although it is getting better as I grow older) but I know that those 3 little words I learned from my loving dad "This is this" has stopped me in my tracks when I read His Word.

Funny how for me today, right now, I listen to all the haggling going on in Washington over important issues and if just one of these politicians said, "This is this" I'm not sure I would believe a word. I don't know who to believe anymore in Washington, but this I know... my dad was a man of his word. Moreover, I know that God is true to His Word and that has moved me, challenged me, helped me, caused me, worked in me, chastened me, bent me, pained me to get past asking the why or I need to know everything before I obey, or I need to have it make sense in order for me to follow.

Looking back at my little ole life, I will be honest-- I do have regrets and one of my regrets is the stupid, head strong, sinful way that I once said to God and to myself, this doesn't make sense so I'm not going to obey, I'm not going to listen, I'm not going to believe unless it all makes sense to me. Sometimes in this present day, I get the sense, I feel the pain, I see the destruction of those that believe that unless it all makes sense, unless it fits their "thing" unless God's plan is completely understandable, they (especially) students aren't going to follow anybody, anything let alone God.

The Scriptures do speak of "This is this". God does say "This is this" and it may not make sense, and I may not be able to explain everything to everyone, or even understand for myself, but that does not diminish Him or His Word.

Thanks dad for using those 3 little words, it has helped when I struggled and struggle in this life. I can almost hear you saying it. "This is this" in your Chicago, polish, way. Thank you God for your Word that is true, alive, and applicable to everyday living.

...another Raft Trip down the New River

Another Raft Trip done. Same river, same rafting company, same outcome. Great day, fun on the river, a couple of good scares, students enjoying God's creation, another student baptized at lunch, another wild day of laughs, swimming, falling out and on and on. I have been on this river so many times (all the way back to 1994) I know when to jump out into a rapid, I know a section in a swimmers rapid that pulls you down and then spits you back up. I love the raft trip. As long as I am a youth pastor, this trip will happen.

Student ministry is much the same really.

When I first started doing youth ministry I thought that every night was huge. I thought that every talk was so so important. I thought that everything we (I) did was significant. I thought that everything was continually new and different, that that I could make a difference in the moment, that the event or the night, or the talk, or the music, or the whatever was so so major and significant.

Last year on the same raft trip, maybe the year before, maybe the year before I started to think-- hmmmm everything is the same. Going down this river has so much to offer and yet to me it is so much the same, so goes student ministry really. Really? Yes. While there are different students on every trip, the same thing happens. Students get away, bond with each other on their raft, have fun working together, have fun swimming, enjoy all the great scenery and come off the river drained, yet exhilarated, tired, yet smiling and talking about all the great moments on the trip.

So goes student ministry. I used to get caught up believing it was about the moment and that moment would be different because of the talk, or the scenery, or all the time I put into it, or that this talk is more important than the next, or that this moment could be the most important moment in the life of a student. Well, after years of the same stuff (good stuff) I have come to the conclusion that actually student ministry is not about the moment as much is it about the process. That is right. The process, all that we do that helps the student learn the rapids, learn the difficulties, learn when to swim, learn when to hold on, learn how to trust the guide, learn how to maneuver through life and be prepared for the day when they graduate and move into college, into adult life, into uncharted waters-- life.

You see, I know that I tried to prepare my own 2 sons to get ready. I haven't always done it right, I haven't always even been right. But, watching them struggle through life, I have looked back at the times I may have concentrated more on the moment rather than the opportunity looking way ahead. Sometimes I looked for the right answer instead of the process they needed to go through to get to the correct attitude and answer. Sometimes I pushed to hard for my way, instead of the process that they needed to experience to get to a good and right resolve for themselves.

Let me explain. Yes, Student Ministry has the same ingredients it has had for years. Opportunity for knowing Christ, growing in Christ, reaching out to others, fun, music, games, application for everyday life, and on and on. Really it is the same river. Same good things for 4 years. Then it is time to move into a new chapter in a students life. I still teach the Bible, I still talk about the same Jesus Christ I talked about when I started, small groups are still important, building a ministry that has value, is relevant, and deals with all the stuff that High Schoolers deal with is still utmost. Not much has changed. Different students but the value of the ministry has not changed in 25 years for me. Students need to know Christ. Students need to know and love the Scriptures, students need to learn character and integrity, students need to learn to love, build healthy boundary's, develop self esteem, students need the process to prepare for life, all of life. The future is ahead and preparation is key.

But because I have done this so long in the same area I have seen first hand how many students have gone through the ministry finished and then-- bam. What happened to how they felt of Christ? What happened to how much they knew about God? What happened to how they trusted Christ? I have also seen the damage or fallout of those that were part of the ministry that faked it all the way through only for their true colors to come out as soon as they step into the "new" life of college.

Not much has changed indeed. Just like the river, I have been over the same rapids for years, I love to surf the same rapid every year. I love to swim the same rapid every year, and just like the river I know that what I do must continue to pursue the same stuff. That Jesus Christ can change lives, that the Bible is relevant, the scriptures are alive and applicable for everyday, that friendships with others of faith is a high value, that students get more out of honest talks then just Bible stories, that students need small groups, that students need vulnerable leaders leading music, that students need to love the church, that students need to love their parents, that students need to go through the process and we the student ministry staff need to be more than a friend, that students need the truth, that students need to be called out, that students need to be forgiven, that students need all the same stuff we (I) have been doing for years. All that to say that yes, there are some of the same things going on, and yes the river does change in levels and speed and while it may seem the same, the result is to be prepared, finish alive and well.

The bottom line is that over these years I have learned that it really is about preparation. In truth I no longer believe that the ministry is all about the moment. The ministry is actually all the moments, one after another after another. It's about preparation for the future-- for the times in life they will face that are unlike those they have faced. For the time ahead in which they will face hard questions, for the times ahead that they will face difficulty when the consequences won't be just a reprimand or a harsh scolding.

Yes, the longer I raft this same river, the more I recognize how important it is regardless of how much the same it is to prepare students for getting through the river called life. Rapids will come, fun will come, danger will arise, times to trust are around the corner, times of difficulty are coming, time to relax and just swim are all part of life. Yes, it may be the same ole "New" river, yes it may be student ministry, not much changes, the values of student ministry never change. It's not about the moment as much as it is about the process.

This last trip was a blast. I can remember many smiles, laughs and all that goes with it. This trip of Student Ministry called leading the NextGen is a blast every moment.

I am FREE

4rth of July weekend. One word comes to the forefront of my mind this weekend! FREEDOM

Yes, Freedom is what I am thinking about! Freedom! Being Free in America to say what I want to say, be who I want to be, think as I want to think, do what I want to do. I am FREE! On July 4, 1776, we claimed our independence from Britain and Democracy was born. Therefore, as a citizen of this great nation-- I appreciate America this weekend. I appreciate the truth that over 200 years ago, brave people came together and broke away, established a new country in order to be free.

So much could be said about our history, our patriots past and present. So much could be said about the declaration of independence, our heritage of freedom, from the founding Fathers to great men such as Martin Luther King, to those that have stood up in order for freedom to be for all people.

I am thinking about my freedom tonight that I have through my faith in Jesus Christ, his death and His resurrection. The freedom I have experienced throughout my life as I have moved from believing in a list to bring righteousness, to being bound up by others opinions, to being captive by forms of spirituality, to being bound to regulations of those that so much enjoy telling people what they can and can't do.

While it is so true that I am free, it is also true that I am bound to something much greater. That is that I am bound to Jesus Christ. He is my example, He is who I follow, He is who I pursue. So the rub on this independence weekend is actually that while I am totally Free to live-- I am totally bound to Jesus Christ. Is that FREEDOM? Really?

Experience first. I know that there are many, many people that don't like me because of my freedom. They judge me for being free to dress like I do. I am judged for the way I speak. I am judged by others for the things I stand against. You see, while I am bound to Christ Jesus as I follow Him. I am also bound to Him to stand for Freedom with Him. I know that it is "Man that looks at the outward appearance and that God looks at the heart." Therefore as a follower of Christ, what I dress like is no big deal. Therefore, I live free to dress the way like to dress... What people think is no big deal right?

I also know that the Scriptures teach: "I have the right to do anything," you say—but not everything is beneficial. "I have the right to do anything"—but I will not be mastered by anything." 1 Cor.6.12 I know full well, that I have the right to do anything. But there are many time, many, many times daily that because of my relationship to Christ I make the choice to not do whatever I wish. I made a choice one day to follow Christ, I make the choice daily to say, "My life is now yours, so help me to live it like you would want me to live."

Here in lies the real Freedom! I don't always do it right. As many times as I have chosen to do and be like Christ, I know that I don't do it perfectly, always correct, always like Him-- and that is Freedom. Freedom brings honesty. Freedom builds character. No longer do I live for other people's rules and regulations-- (I know that drives the pharisees of this day crazy) I do know that I don't live a perfect life, nor do I believe that my relationship with Christ demands that I do it perfectly. If I could, I wouldn't need Christ period. Freedom has produced in me a dependence in Christ Jesus alone. I know, it is crazy. How I wish others could get free. Get free to enjoy life outside the false righteousness of works, and dress, and the special list that each community of "Christians" has established for their tribe. I know, I broke free of that dependance and moved on to a dependence on Christ and His work on the cross to deal with all of my inadequacies, and flat out sin.

It's funny how many times I run into people that turn up their nose to me, like I'm some kind of twisted person because I don't do it their way. What is tough on me is that most of the time they are church people. It's funny that every once in awhile I am bothered by those pharisees like I almost want to jump through their hoops again so that "I can be like them" and then I recognize the bondage of that way of life. No thanks. I am bound to the one that brings me total Freedom, even freedom to fail.

How free am I really? I am in my 18th year of sobriety. Yes, look how free I am, I'll admit this 1 short coming, I am an alcoholic. I can't ever just have one drink. While others can, while others can enjoy a good wine or a beer, I can't. Do I ever judge them? No way. But, as I admit my short coming how many will judge me? "Oh that Youth Pastor is a drunk." Oh, man like I said, that is just one little short coming... this blog isn't long enough to list my sins, my failings, my total disaster of choices I have made. But I am FREE! I don't really care to much what others think anymore.

By the way, how many of those that judge me would ever admit that the way they talk about me, or behind my back, or about my past, is gossip? How many are free to say-- o.k., I admit it, I'm a gossip, I judge others, I don't like certain things about Him or her or them. How could they ever admit their sin? They can't, they are bound to playing a righteous game. They are bound to a form, but the substance proves who they really are inside.

You see, for those that don't like me or others being free it's because they are still bound to something that will never set them FREE.

King David says it like this: Psalm 119.44-46
I will always obey your law,
for ever and ever.
I will walk about in freedom,
for I have sought out your precepts.
I will speak of your statutes before kings
and will not be put to shame

I have found these words to be so true... as I read, learn, get into the Scriptures, I find so much freedom. When I obey the Scriptures, other peoples stuff goes away. Other peoples rules and dependence on doing it the way they think it should be done goes away.

Jesus said it like this:
"and you will know the truth, and the truth will set you free."
"So if the Son sets you free, you will be free indeed."

Yes! I celebrate my FREEDOM this weekend. My Freedom living in America to live, to love, to worship, to work, to enjoy life.

Yes! I celebrate my FREEDOM in Christ this weekend. The freedom I have to be who He made me to be, the freedom to make a choice every day to follow Him, the freedom to live my life as unto Him. Yes, I am Free to fail, to learn, to blow it, to seek Him, to be honest, to allow Him to develop my deep yearnings for Him. I am Free as I am bound to Him!

I love this song by Newsboys

Through you the blind will see
Through you the mute will sing
Through you the dead will rise
Through you all hearts will praise
Through you the darkness flees
Through you my heart screams
Yes I am Free,
Yes I am Free!

I AM FREE TO RUN
I AM FREE TO DANCE
I AM FREE TO LIVE FOR YOU
I AM FREE
YES I AM FREE

Through you the kingdom comes
Through you the battle's won
Through you I'm not afraid
Through you the price is paid
Through you there's victory
Because of you my heart sings
I am free
Yes, I am free

Sad that many can sing that song and not enjoy the same Freedom they sing about!
I'm singing it, I am living it. I am FREEEEEEEEE

Freedom and a lil more Bonhoeffer

Continuing to think and contemplate Freedom, my freedom, America the Free, Freedom in Christ, I found myself going back to a book I have read and reread several times. You see, I finished reading the book Bonhoeffer, Pastor, Martyr, Prophet, Spy by Eric Metaxas a few months ago. I still enjoy going back to the book occasionally for quotes and to just read of Dr.Bonhoeffer's life experiences.

I will never be the same after reading Eric Metaxas' work on Bonhoeffer. I was moved to tears, to joy, to resolve for more love to the Christ, for more of the likeness of Jesus in me. I have read some of Bonhoeffer's works some time ago. I know, I didn't get it. Maybe I was not ready to read The Cost of Discipleship. Nevertheless in span of about 2 months of reading, I kept running into the the man Bonhoeffer. In the book Hitler's Cross by Erwin Lutzer Dietrich Bonhoeffer is more than mentioned. After all he was a very small part in the Valkyrie plot to assassinate Hitler as Hitler was at his fortified bunker and ultimately paid for his part in the botched plot and because Bonhoeffer was a leader in the underground church called "the Confessing Church".

But... this book hit me hard. I found myself relating to him so much—and yet—I have never witnessed what he witnessed— watching Hitler destroy the Jews, destroy disabled people, destroy the church, destroy families, destroy a nation. I cannot fathom what this Godly man experienced. To die by the gallows for being such a humble, loving servant of God, to die by the gallows for being part of a conspiracy to rid the world of evil, to die for what he believed, I cannot comprehend. I can relate to his attitude toward—some of the things I have struggled with as a pastor of over 20 years.

Remember, Dr. Bonhoeffer prior to the reign of the Third Reich was free to learn, to teach, to preach, to pursue Christ... Freely through out his country Germany. But the National church sold out to Hitler and the days of Freedom to worship as a Jew, and as Christians ended quickly.

Bonhoeffer said—"I have long thought that sermons had a center that, if you hit it, would move anyone or confront them with a decision. I no longer believe that. (Me too--) First of all, a sermon can never grasp the center, but can only itself be grasped by it, by Christ. And then Christ becomes flesh as much in the word of pietists as in that of the clerics or of the religious socialists, and these empirical connections actually pose difficulties for preaching that are absolute, not merely relative."

In other words, Christ must come alive in the Word and from the Word. Speaking, preaching, teaching God's word is not so much about delivery, but about Christ coming alive in and through the message. Now that is heavy.

On the other hand—when I read of this man's life—his theological insight—I cannot help but think that here is a man, and only a man, that dedicated himself to understanding completely that point. That outside of the Christ alive through the Word, preaching, teaching may not do much at all. I have often wondered "Who is getting what I'm speaking about? But this not why Bonhoeffer lost his life. He lost his life not because he was a theological man with much much knowledge. He was killed because he did what he knew. He knew the Word as the Alive Christ and could not watch the Jews murdered. He acted upon what he knew.

"A major theme of Bonhoeffer was that every Christian must be "fully human" by bringing God into his whole life, not merely into some "spiritual" realm. To be an ethereal figure who merely talked about God, but somehow refused to get his hands dirty in the real world in which God had placed him, was bad theology. Through Christ, God had shown that he meant us to be in this world and to obey Him with our actions in this world."

With the above quote—I totally go crazy in yes yes yes. Ministry, Student ministry, church is to the many—a place to teach, to be safe from the world a place to band together and treat the world with disdain (while treating some in the church with the same disdain.) But I—yes I have felt since my days in High School—then studying for ministry, and now serving in ministry that—yes—our biggest failings as Christians in this world is that we—have failed to help, to teach, to prepare followers of Christ the *how to live* in this lost and dark world—and actually have done more damage by separating the "spiritual" with everyday life.

While I consider Freedom this day, I think of how in just a very short time back in the 1930's and 40's a whole nation's freedom, the ability to worship God, the Jew, the Lutherans, evangelicals of the day disappeared. Had the church just buried its head, become safe, decided not to deal with the culture, and abandon the truths of the Scriptures so much that it did not even see what was going on? How could so many followers of Christ give in? Did they? One man didn't. Dr. Bonhoeffer continued to teach the truth that Jesus is alive, that the Scriptures have meaning for living, and that mere words won't cut it. He lived the truth that Jesus is alive, He changes lives, He is the author and perfecter of our faith.

Again, Dr. Bonhoeffer believed "every Christian must be "fully human" by bringing God into his whole life, not merely into some "spiritual" realm. To be an ethereal figure who merely talked about God, but somehow refused to get his hands dirty in the real world in which God had placed him, was bad theology. Through Christ, God had shown that he meant us to be in this world and to obey Him with our actions in this world." Now that is Freedom!

Thank you Dr. Bonhoeffer for your life example to me. I can not wait to meet you in heaven.

the Gospel. Is it still powerful?

Can we talk? Can we talk about something really tough to talk about? How P.C. Are you? What really changes people? Can people change their hearts? Does the Gospel mean anything to you? Is it more important to change society with money, food, nails and hammer? Does the Gospel play any part in what the world actually needs? Does it really matter?

 I grew up playing pee wee baseball and pee wee football. I played hockey on a rink made in a park, on a creek, on a river, the street, the gym floor...where ever we could play. Oh, and we kept score. My friends to this day talk about all the fun we had. I played park district baseball. I didn't play alone, all my neighborhood friends played on separate teams. When I stepped up to the plate and my very good friend was pitching he would throw big curve balls because he knew I couldn't hit them. I wiffed 3 times-- struck out by a very good friend. Did we laugh back then? No. Was it fun for me? No. In the moment was I glad I struck out? Of course not. Nevertheless I ultimately grew. I had to learn how to hit a curve ball. We kept score. We talked about it. We poked at each other about which team was winning more games and so on. Personally, competition was extremely good for me. I learned how to win graciously. I learned how to lose without hanging my head. I learned how to cooperate within a team for a common goal-- winning. I learned some very important things through winning and losing. Frankly, this P.C. ideal about not keeping score- about not hurting kids feelings is just plain screwy! Is it not okay for a youth worker, youth pastor, or anyone to say-- "Be quiet already. I'm not following this way of thinking"?

Does anyone remember when calling a friend out for "bad" behavior was a good thing? When talking to a friend about their choice of friends or unhealthy behavior was part of being a friend? When talking about things that were "not acceptable" was a good thing in relationships and was the right thing to do? When going against the flow was considered "righteous"?

Does anyone remember when talking about sharing the Gospel was part of growing in one's relationship with Christ? That sharing the Gospel was part of what a youth ministry held as a high value? That reaching all students was part of the "why" one did this thing called youth ministry? That campuses were to be reached? That all students needed the Lord? How about this - when did youth ministry become about making everyone happy? Or keeping students safe? Or keeping the Christian student out of trouble? Or just taking care of the Christian student and leaving out doing ministry for those outside of the walls of the church? Oh, has that not changed? Are our youth ministries still about reaching students? Really? Or is that something that is done by a short term mission project where you go overseas for 2 weeks? Or by going to the homeless shelter once a month? Or by giving out food on a monthly basis? Is that really reaching out or is that something that we do because everyone else is doing it? Is doing all the above about really touching the lives of people or is it what we are supposed to be doing?

The question that keeps running through my mind and heart is this: Has P.C. entered into our ministry and we just don't know it? Maybe being P.C. is actually a new legalism that speaks of doing, and doing and doing without sharing the life changing Gospel that actually transforms lives. Maybe some have gotten past the Gospel because "that may offend people", so just do and maybe they will see we really care. Don't offend people with the message of the transforming power of the Gospel. Get close, but God forbid, don't offend people with the message. The street corner preachers of the past have hurt us by their rants, their calling out sin, and their brashness. So now, we've gotta be cool. We've gotta be relevant. We won't step on toes. We 'll get our hands dirty and share all our stuff, but sharing the Gospel is too confining. Sharing the Gospel may mean that people won't take our stuff. That they won't accept our "doing" for them. After all, isn't it better to take care of the needs of those in need? The end result is not to know Christ but to make people less miserable. Is that too harsh?

Now, I know that rubs hard at some people. But many today forsake the transforming power in the Gospel (that will offend) to "doing" because "doing" is less harsh and provides earthly needs. In this P.C. world we think we can share the gospel later - but is there really a guarantee of later? No doubt it's easier to "do". Isn't it easier to get students to fill bags, give a few hours a week, go away for 2 weeks rather than live out their faith daily as they share what makes them tick-- the transforming power of Jesus in their lives? Or is He really transforming them? Is He really giving them the burden of the lost world? Is He really working in them to care about not only the needs of people but also the hearts of people?

In principle what the world is doing today is what we Christians are now doing. While we have the message, while we have the answer to the world's darkness, the P.C thing is to not rock the boat. To not be like those from the past that came on about sin and all that-- preaching the Gospel but not taking care of the needs of people. My mind and heart says that an effective student ministry teaches, demonstrates and helps students see that the people outside the church walls matter – both in their separation from God and their brokenness in their poverty, their loneliness, their need of help in the state in which they are living.

Is it now too harsh to believe like Paul...to be like Paul....and actually live out this truth?
"For I am not ashamed of the gospel, because it is the power of God that brings salvation to everyone who believes: first to the Jew, then to the Gentile. For in the gospel the righteousness of God is revealed—a righteousness that is by faith from first to last, just as it is written: "The righteous will live by faith." ~Romans 1.16,17

Has P.C. Entered into student ministry? Do youth leaders today feel the Gospel is actually irrelevant. That the only way to reach people is by doing? That the transforming power of the Gospel is something that those old time holy rollers, those right wing people did back in the day? Is the gospel just too politically incorrect?

Does Jesus still save? Do we still contend for the Gospel? Are we building student ministries that care only for the outside stuff that people desperately need while holding back on the only thing that can actually transform people? Is sharing the Gospel only about going to heaven or not going to heaven? I don't think that is the only main reason. Doesn't the message of the Gospel when received actually connect broken humanity to the living God? Or is that really not important? Is there another way? Is good deeds the life changer? Or is good deeds a result of a changed heart? Really.

Has the day has arrived, that the complaints of the disenfranchised with the church – those that have said "we don't like the church", "the church doesn't really care, they just preach about how bad we are or how Jesus is the answer or how this or that is missing" caused us to change and become P.C. in order for our message to be heard. Is the message gone now? Are we practicing a new outward appearance? Are we now teaching students that the only thing that really counts is how we "do" things for others and neglect going for the tougher thing that may turn people off, the sharing of the Gospel.

We live in a very tough time. A time of being honest enough to raise this issue, but also offending those that have made the crossover from caring about peoples broken relationships with Christ to only dealing with their external brokenness. A Christ follower lives out the life of Christ for sure. I know full well that reaching out to people, feeding the poor, taking care of those in poverty, "doing" for all people is vital to sharing the Gospel. But is the Gospel being shared? I'm not talking about making people better on the outside. I'm not talking about transforming the outside. I'm talking about sharing the Gospel so that people's hearts can be transformed or at the very least give people the chance to decide for themselves if the gospel is relevant.

Isn't it true that in the end we are taking nothing with us? That all people will be faced with how they responded to message of the Gospel? That in the end, all the "stuff" in the world will change no one? That God wants a relationship with all humanity and we have that message? Isn't it true that every day we walk into a student ministry room or someplace where we face students that say they love the Lord but have nothing to do with Him during the week at school or at home? And then they go out and give to the poor, take care of the needy, do all the stuff and could care less about the why they are there... to share the Gospel. But are they? If the answer is no, is that okay? Is it really the role of Christians to right the wrongs perpetrated on those that are without, those that are poor, those that are in need? Is the Christ follower obligated to only fix the injustices through out the world and not to share the Gospel?

Back in my day, (High School) I did all the stuff. I went to church, I dressed the right way. I memorized the scriptures. I did everything I was supposed to, but I didn't know the Lord at all. I was taught all the stuff without any understanding that I needed the Lord to transform my heart. After all, I could transform myself. I did all the stuff-- until it was time to leave for college. Then, no one was around to see my outward stuff anymore. I went big. I went for it. My heart was dark. I was a product of the youth group mentality. Do like we do and you can belong. Be like us and you are one of us. Do all the right stuff and I may just be able to save myself by my good deeds? After all, if I could do and be righteous by keeping all the "laws" of our group-- I actually became as good as everyone else. At least that is what I believed and that is how I lived.

I believe we have a new thing but the same old problem. Do what is deemed important and that proves you know the Lord. Do the P.C. stuff... take care of all the right stuff and you are walking with Christ. Now it's not about dress, rock and roll and all that stuff, we all got over all that. Now it's about transforming the world by "doing" but isn't the Power of change found in the gospel?

The day is here when people need more than just students fulfilling a giving moment or just "doing" for those that truly in need... but, I dare say that the P.C. movement keeps us from going to the hard level. The daily level. The level of going out and sharing the Gospel with friends, with classmates, outside in their community into their city into the world. "Doing" without the Gospel is considered "righteous". Not offending people is better. At least they will know that we are Christians by our actions, right? The message is now in the deed. But is it? Everybody is doing it. We are a generous people, but do our students really believe that mankind is helpless in their hearts? Do our students know that people, all people, need a relationship with the living Christ?

I have a little rule I have followed for years. Here goes. As the ministry leader I desire to reach every campus in our community. Is that really about numbers? Absolutely not. Am I trying to build a student ministry? Absolutely. Am I just interested in filling a room? Not at all. Do I believe that students actually need Christ to change them from within? You bet. And so, I believe that the students that get the life changing message - that get the reality of Jesus Christ in their life - as they live their faith at home, at school, at parties, on the street, where ever they live, they are ready to go and do the things that flow from their heart. I know that is not what is going on right now. It is a disservice to followers of Christ to make giving, missions, service projects, etc. that are fulfilled once a year, once a month or once a week the essence of being a Christ follower.

I desire for my team of leaders both students and adults to grab on to the life of Jesus that is lived out every day. I know that it could be argued that mission trips and "doing" are good training opportunities, and they are, but if a student ministry is solely focused on the "going and the doing" without a clear reason to share the transforming power of the gospel aren't we just like all the other non-profit organizations in the world that give, that feed, that reach out? I contend that the church, the Christ followers today have the answer for the ills of the world and that answer is in found in the gospel. Or is that too simple? Too politically incorrect? Too narrow?

Do our students believe that mankind outside of a relationship with Christ is without hope for peace? Real peace. The peace that passes all understanding? The peace of having a relationship with the living God through Christ Jesus? The peace that says in one's insides that God and I are connected because by faith I have received the life changing truth that the death and resurrection of Christ is a reality? That the only thing that can change a persons heart is a relationship with Christ? Or is that now out of the equation?

Why put this out there? Simply stated: I sense that the time is now to diligently do both. Sharing the gospel while reaching out, feeding the poor, and taking care of the needy. The time is now. The harvest is ripe for telling people of the good news that hasn't changed in 2000 years. Yes, we must put the hands and feet of the living Christ in our deeds with the message. This world needs followers of Christ to do both all the time as they live out their faith.

I believe the gospel has power to change people. Moreover, I believe people need to change internally. I believe that sin really keeps people from a relationship with the living God. I believe that it is not politics that will change the world but that Jesus came to change this world through His followers, the message they share, the good deeds they do, and the example they set. Let us not stop sharing the life changing message of the Gospel, regardless of how it is received.

"For I am not ashamed of the gospel, because it is the power of God that brings salvation to everyone who believes: first to the Jew, then to the Gentile. For in the gospel the righteousness of God is revealed—a righteousness that is by faith from first to last, just as it is written: "The righteous will live by faith." ~The Apostle Paul

Living Inside Out

"These people honor me with their lips, but their hearts are far from me. They worship me in vain; their teachings are but rules taught by men." Jesus called the crowd to him and said, "Listen and understand. 11What goes into a man's mouth does not make him 'unclean,' but what comes out of his mouth, that is what makes him 'unclean.' " Then the disciples came to him and asked, "Do you know that the Pharisees were offended when they heard this?" He replied, "Every plant that my heavenly Father has not planted will be pulled up by the roots. Leave them; they are blind guides. If a blind man leads a blind man, both will fall into a pit." Peter said, "Explain the parable to us." "Are you still so dull?" Jesus asked them. "Don't you see that whatever enters the mouth goes into the stomach and then out of the body? But the things that come out of the mouth come from the heart, and these make a man 'unclean.' For out of the heart come evil thoughts, murder, adultery, sexual immorality, theft, false testimony, slander. These are what make a man 'unclean'; but eating with unwashed hands does not make him 'unclean." ~Matt. 15.8-20

I find these words from Jesus Christ so, so uplifting, so life changing, so completely opposite of the way students and some parents think. Maybe the truth is that it actually is much easier to concentrate on what has been taught and communicated over the years. Maybe it is much easier to always blame the outside stuff on what is wrong. Maybe it is too difficult to listen to what Jesus says as valuable-- after all, we can't see Him, we don't really believe that the Word has value, maybe it's too dog gone hard to actually follow the Christ on such basic, compelling, life changing words.

First things first:
What goes into a man's mouth does not make him 'unclean,' but what comes out of his mouth, that is what makes him 'unclean.'

Explanation: Inside is where it starts not on the outside. (Lets stop putting the cart in front of the horse.)

But the things that come out of the mouth come from the heart, and these make a man 'unclean.' 19For out of the heart come evil thoughts, murder, adultery, sexual immorality, theft, false testimony, slander. 20These are what make a man 'unclean'; but eating with unwashed hands does not make him 'unclean.'

So, why does the emphasis always seem to be about the "Outside" stuff?

- It's easy
- Tough to change
- Don't have the courage to look inside
- Less hassles with those that want us to live a certain way.
- Too much pressure
- Just plain ignorant

The reality. The real reasons why Jesus went after those that loved outside issues?

"These people honor me with their lips, but their hearts are far from me. 9They worship me in vain; their teachings are but rules taught by men."

Jesus then, and Jesus now doesn't appreciate people that talk talk talk about living the life of following Him. Jesus says, our hearts matter first and foremost. Oh and as far as the "rulez" go? That's worth another blog. The Pharisees loved their rulez all their rulez without honoring God.

Maybe I should ask myself:

- How do I honor Christ? How's my attitude toward spiritual things?

- How do I live for Him? Outside first or from the Inside out?

It doesn't seem so long ago that the light went on for me-- that I understood that my heart was totally dark, full of sin.
I couldn't fix it myself
I couldn't go to church and get clean
I couldn't get my heart cleaned by doing and doing and doing.
I needed the Christ, the one that I had heard about all my life to fix this broken heart of mine. I realized I was just like the Pharisees that practiced "religion" but cared nothing for the Christ or their God.

I had to allow Christ to check out my heart. I couldn't blame, or try and explain my attitude, my actions any more. I needed Him to tell me the truth.

How bout you?
What does He tell you about your heart?
Allow yourself to look inward– and be honest-- Where is your heart?

Test me, O LORD, and try me, examine my heart and my mind;
~Psalm 26.2

Search me, O God, and know my heart; test me and know my anxious thoughts.
~Psalm 139.23

Isn't this where it starts? Really. Think about all the things that students are doing-- where does it really start? To many videos? The rock and roll? The commercials? Where? And what really can transform students? Where does transformation occur? Outside first? Wrong! Totally wrong. It starts inside and changes the outside, well that is according to Jesus.
Following Jesus for life

- Begins with the Heart
- It's all about what is happening internally with our relationship with Christ.
- It's all about honest introspection, honest confession, honest repentance and then-- once the heart gets cleaned up and transformed, then the outside stuff gets transformed.

11 Rejoice in the LORD and be glad, you righteous; sing, all you who are upright in heart! Psalm 32.11

This is the most difficult truth to teach students in the NextGen. It is also the most rewarding. Once a student finally deals with their messed up heart-- church student or not, once they get real and honest about their heart-- oh man does their life change.

Living by the Internal

"There is nothing more real that a man's character and values. The track record of what he has actually done is far more real than anything he says, however elegantly he says it." ~Thomas Sowell

"The inward area is the first place of loss of true Christian life, of true spirituality, and the outward sinful act is the result." ~Francis Schaeffer

I was looking through my bookmarks on my web browser deally and ran across the bookmark for my AARP web stuff membership. I actually have a spot on the AARP site. Wow! I can't believe I have been around for 52 years almost 53.

What do I think about this? Hmmmm I have been thinking about influence. Influence on my life and the influence I have had in others lives. When I was growing up I continually heard from my mom this statement "what are people going to think?" Some people appreciate that statement—I'm not that keen on it. It's the context from my mom—who is 94 this year. What motivated my mom to continually harp on me about "others" and the way they thought about me was not about the internal things lived out. That statement was actually about the external things – looks, clothes, hair, tattoos etc.,and being accepted or liked if you will because of the external things. Some may say, "that is good" well it may be good if one is working on the internal things first—character, integrity come to mind.

So then, how did I get here (the externals and influence) through an AARP membership and website? I thought of the short life of Jesus. I thought of His influence on the people around him. What made Him influential? Was He motivated by "what will people think?" Was He motivated by simply living out what was internal—His love for the Father, His love for humanity, His choice to pursue the cross? I believe that Jesus was influential because He lived out His passions and what others thought about Him was not the key to His life— obviously some accepted Him and others did not. Jesus did not change so the "others" would—He was driven by what was internal. After all, Jesus was known for being a friend of drunkards and gluttons... "a friend of sinners." Yikes

I thought about this stuff last night—in this day of Facebook, twitter, blogs, YouTube---I have connected and reconnected with people that go all the way back to high school—35 years later—what really do they think of me? I don't look the same—older, hair color has changed and gotten thinner, some scars, getting shorter—do they really care about the externals? I don't think so. Do they notice the externals? Sure. But what they know most about me is from the inside out. Do I have character? Do I have integrity? Do I care about what people think of me because of fear? No, I have chosen to Follow Christ over the years—just like the first people that Jesus asked to "Follow me" without worrying about what others would think-- just going for it! (I have seen over the years what people pleasing does to many of my friends and on occasion myself)

I have come to the realization that "Following" Christ is a process and had I been worried about what others thought—I may have not jumped in, engaged Him and followed with all that I have. Now looking back-- Oh you bet I haven't done it right. You bet I have failed along the way, you bet I have blown it—but I have chosen to be transparent and tried to be honest enough to not care so much about what people think of my external stuff – but choose to live from the inside out—and hopefully people have seen the Christ in me.

The ministry I lead, the students and families I work with are so important to me because I know the value of the internal-- how important it is for all to live by what God is doing in them through their relationship with the living Christ. Moreover, how much more does Jesus the Christ care about each student, each family, each person? This stuff matters to God, therefore it does matter to me. I know what can happen when people live out what Jesus is doing in their heart which begs the question-- Is He? Is He doing something in our hearts? That is where the action starts!

I witnessed the other night 2 students that came to terms with this truth. That their hearts needed fixing and that the only fix is by faith in Christ Jesus. You see they have tried to do it themselves. They have tried and tried and tried only to always fall short (just like the Scriptures say) These students came to Christ with the knowledge of watching peers try, watching adults try only to see themselves and others as on the outside, still broken, tarnished, full of angst and hurt. It is the heart that needs transformation by the work of the Living Christ. Then there can be hope life and life full.

"The inward area is the first place of loss of true Christian life, of true spirituality, and the outward sinful act is the result." ~Francis Schaeffer

"These people honor me with their lips,
but their hearts are far from me.
They worship me in vain;
their teachings are merely human rules." ~Matt. 15.8,9

Distractions

Distraction: That which diverts attention; a diversion. A diversity of direction.

 Now that my sons are at College (almost a week now) It seems like time has slowed down a bit. When I get home after work there is no one here except the cat. When its time for dinner its just Marcie and me. After dinner its just Marcie and me, oh and Ranger the cat hangin out on the couch watching T.V.

One of the things that I have noticed recently is this: Distractions. Before my 2 boys left for school we talked about the distractions that could take them off course. You know? Distractions. The things not many of us care to deal with, but contend with everyday. Distractions. Like the cell phone. Like emails. Like twitter. Like Facebook. Like the inter web, music 24/7 via ipod, a new this or a new that. Distractions. The need to have every minute filled. The need to know everyone's business. The need to be the life of the party. The need to be in control of life. Distractions. You know? The distractions that seems to interrupt, the distractions that we allow to interrupt. The distractions that cry out for an urgent reply then take us out of the groove for an hour or two.

What I'm talking about is simply this: I have noticed that not too many of the things I used to think were huge, now seem to not matter very much. I'm not as distracted. I'm not as pulled away from "stuff" by "stuff" any more.

The interesting thing that I have found is that first as a father, and as a youth pastor, I can see more clearly the plight of distractions. I know what they did to me. I know how distractions robbed me of a couple of things back in the day of High School and early college days. I have recognized for years my personal distractions. That also means that I (as a father) know the distractions that my sons deal with and they are not to different than those I dealt with. I see what High School students deal with when it comes to distractions and those are not much different than the distractions I also dealt with.

Thank God I didn't have a cell phone in high school. I didn't have the Facebook in high school. I am thankful my mom couldn't call me anytime of the day and that my girl friend couldn't call me anytime of the day either. Yes, I didn't have x box or a lap top. I did have a car, I did have friends, I did play an instrument, I was involved in sports, I worked, I had to go to school. So? Well the distractions I'm talking about are the things that take us away from the "important" things. The things that matter. The things that if I would have learned back then, I wouldn't have had to bang my head against the wall later. You know? The distractions that took me away from dealing with the inner angst I felt but pushed aside with the distraction of more busyness. The pain I had because I didn't feel adequate, so I found things to do that helped me to feel adequate while in truth those things were just distractions from the real issues.

The real issues? I know what they are for me. I know they are not the same for everyone, but maybe quite similar. I watched my 2 sons get distracted from pursuing their passions and gifting by what is supposed to be normal things-- putting relationships in front of the time to hone skills for the future is really just a distraction to doing the hard things, taking the pain up front, like saying no to something now because in the long run what seems so important in they end won't amount to much. How many of us know first hand the time we wasted on distractions and yet would rather talk about, preach about all the other big ticket items.

Distractions aren't talked about much it seems to me. With the Youth Pastor hat on it seems many would like me to deal with the "sin" things like drugs, sex and rock and roll. Not many parents it seems want to deal with the real issues of distractions. Maybe the real issue is that in life distractions aren't talked about because we all deal with them and to many distractions may be harder to deal with than all the quote "sins" we are all familiar with.

I think parents, myself included must help students, our students with what we know of ourselves. That distractions take us away from important things in the now and for the future. Example: David and Bathsheba. Think about it. King David is to be on the battlefield with his warriors. Instead, he decides to stay away from what he is supposed to be doing-- it is then that he is distracted by Bathsheba as she bathes on a roof top. Had the King done or been where he was supposed to be, Bathsheba would have never been noticed. I know personally that I have let distractions take me out of stride. I know that distractions have affected my 2 sons. I know first hand that many students over the years have been distracted to the point of losing focus, losing their joy for good and right things, losing their stride because of distractions which ultimately turned into much pain, much hurt and some destruction.

Maybe the bottom line is this: That the distraction of let's say the social media today or in my day was literally social living-- out every night, hangin out, being out, being with friends-- that the distraction of the "social" stuff actually leads to believing and living with the belief that without connectedness a person is not whole. Which in turn could easily lead to moving to the next level-- the intimacy we all think we need, which leads to unhealthy relationships which leads to a desire to connect which leads to a relationship that goes beyond what God intended for 2 people that are married. Could it be? Could it be that we continue to avoid dealing with distractions because they seem to be a normal part of our lives, while all along this inner voice continues to cry out to us that "I am here, I am the source of contentment through a relationship with me." To those that know Christ personally He continues to knock at our hearts door to as He says "to sup with us" that we would rather find satisfaction in any distraction other than intimacy with Him the living God, the great mystery, Christ in you.

This little diddy today is just to encourage us all to look deep into the distractions that are actually hurting us. Maybe we all can do a better job at talking with students about the things that aren't the big "sins" and start talking about the little things that get students distracted enough to get them away from the more important things and ultimately turn into the big sins.

Distractions are all around. Be careful.
Last thing. I do know this, that everyday when I start my day I ask God to help me know the things that I need to pursue and help me to let go of the stuff that doesn't matter. Maybe the truth is that what seems to be just a "small" thing, a distraction, is actually the beginning of the loss of focus on what is important, good, right, and valuable for us.

"Therefore, since we are surrounded by such a great cloud of witnesses, let us throw off everything that hinders and the sin that so easily entangles, and let us run with perseverance the race marked out for us."   ~Hebrews 12.1

Good "Ole" Rush St.

I had a great weekend in Chicago. Chicago is where I lived my first 24 years of life. I love that city. For years going back home to Chicago meant staying with family or friends. I have always wanted to spend a weekend downtown with my wife Marcie. Now that our sons are off to school it was time to head back home and stay right downtown at the Drake Hotel. What a magnificent hotel. Right on the corner of Walton and Michigan Ave.

As we were downtown walking some of my old favs-- Rush Street, Division, Michigan Ave, I had some old memories-- good and bad come back. I thought of the many times I would ride my motorcycle down to Oak Street Beach and sleep the morning away after working all night at the Jewel. I must have done that everyday for at least half the summer. I remembered the drives downtown to some great places to eat. My short stay at M.B.I. My time working downtown for an electrical contractor, so there were many places I remembered going to on service calls. Oh I have so many great memories of Chicago.

I also have some not so good memories from my downtown times in Chicago. "Holy Cow!"

Which actually leads me to this little blog today. When it comes to parenting, being a youth pastor, being around students much of the past 20 years I think of this: "Therefore, if anyone is in Christ, the new creation has come. The old has gone, the new is here." 2 Corinthians 5.17

Yes, walking around my favorite places brought back this truth-- and I know it full well-- I have seen many students go the direction of "partying hard, living the dreams of having it all". I have tried to share my story as best I could and have those looks from students and even my own 2 sons-- you know, the "Man you don't know what you are talking about. I'm gonna go do the stuff that everybody does, I don't need your input or your view. Besides, that was years ago. I want the life of bright lights and fun times. I can handle it."

Being back in Chicago this past weekend was a blast for sure. I was able to relish in the new rather than the old. That was fun with a huge reminder of the past and the transforming power of what God can do in one's heart.

There is hope for those that are looking for "glitter and gold" only to find it wanting. There is hope for those students deep down inside that finish a night on the town and ask-- "Is that all. I want more." There is hope for the people like me that decide that life is a party and I want it now.

But there is something much greater.

"Therefore, if anyone is in Christ, the new creation has come. The old has gone, the new is here."
2 Corinthians 5.17

A sad day in the I.C.U.

I was at the ICU unit today visiting a family whose daughter is on life support because she was with her intoxicated boyfriend as he drove into a light post. (this is the second student in 6 months, same ICU, same issue) both direct results of alcohol. I don't know all the details, but this I know-- that this young lady was a passenger in a car driven by a person that was drinking (an open container was found to be in the car.) I write this blog tonight with a heavy heart for her and her family. I write this blog because I work with students that continue to use. I write this blog not to place guilt or shame but to keep in front of all that would read this blog the truth about alcohol, and the truth that choices have consequences.

When I walked into her room I could not help notice the 12 I.V. bags, the life support machine doing the breathing for her, the blood continuing to drip from her mouth, her half shaved head, her bruised face. I was speechless. The only thing I could do was pray silently for her, for God to perform a miracle, for God's help in this great time of need. I prayed with her brother who is part of the NextGen ministry, a servant, a kind hearted young man who is devastated. It was just Friday morning her brother and I prayed about his sister and about her relationship with the young man that was driving. Early Saturday morning the accident happened. As a youth pastor there is nothing harder than walking into a waiting room with families hurting, heavy with pain over the loved one that is struggling for life itself. Even now after hours have passed since visiting my heart aches for this family, for this young lady.

While in the waiting room at the I.C.U. I received a call from another student that was upset for the partying they did last night hours away. He shared with me his known inability to not partake, his inability to say no to a night that he knew he would end up drinking which ultimately led to being drunk. I told him where I was... ICU with a family that has a daughter on life support due to the same issue by which he continues to struggle. This alcohol lifestyle is killing students daily. It may not be today, but the outcome is surely around the corner. Partying is just an escape period and for those that don't want to deal with it or speak about it or face it there aren't any options any more. We must face it! We that have sons and daughters, we that work with students daily can never stop speaking about the consequences. We can never stop speaking into their lives. We may not be liked, we may not be treated kindly, we may be called all sorts of names, but we must intervene.

The idea that alcohol is a "right of passage" or part of "being a teenager" is a flat out lie from the pit of hell. First, the student is underage. Second, alcohol is another drug, 3rd being buzzed, drunk, high, brings with it consequences that one may not be able to overcome. As a youth pastor it really is time for those of us that see it, feel it, deal with it weekly to speak up, to never ever stop telling the truth that the lifestyle of partying has nothing good about it! Absolutely nothing.

My heart is heavy today. For you see, I know the answer. I know the truth and I know not many are listening. I wish I could help. I know the truth though, that a person will continue to use until they come to their own reasons to quit the partying and that just may be too late. There is no way to speak cute about it, or PC about it, or even glamorous about it. Which leads me to another issue within the issue. While the world says drink to be happy, while the world says be cool and have a Bud, while the world says in order to be accepted you gotta be a party animal, while the world says it's o.k. it's part of growing up, it's cool, it's what you are supposed to do. While the world pontificates about the religion of using, there is a problem. What about those that claim to follow Christ? What about those that desire to follow Him with all their heart? I know full well of the days I partied. I know full well how much I appreciated a good buzz, getting loose, getting crazy. I know full well that in those years the last thing I cared about was walking with God or following Christ. I didn't care one bit. Oh I felt guilt and shame continually and that is why I drank again and again and again. The cycle went on for a long time until I came to the bottom. I wasn't sparred the consequences, I wasn't sparred the distrust from those around, I wasn't sparred an accident that should have been my wake up call. It didn't take long to form my dependence on feeling good, blocking out pain, being in and at the party even if I was by myself. I was addicted and nothing was going to stop me except my brokenness and my will to stop and my complete and utter reliance on God.

I finish this blog tonight with a heavy heart for this young lady. I find myself praying for her and her family often. To my friends in Christ that may gloss over this issue, to my friends in Christ that struggle with the courage to face the problem, that is the problem of living in this world and not "offending" or continuing to love the party life, or that continue to live their life like following Christ and getting ripped is o.k. I have a few questions: Is that the life the Lord wants of His followers? To live as if their life is still their life and theirs only? To live as if their actions are only their actions? Is it really right to think that the "I can do whatever I damn well want to do" is actually how a follower of Christ lives? Is it really o.k. to think that this is just a phase, that it's o.k. to flip following Christ off for a time? Oh is that not how it is? Students that know Christ that make the choice to party, to use, to live like they want, isn't flipping Him off? Better check deep down inside for the answer to that question. Those are the tough questions of a NextGen pastor.

Maybe I've been in my field too long. Maybe I'm just tired of watching students self destruct due to using, maybe I have had enough of the pain in my own life, I don't know-- but I do know that doing student ministry is where I reside, that student ministry has a high value, and that doing student ministry means that I must tell the truth. Maybe this day, this tragic event and the phone call from a student brought the reality of this issue back to the forefront for me.

I want to remind readers today that there is an enemy that wants to destroy people. He is evil, he is ruthless, he hates God, he hates everything about God's purposes. Reevaluate everything. For the devil is coming after life in huge ways.

9/11 Changed things

9/11 2001 I was on my way to my new office, doing a new ministry role as pastor of a church plant, listening to talk radio driving down I-75. A news bulletin came from the talk radio show host of a plane that hit the twin towers. I got to my office called home as the second plane hit the second tower. A friend from the church working in the same office complex came over, we found a t.v. set and watched the horrible day unfold.

During that month my father was critically hurt in a car accident with my mom and in November my father had a life ending heart attack due to the accident. No question from 9/11 2001 through November, 2001 I was ill prepared for all the changes taking place in my country and in my little life. In truth, life hasn't been the same since.

When Cooper and Alex, my sons were maybe 8 and 10 I used to tell them to enjoy Saturday cartoons because the day is coming when Saturday's will change from sleeping in, watching cartoons to early rising and heading to work. Life is going to change boys, so get ready.

9/11 2001 changed many things indeed. The last 10 years many things have changed. The job situation has changed not just my job but the opportunity to even have a job, the investment of a house has changed many houses are now upside down, the economy has changed, the price of a gallon of gas has continued to change.... life as an American has changed, that can not be denied.

This great Nation where I live has faced huge changes over time for sure. The tragic day of 9/11 brought change in many things and one stands out for me today. I don't ever recall telling someone, anyone that they must put their faith in Christ or face possible jail, torture or even death. I don't ever remember in my life time the idea that there were people that were willing to destroy humans for their religious point of view.

That did happen during the reign of Hitler as he wanted what was called "the solution" to the Jewish problem. While many will choose to deny the connection, the truth has been documented. Hitler murdered millions of Jews because of their religion and their nationality. Today, the change has come. While it is true that this Sunday the 10 year anniversary of the deadly day of destruction took place from those that want to destroy any faith, any religion other than their own. That cannot be denied. And as our economy struggles, our job situation struggles, our government struggles – the rerun of Post WWI Germany comes to mind as the man Hitler came to power as Germany cried out for a new regime to take care of the mess that Germany found itself. Hitler was able to bamboozle the country for the sake of security, new money, new jobs and a strong Germany without the freedoms it once possessed. Germany was willing to lose much in order to gain economy, security, jobs and a better life. Change came to Germany with a high price. Change is coming and I fear many will throw away what was once a high value in order to have what is perceived to be security, a better economy and even a false better way of life.

To me 9/11 brought much change to our Nation indeed. Moreover it brought change to me, a father, a pastor, a follower of Christ. I believe those that follow Christ will have much to stand up for in these years ahead. I believe those that follow Christ will have much to live for when it comes to their faith in the living Christ. There may come a day when a follower of Christ will be considered the problem. That the follower of Christ will have to say no to a mandated religion. The follower of Christ will have to say no to those that want followers of Christ to be quiet, to follow another, to even renounce their faith.

Far fetched? To some no doubt, but the change is here.

Jesus said it like this in His prayer for His disciples: "If the world hates you, keep in mind that it hated me first. If you belonged to the world, it would love you as its own. As it is, you do not belong to the world, but I have chosen you out of the world. That is why the world hates you. Remember what I told you: 'A servant is not greater than his master.' If they persecuted me, they will persecute you also. If they obeyed my teaching, they will obey yours also. They will treat you this way because of my name, for they do not know the one who sent me." ~John 15.18-21

Yes, our world is changing. Yes, life seems to be much different these days. Yes, there is a new angst in this world. But one thing will never change. "Every good and perfect gift is from above, coming down from the Father of the heavenly lights, who does not change like shifting shadows." James 1.17

"I the LORD do not change." Malachi 3.6

The older I get, the longer I live, the more I see, hear, witness the changes all around, I recognize how much I need God. How much I need the steadfastness of the Lord and how much on this 10 year anniversary of this terrible day how much people need more than the security offered by this world. I know many today that long for change or as is now the catch phrase "transformation". What kind of transformation? Kindness? Newness? What? The Scriptures speak of transformation. The changes this world needs is not in new government programs, new ideology, new this or that. The change, the "transformation" this world needs is not found in the people that fly planes into buildings or kill people that don't believe in their laws or ways. That is garbage.

The Bible speaks of mankind's complete and total depravity. The pharisees tried to live externally and called on others to live "changed" lives by practicing this external way of life but the law pointed out the complete and total depravity of the heart. Jesus Christ is the only one that can change a persons lost and dark heart. Yes, change is coming as those that know Christ continue to share, and live out the Gospel. One by one as people place their small faith in Christ, the only one that can transform a darkened heart, transformation will occur. Many would like to leave all the above behind and go back to pushing externals leaving behind what to many now is considered archaic and even outdated. Transformation, true change of heart and behavioral change takes place through the salvation offered by the only Savior-- Christ Jesus.

To those "followers" that believe in some other form of "changing" this world I freely, openly disagree with that ideal. For those followers of Christ that believe that mankind can "change" themselves, or believe that they can bring a new kind of Utopia to the world without the power of the Gospel, I respectfully say you are mislead. Maybe the biggest change through the past 10 years is actually those that have been f00led into believing any thing other than this truth that mankind without the Savior, without God will perish, that sin is killing people, that the world desperately needs Jesus Christ and His transforming power.

I will never forget the destruction of 9/11. Nor will I ever forget the truth of how much people need a transformation of their heart. May God by His matchless Grace continue to reconcile people to Himself by the power of the Spirit through a relationship in the only Savior Jesus Christ.

Today I honor 9/11 by freely going to church. I honor 9/11 by exercising my freedom to worship the only true God, the only Risen Savior! Today I remember 9/11 by living free, speaking freely and living out such a great Salvation.

Who cares about apathy?

"By far the most dangerous foe we have to fight is apathy – indifference from whatever cause, not from a lack of knowledge, but from carelessness, from absorption in other pursuits, from a contempt bred of self satisfaction." ~William Osler

There really is nothing much harder than doing ministry with people that don't care. Apathy is all around students today. Maybe it's the deep down inside feeling that students have about a world that seems to be uncontrollable. Maybe a student feels like their voice doesn't matter. Maybe a student has been taught at home by parents, or others that their struggles or hardships will be managed by someone else. Maybe students today really don't care about their world, the happenings around them really don't matter. Maybe they just are involved in so many other things that to care about something may be just added energy that they just don't have to give. Maybe apathy is just easy.

Apathy: A lack of interest or concern, a lack of feeling or emotion.

Apathy is one of the hardest things to help students overcome. I know personally what apathy can do because I was a student back in the day that chose to "not care" so that I could do whatever I wanted to do. Not caring allowed me to think that what was supposed to be important in my world wasn't important because I just didn't care. The end result was that what was important stayed important regardless of my "opting out". Only to make what I didn't care about to at some point as I woke up, I realized it was important and I had lost much ground.

I work with students that are apathetic all the time. But, apathy towards spiritual things, more importantly towards their relationship to Jesus Christ is hard for me to deal with. I mean, I can't yell it out of them. It is almost impossible to reason with them about their apathy. It is even harder to convince them of their apathy. I can't entertain them out of it. I can't speak it out of them. I can't will it out of them. What then?

Well, I take a lesson from my own life. The greatest wake up call was that as life was passing me by because "I didn't care" I began to realize my apathetic state. There were people around me that I saw moving forward, taking a stand, speaking out, living out their passions and I wanted to be part of something that was greater than just hangin around, complaining and just going through the motions.

The hard part of doing student ministry is that many think that a program filled with all sorts of stuff will make the difference. Many think that more and busy and more will keep students from being apathetic. But I'm talking about a relationship with Christ. So, how does one help a student to move out of their apathy? Working in church means that there are plenty of students that at some point came to a place when they said "I want that, I want a relationship with Christ Jesus but right now I really don't care." Now what?

Does a student ministry entertain so that the student will care more? Does a student ministry do things so that a student will want more of Him? We all know that doing "Chubby Bunnies" doesn't cut it. We all know that just a Bible lesson ain't gonna cut it when those hearing the lesson "don't care." Apathy is all around. Apathy keeps students from calling out evil in their own lives. Apathy keeps students from caring about those without Christ. Apathy keeps students thinking about "their" needs. Apathy keeps students from caring about ministry, the church and other such spiritual things.

Francis Schaeffer said it like this: "I have come to the conclusion that none of us in our generation feels as guilty about sin as we should or as our forefathers did." Thus, the problem of not caring about the real issue. Sin. Sin is the real culprit isn't it? If one is apathetic, then why care about anything that may point inward. Why care about what God think is sin, if it is sin "I don't care." The "I don't care" about it is actually at the core of many of our problems and issues.

I'm praying for a breakthrough. A breakthrough for students to see, to feel, to desire Jesus Christ with all their heart. It's no wonder that Jesus said, Hot or cold but lukewarm is no good. Or the image of the Christ talking about salt losing it's saltiness-- and when that happens that salt is only good for a pile of garbage.

Recently a father told me this story. His daughter was dating a young man that the father knew (and so did his daughter) was not a good guy. This young man had already hurt his daughter. This young man had a proficiency toward alcohol and other substances. This young man was not good for his daughter and he told her so. He said "this guy will hurt, he will not be good for you." The daughters response? Apathy says-- "I don't care" and an "I don't care" mindset will ultimately hurt anyone in the long run and an "I don't care" to this situation actually did end up exactly how this loving father said it would. Apathy is deadly.

"Apathy is the glove into which evil slips its hand." ~Bodie Thoene A sobering quote and a sobering truth.

The end result of apathy is a life that is standing still, just going through life with not much joy, not much hope, not much faith in anything but opting out of a life that can be so much more. Praying for a breakthrough!

Just a blip on the radar screen of life, but not easy.

One of my favorite things that I have the privilege to do is to hang out with parents of students. Really? Seriously. Yearly I get to lead and be part of an 8 week session called "Dealing with today's teens" a DVD series by Mark Gregston.

I'll admit right up front. That my time with my 2 guys going through teendom was tough. Actually there were days, many days that I was absolutely clueless. Which leads me down the path to when I started student ministry oh 20 years ago or so. I was absolutely clueless then and I didn't even have my own kids yet. Interesting that I really couldn't understand no matter how many books I read, or seminars I listened to, how lonely, how out there parents feel when in the midst of going through the crazy teen years.

So I lead this session with oh anywhere from 25-30 parents. Great people that love their kids no doubt. I know their students. I know some students are way out there right now. I know that their students are struggling with peer stuff, image, temptations, the media blitz, the bad attitudes all that goes with growing up in this brutal, lost world.

My role to parents, all parents continues to be that of Pastor, friend, and mostly peer. Even though my 2 guys are out of the house I still feel raw from this past summer of watching my 2 guys struggle with all that students struggle with and much more. Yes, being with this group of parents is always a joy for me. Kinda like an opportunity to make sense of my experience with my 2 and the years of student ministry and like giving this group of people a gift from a parent, a student pastor with lots of miles of experience, and real, I mean real empathy!

Yes, I really do appreciate parents today as I lead this ministry called NextGen. One of the difficulties of the student ministry is the many parents I know that must be hurting, struggling, praying, feeling lost that just aren't connected to the ministry or even me.

So I will keep working with parents, telling the truth, trying to help them as they go through some tough times. The best thing I can say is simply this: This time called teendom, adolescence is really a bump on a long road for sure. So continue to love your student no matter what, continue to move from trying to be their friend, cease to enable, and prepare them to go, continue to always tell the truth even if you are not liked.

Oh I know I haven't arrived, and I know that there is still much to do when it comes to raising my 2 guys, let alone what other parents are going to continue to experience. This I do know: I'm not the same person I was when I was a teenager. I look back at these past few years with my 2 guys and yes some of that time was absolutely crazy. But most of those years made me a better man, parent and youth pastor and it is true that as tough as those years were I'm beginning to see and understand that it really is a little blip on the screen.

Tangled up

Enmesh: to catch or entangle in or as if in meshes

What is "enmeshment?"

"Enmeshment is a description of a relationship between two or more people in which personal boundaries are permeable and unclear. This often happens on an emotional level in which two people "feel" each other's emotions, or when one person becomes emotionally escalated and the other family member does as well. A good example of this is when a teenage daughter gets anxious and depressed and her mom, in turn, gets anxious and depressed. When they are enmeshed the mom is not able to separate her emotional experience from that of her daughter even though they both may state that they have clear personal boundaries with each other. Enmeshment between a parent and child will often result in over involvement in each other's lives so that it makes it hard for the child to become developmentally independent and responsible for her choices."

What causes two people to become enmeshed?

"The causes of enmeshment can vary. Sometimes there is an event or series of occurrences in a family's history that necessitates a parent becoming protective in their child's life, such as an illness, trauma, or significant social problems in elementary school. At this time the parent steps in to intervene. While this intervention may have been appropriate at the time, some parents get stuck using that same approach in new settings and become overly involved in the day to day interactions of their children.

Other times, and perhaps more frequently, enmeshment occurs as a result of family patterns being passed down through the generations. It is a result of family and personal boundaries becoming more and more permeable, undifferentiated, and fluid. This may be because previous generations were loose in their personal boundaries and so it was learned by the next generation to do the same. Or it may be a conscious decision to stay away from family patterns of a previous generation that felt overly rigid in its personal boundaries."

~David Prior, LMFT. Prior is the executive director of Sunrise RTC, a treatment program for adolescent girls known for its effective work with enmeshed family relationships.

Here in lies some of the difficulties of building and doing "new" things, work "new programs" in the NextGen ministry. Enmeshment may keep people from moving beyond different approaches because they may be so enmeshed in what they perceived to be an outstanding way of doing things, or developed unhealthy boundaries with leadership, or through time connected-- actually becoming enmeshed if you will, to "the program", a person, or a belief system.

I understand because I am a father, youth pastor and leader. I know first hand how difficult it becomes to try to make changes or do something "new" if you will, if people are concerned more about "the way" and what they are accustomed to. As a father I have had to always be the "dad" and not "the friend" because I have seen first hand what happens when parents are considered and even proud to be their high schoolers "friend" rather than being the parent. When the "friend" as the parent remains the "friend" unhealthy boundaries arise and can turn quickly into an enmeshed relationship.

As a youth pastor I know first hand how parents and students get stuck in the way "its always been done." There are some students that become too close to a youth pastor, and the youth pastor too close to their families and soon unhealthy relationships are developed. As a parent I did not want to be either one of my son's friend knowing that being their friend would hurt them in the long run. I also know that in youth ministry me being connected to students as their friend is also unhealthy. When Jesus the Christ says to His disciples that He is their "Friend" He is their friend. He is also our friend. Yet, He Jesus while being our Friend is also at the same time our Savior, our Lord. When the line of Friend and Savior/Lord gets fuzzy then the possibility for treating Him as just a pal with diminishing respect and adoration will occur. Enmeshment means that I as a leader/youth pastor would be tangled in students feelings, attitudes and behaviors. I am here as a youth pastor to help them, to teach them, to show them the truth and live it in front of them. Enmeshment causes leaders and parents the inability to do the "hard" things. Enmeshment is a possibility for all those that do youth ministry, leadership and of course for parents.

As the leader of the NextGen ministry my first concern is always for the total ministry. Are we being effective? Am I teaching, leading, the way God is asking me, calling me, directing me? Dealing with many different families, students, situations means that as the leader I am not a friend to 100 students, 50 students or even 5 students. I have a ministry to lead and I must not get enmeshed with any student or family for that matter. Yes, as youth pastor, I care for all students and families, not just a certain "type", or for those that agree with a certain style or for those that are doing well, or for those that "get it". A student ministry that will grow, reach students, minister to many high schools, many families will not grow if enmeshment is occurring.

Finally, it is crucial to point students to Jesus the Christ as the one that understands completely who they are, what they are feeling, what they are going through because He does understand fully our humanness, our issues and everything about living in this fallen broken world. At the same time Jesus takes us as we are that is not the ending point. He desires for us to "turn" repent from the things that He is revealing to us in order for us to be more like Him.

"In order to meaningfully repent of the ways in which we violate love, we must recognize them. We won't recognize self-protective patterns of relating as sinful violations of love until we face the disappointment in our soul we're determined never to experience again." ~Larry Crabb

Love one another. Doable?

"A new command I give you: Love one another. As I have loved you, so you must love one another. [35] By this everyone will know that you are my disciples, if you love one another."   John 13. 34,35

 "Get rid of all bitterness, rage and anger, brawling and slander, along with every form of malice. Be kind and compassionate to one another, forgiving each other, just as in Christ God forgave you." ~Ephesians 4.31,32
Kindness: n. the practice or quality of being kind. a kind, considerate, or helpful act

You are walking home from school or leaving the store or riding your bike when all of sudden a person walking towards you trips and falls and bumps their head on the cement. What will you do? You are at church and a person that you don't like falls and bumps their head, right in front of you. What will you do?

You are with a bunch of your "Christian" friends and a person that you hardly know, but you see on occasion walks by you. Will you say hello? Will you extend your hand for a hand shake? Will you ignore them?

One more. You are with a group of "Christians" and they start complaining about a person, what will you do? Will you jump in? Will you walk away? Will you tell them you are not interested?   hmmmm

Interesting don't you think? Really. I'm a follower of Christ and I do ministry. I do this ministry called NextGen so I come in contact with many, many students on a weekly basis. I see how they treat others. I see how cliquish they are. I know that many know better. I also know that many watch adults mistreat others. They have heard things said about others from adults that don't need to be brought up, talked about to anyone period. They see the meanness out there. What are they supposed to do? After all, by now we all know what the "big" sins are right? If you don't do the "bad" things, the big sins, what could be so bad about ignoring, blowing off somebody? Right? Isn't that the way it is? As long as I'm not doing this or that I can be a "christian" snob. I can treat others the way I want to and it's none of your business. After all, I'm better than those people that don't think like me, do it like me and aren't as good as me.

I'm willing to step into this whole discussion because I see what is going on all the time. "Christians" now love to talk about feeding the poor. Taking care of those in need (they don't know) Doing "kind" things to people outside the doors of church. That is cool. That is important. That is what God wants. That is what Jesus expects. As far as the brotherhood or sisterhood, don't worry about your brothers and sisters, don't care about those you see walking the halls. Don't care about those in the brother and sisterhood that are struggling, have failed, don't talk your lingo, don't do it like you. Forget them. Go to the shelter once a month, but don't worry about talking behind backs, don't worry about putting others down, don't worry about "those" people in the brother and sisterhood, you just care about the people you like or at least that you care about once a month.

Lets go a step further. In this day and age to talk about this stuff is almost like talking about something that is off limits. Talking about the "not to's" about sex is o.k.(almost) Talk to the kids about drugs, talk to the kids about underage drinking and smoking, but talking about behavior that people deem "their business" is off limits. Do you see it yet? It looks like this: Picture a student that is wondering what it looks like to follow Christ with all their heart and life. This student has said in his heart and mind that Jesus Christ is worth following, this student understands what it means to receive this great truth that Jesus forgives them and following Him is worth everything. So this student meets some "christian" students and because they don't know him, they ignore him, go around him and never engage him. Is that cool? Is that o.k? No. It's not o.k. Where are these students learning that behavior. School? Church? Home?

The Scriptures teach much more than don't smoke, don't drink, don't have sex, don't whatever. The scriptures teach us how to live with each other. The scriptures teach us to live in community with one another. The scriptures teach us to love one another. The scriptures teach us to care for one another. The scriptures teach us much about living this life called "being a Christ follower" being "saved" being a student in a lost world, being an adult in this lost world.

"Get rid of all bitterness, rage and anger, brawling and slander, along with every form of malice. Be kind and compassionate to one another, forgiving each other, just as in Christ God forgave you."
~Ephesians 4.31,32

As a the leader of the NextGen ministry it seems that there is something missing. Students opt out of coming to events and getting involved and I wonder what is going on? Is it me? I would like all students to come to all the events and things we do no matter where they are spiritually. I would love to see students embrace and engage the ministry. Moreover, I would love to see students engage God, embrace each other, and love each other. I would love to see adults love each other, not just their little clique. Not just all those that agree with them. How bout embracing and engaging all followers of Christ? Is that not possible?

I just wonder if adults can't do the above, how are our students gonna do it? This is a perplexing situation indeed. For I know that there are many students that want to grow in their relationship with Christ. I know that there are many students ready to get well past the pettiness of their peers and from some their parents cutting down others, treating people poorly and just neglecting the values that Jesus teaches. I am continuing to pray for a break through in the NextGen ministry. Continuing to pray for parents and students that God would give them His heart on this matter. That people needs healing. That some followers of Christ need examples in theses matters. That being kind, taking care of people, loving people, caring for people actually starts at home and in the church. A friend of mine once told me that the hardest place to live for Christ was at home. He was right and I'm not going to stay silent about this high value.

Personally this instruction about "forgiving each other, just as in Christ God forgave you." is serious business. I happen to know many over the years that have not yet forgiven somebody and continue to act as if that is o.k. Well, is it? Paul's instructions are for all to all and it's not conditional. How bout this? When the opportunity to be kind to anyone comes along today, go for it. When the Spirit reveals the who to forgive today, forgive them finally. When it's time to move away from the "clique" and engaging those you may not "like" how about being the one to set the example?

"A new command I give you: Love one another. As I have loved you, so you must love one another. [35] By this everyone will know that you are my disciples, if you love one another."   John 13. 34,35

So you don't do all the "bad stuff" and you don't do the above. What does that say? Really?

"Now that you have purified yourselves by obeying the truth so that you have sincere love for each other, love one another deeply, from the heart."
~1 Peter 1.22

on being Thankful

Colossians 3.15
"Let the peace of Christ rule in your hearts, since as members of one body you were called to peace. And be thankful."

Another way to read this verse

Check it out

When you let Christ rule—peace is real—and because you belong to the family of God, letting Christ rule with peace is your calling. So be thankful.

Who should live like this?
The People of God
The Church
The Family of God
The Brothers and Sisters
The Followers of Christ
Those that understand such an awesome great
Salvation!

Thanksgiving day is 24 days away. Are you Thankful? Hopefully this little blog will help turn you and your heart toward Thanksgiving.

Question:
Who is ruler in your life?

Out of His rule comes peace.
Out of His peace comes a   Thankful Heart

Giving Christ his place—Lordship

A choice? Act of the will
To let Christ rule
Which brings--
Peace
Gratitude
Inner Joy!

And then

The ability to sing
The desire to love large
The ability to care
The desire to help each other

You see – God's people

Are Thankful people

Thanksgiving: a Heart issue

Thanksgiving

The benefits of a thankful heart

The benefits of a thankful life

 Questions:
What do you delight in?
What brings your life good vibes?
When are you most thankful?

Just a few weeks before Thanksgiving Day

We can learn a couple of things about...
God. His delight? In what does God delight?

We can also learn a couple of things about us

So, what does God delight in?

Psalm 51.16,17
"You do not delight in sacrifice, or I would bring it;
you do not take pleasure in burnt offerings.
My sacrifice, O God, is a broken spirit;

a broken and contrite heart
you, God, will not despise."

Sacrifice? No?
Noun—The act of offering

In context
The act of offering of an insufficient burnt offering
To remedy our own issues, shortcomings.
A substitute
A false front
A kind of doing
A possible outward show

David is writing about
The motive behind the sacrifice.

What is God saying?

God is saying that He delights in
The matters of the heart.
The internal

Our motives matter to God!
and He delights in...

The sacrifices that God delights in are

- Brokenness
- A contrite heart

Why?

Brokenness and a contrite heart
Prove ones:

- Trust

- Clay like position

- Sense of need

- Humility

- The NEED for God in our lives. God delights in our consistent, honest need for HIM

So this month-- I ask myself... What do I delight in? Is my thankfulness due to my constant
need for God. Or is it due to what I get? Or what I think meets my needs? I really do know...
I am a broken man that without the Lord I would be even more of a disaster. How bout you?

All to start the movement towards a Thankful person.

Thanksgiving memories led me to Grace

Thanksgiving. Thanksgiving day is soon approaching. I have celebrated lots of Thanksgiving's that's for sure. I remember many of those thanksgiving days. Such great memories. So many uncles and aunts and cousins and man, it was fun.

I had no idea as a kid what family life was all about. You know? I just knew of my mom's side of the family and my dad's side of the family. We were all different, we were all kinda the same. Celebrating Thanksgiving brought us all together for food, for football, for talking, and laughing and carrying on about all sorts of stuff. It seemed from my kid kind of view point that life was pretty simple, pretty easy, pretty fun, pretty much normal. From my kid eyes and view, I had a pretty neat family. Ahhh yes, thanksgiving day was pretty cool indeed.

Life moves pretty fast. Life brings with it all sorts of changes. Some of the changes are good, and some well, not so good. Three of my dear uncles have passed away, 1 of my mom's brothers and 2 of my dad's brothers are gone, along with my dear grandmother and my grandfather but my memories are still alive and well. Yes, thanksgiving time with my family growing up was a blast.

The year was 2001, it was late September and I was away at a conference. I got a call that my father and mother were in an accident. My father was in the hospital in Goshen, IN and I needed to get there to see him. Skip forward to November of 2001. I was doing the Sr. Pastor Church plant thing, it was a Monday night and I was at a friends house in Dayton. I was as usual thinking about ministry stuff, my sermon for the coming weekend so I headed to West Chester to do a little work in my quiet office. I wrapped up the night and headed home. When I walked in the door, I noticed some friends on the couch and then Marcie told me something bad had happened-- My father died. He had a massive heart attack.

Yes, life changes, life is tough. I hadn't really noticed that over time so much outside of me was changing along with what was going on inside. Maybe years of struggling through my own sinful addictions. Maybe the struggling with trying to be a Sr. Pastor. Maybe the struggling with working with people. Maybe the struggling of trying to figure out life. Maybe the struggling with me, with others, with life was like a frog in a kettle. I don't know, but sometime during all this stuff I may have gotten a little messed up. Oh I have been sober for 19 years, but I'm not talking about that. Oh, I have made it through some tough times looking for work. I'm not talking about that. Oh, I have made it through some tough situations. I'm not talking about that.

Somewhere, sometime, something happened. I thought way back when I started sobriety that I had come to the end of myself, the bottom. I think, what I'm dealing with as I approach thanksgiving is simply this: I am thankful for so much. I am thankful for the little things. I am thankful for my life. I am thankful for so much and this month I am focusing on the years gone bye, and I am truly thankful. I am thankful for so much of things that are gone and so thankful for the life that I have been given. What I'm saying is that as I reflect on thanksgiving, I am becoming-- becoming mindful, becoming grateful, becoming thankful for what I have been given

I am thankful for my birth mom, for she gave me life and set me free. I am thankful for my neighborhood friends. I am thankful for the place I grew up. I am thankful for so many of the little things. I am thankful for the people in my life that loved me. I am thankful for my parents Ray and Ruby. I am thankful that my parents adopted me. I am thankful for my adopted sister Kathy. I am thankful for my wife and her family. I am thankful for my sons. I am a thankful man. Funny to me that my thankfulness has come out of the grind of life. The tough things. The hardships. For the hardships, the tough times have shown me how much I have been given. I can't help but be thankful.

And so, this coming thanksgiving I am reminded again of what I have been given from birth. I was given a great life. I was given everything I have needed. Not one great thing did I earn and I am much more aware of what I have been given period.

Which leads me to the final little thing today. I am truly grateful for the largest greatest thing I have. My relationship to Jesus Christ came freely without me earning one thing. It was by Grace and Grace alone-- freely given to me.

"For it is by grace you have been saved, through faith—and this is not from yourselves, it is the gift of God— not by works, so that no one can boast." Ephesians 2.8,9

So this thanksgiving I am reminded again. The economy is nuts. People are getting crazier. Life is flying and I am thankful. My thankfulness is due to my relationship to Jesus Christ really. Life has changed hugely over the years, and I find Him to be everything He said He is, would be and will be. I could listen to all the haters, all the complainers, all the garbage, all the blame, all the angst, all the crap, but I'm making a choice to focus on this one thing-- Jesus loves me and for that I am thankful.

Interesting that my thanksgiving memories pointed me right back to the most significant thing I have and know-- and because of Him I am thankful.

Thanksgiving produces Giving

So, Thanksgiving is right around the corner. Family together, good food, good times, giving thanks, for each other, for all the good gifts, there is so much to be thankful about. Unless of course you resemble Ebenezer Scrooge?

You know what? Christmas is also near. So I generally combine my thankfulness for life and for the Christ that brought me salvation. Really I do. I think it has been many years now that the combination of thanksgiving and Christmas brings to me much Joy for life, for family, for friends and for my relationship with Christ.

Yes, there is no doubt that "culturally" we all are bombarded with the commercialism of the season. No question about it. That being said. So what? Really. Thanksgiving, my thankfulness is not determined one bit by the culture. Really. The second part of this little blog is simply this. I'm really not into hearing everybody knock the season "of giving" because of the commercialism. So what. Giving gifts is a privilege and an honor. I have become a giver of gifts as I am more and more thankful for what God has given me in Christ Jesus. I actually enjoy giving gifts!

Do I have to give to everyone? Can I only give to certain people for my giving to be of value? Do I have to do it the way "others" say it should or shouldn't be done? Please. I get the strange feeling that many that don't want to give to anyone or anything because they say "its all about commercialism" are actually miserable inside, stingy, holding on to their cash money and lording over others their opinion believing that not giving or only giving to those that are now deemed worth giving to has become the new self righteousness.

I give gifts to many people. I give because I want to. I give because I'm not holding on to "everything". O.k. I do hold on to money, and things. At least I admit it. That being said, I love giving to many people. My family. My friends. The poor. Those without. I love to give. Does that make me better than anyone? Absolutely not. So you don't like commercialism? So you don't like gifts on Christmas or giving thanks on thanksgiving? Aren't they both connected? A thankful heart can't help but give out of thankfulness. A thankful heart gives because they are filled and want to give to others.

So, for all those that believe that giving is only valuable if it fits a "certain criteria" I say ba hum bug. If you don't want to give gifts. If you don't want to give except to those you deem deserving, fine, but don't blame your issues on commercialism. Just tell the truth. That you may just not want to spend any more of your hard earned money. Just say it. Say that you want to save your money, keep your stuff and only give to whom you deem worthy to give. Isn't that the way it is anyhow? Really. We all give to who we want to give. The problem is that giving will always be to some a "do it my way" kind of thing.

I will continue to give. It may not look like all the new "givers". I may not do it like everyone else does it, but I like giving to whom ever I feel like giving, and when I die and I am gone, I'm planning on going with nothing in my pockets. Oh, there will be stuff on my walls, there will be some nice clothes and you can have em all. In the meantime, I love thanksgiving and I love Christmas.

Commercialism hasn't hurt me one bit. I still like the old Andy Williams Christmas shows, I still like the old Christmas Carols, I still like Christmas. I know what Christmas means period. If you don't like giving thanks because of... If you don't like giving gifts... fine. Ebenezer Scrooge has been around along long time since around 1843 and there is nothing new about those that love to keep their money and stuff to themselves and then talk badly about others that enjoy giving thanks which turns into a generous life of Giving.

By the way, the Scriptures tell of the Father as being a giver of "Good" gifts.

I know why I like to give, and I know that giving hasn't always been my nature. I know that there are some that have decided to forgo giving to family and others to give to those that are less fortunate. That is fine. But, this whole notion of only giving to certain people, when actually chopping down the list and actually saving money is not as generous as some would like to portray. If one says that they aren't giving anymore to family and friends and only to certain causes while still living in big houses, still driving nice cars, spending money on self, checking the bank account everyday is easily seen for what it is. Don't you think? I suggest that we all take a long look into all that God has done in them through Jesus Christ and by Christmas maybe there will be a reason to give out of such a huge grateful heart. Holding on is not so generous under the guise of good "stewardship". I actually think that giving should hurt my check book and bank account.

C'mon, isn't true that when we realize how gracious, how giving, how awesome God has been to us through giving us His son Christ Jesus, that we can't help but become gracious, and giving? Isn't that true? I suggest that many that have lost their way about this, just spend some time considering the greatest gift given-- "for unto you a child has been given". Yeppers it's getting close to Christmas and I'm getting excited.

"Give, and it will be given to you. A good measure, pressed down, shaken together and running over, will be poured into your lap. For with the measure you use, it will be measured to you." ~Luke 6.38

Let Love break through again in your life!

My Dad-- Ray

Raymond A. Solin
3/24/1921 - 11/08/2001
US Army, PFC WWII

I'll admit right up front. I don't often think of heaven. I don't often think about the end of my life. I know, why am I bringing this up? Right? For starters this month means that 10 years ago my favorite man passed away. My dad. My friend. The man that taught me so much about the Grace of God. He really did. His name is Raymond Alexander Solin (Solinski) I love this man for showing me, not really telling me about it, but showing me the Grace of God.

One of the reasons I love, enjoy the fact that I'm adopted is that I ended up with Ray. How I got there? How it would be with him? How? Only by God. Only by the movement of God and for that I learned a little about Grace. Never did I hear from my dad that I had to earn his love. Never. Never did he yell at me for not being his dream, or his period. I always felt to my dad, I was really a gift. That showed me a little of God's grace.

Interesting that I never felt I measured up. Truth be told, he didn't do that to me. I felt that way because I know full well that I was failing as a person, as his son. So, in the midst of a very dark time in my life I felt, I felt it was time to leave. I didn't deserve his grace, I didn't deserve his love, I didn't deserve his gifts, his care, his being my father.

So, one night I decided to pack up my stuff and go somewhere. I had no idea where, but I was going. As I loaded up my car, Ray waited for me at the front door. "Where are you going?" He asked. I went off on him and it turned into me and him actually swinging away, I connected, he connected, and we fought on the front porch. Finally he connected with me and brought me to my knees and woke me up. I said, "Dad, I'm sorry, I'm leaving because I don't deserve to live here. I have let you down, I have hurt you, I need to go." He said words I will never ever forget. He said words that I heard a times before from the scriptures, from people trying to tell me about God's grace, God's love... He said,

"Don't you know that there is nothing you could do that would make me stop loving you? Nothing"

It was that night, that moment that it all clicked. His love for me was an image of God's love for me. Ray told me a truth that I only understood with my head and that night, I got it with my heart. That God loved me even though I was the ultimate sinner. My dad loved me as much as a human being could love me like the Heavenly Father loved him, now Ray loved me the same. I finally got it. My adoption to my dad was a shadow of God's adoption of me through Christ Jesus.

You see, it's not about measuring up. It's not about perfection. It's not about doing to be loved. It's about God's unconditional, unrelenting Grace.

Thank you Ray. I love you, I miss you, you showed me God's Grace! I so look forward to seeing you again.

Love broke through

Like a dreamer that was trying to build
A highway to the sky
All my hopes would come tumblin down
And I never knew just why
Until today when You pulled away the clouds
That hung like curtains on my eyes.
I was blind all these wasted years when
I thought I was so wise.
But then You took me by surprise.

Like waking up from the longest dream
How real it seemed
Until Your love broke through
And I was lost in a fantasy
That blinded me
Until your love broke through.

All my life I have been searching
For that crazy missing part
With one touch You just rolled away
The stone that held my heart,
Now I see that the answer was a simple
As my need to let love in
And I am so sure I could never doubt
Your gentle touch again
It's like the power of the wind.

Like waking up from the longest dream
How real it seemed
Until Your love broke through
And I was lost in a fantasy
That blinded me
Until your love broke through.
~Keith Green/Randy Stonehill
Love the Keaggy rendition

I was waxing this morning to the words of this song. It was weird, in
the middle of listening to the Keaggy version on Youtube I went right
to a spot, a time, the time, the moment...It was crazy—I went to a

time when realization occurred. Weird though, I can't remember the day, or the circumstances but it was like I went to the spot, the time, the moment, when I realized how broken, how off, how hurt, how messed up I was. It was like I went to the spot, the time, the moment when my depravity hit me right between my eyes, my heart was empty—oh I knew the stuff, the schtick, the answers, but I was lost, trying to find my way by doing, by getting, by making changes by this and that and this and that. I kept running into the same old wall....
ME

I listened to the words again this morning and was moved, I went right back to the spot, the time, the moment His love broke through my heart. It was a gentle touch, it was an incredible thing, and I went right back to the spot, the time, the moment, and it was back then, and it has been, and it is, and it happened again this morning—His love broke through—His gentle touch reminded me again of His love for me and my utter, broken, sinful heart. His love broke through, it's like the power of the wind and it happened back then, and lots of times in between, and this morning. Love broke through! You know?

Oh man, I can't explain it, I went right back to the spot, the time, the moment and it was this morning that I felt His touch. I felt Him. I felt Him say-- I love you, I forgive you, I am taking care of you. Love broke through all my busyness, all the work, all the pain of my mistakes, my sin, my aches, life. Oh that students and parents would feel his gentle touch, that He would take them back to the spot, the time, the moment, when love broke through. Oh that He would do that again for His people it's like the power of the wind.

Love broke through, love breaks through!

A farmer went out to sow his seed

I remember my first full time youth ministry call, job, all the way back to the late 80's. Wow. Seems like a long time ago. I had a few things in my bag of newly graduated youth ministry degree materials at least I thought. Plus I had a great experience as a student of a youth group turned to youth ministry way back in the 70's. A couple of things though that may seem existential to some of my contemporaries, nevertheless they may have some merit.

First I have often wondered how I as a kid, growing up in a great church, surrounded by great young men, with great youth leaders ended up at some point walking away from "my faith" if I can say it that way? For one, I don't believe that I ever really by faith knew Christ personally. Oh, I made my profession, I was even baptized but when it was time to live it out at my first college experience I failed miserably. Oh I hung around a group of fine students from Campus Crusade and I knew the right things to say and do, but I really had no interest in going and doing what they were doing and soon I was hanging out with people that were more fun and interesting. Did I get tired of the "mantra"? Did I get tired of "knowing" all the "right" and "wrong" things? Did I backslide? Did I do all the stuff I did because I was rebelling? Did I just go south for awhile? Was I an 80's prodigal?

Interesting that I can go back over 25 years of being around "churched" students, those that "claim" to know Christ, know plenty of the "right" things and the "wrong" things. I have witnessed students that graduated from High School that once claimed to love Jesus and go to a very dark side and unlike me do not return. I know students now that are well into their 30's that at one point were part of the youth ministry I led when they were freshmen and sophomores. I have seen many, many, I couldn't tell you how many, but it is a large number of students that left the church, left their faith to never at least not yet return.

This subject I am going to pursue over several blogs so this is just the beginning of my journey through why student ministry is valuable, why mentors are valuable, why just raising a hand, just walking an aisle, just hanging out at youth group, just reciting and saying "right" things may very well be part of a not so new problem. There are many books out there right now about this very thing. As a matter of fact I'm bringing in the author of "Generation Ex-Christian" Drew Dyck to speak to parents in March for the NextGen ministry in which I lead. The Barna group has much out there right now about this very issue. Interesting though that I left all my church, faith, friends, mentors moorings way back in the late 70's and it seems to be the talk of many today.

I personally have come to a different conclusion for my story. I contend that I never ever knew Christ Jesus personally. Oh, again I knew all the answers, I studied Scriptures, I did everything "right" to a degree, and when it was time to flex what I knew, when it was time to live it out, when it was time to do it on my own? I didn't, I couldn't.

I see many, many students like myself, over and over and over again. I can't get them excited about the Lord. I can't get them to get involved. I can't do anything to move them either which way. By the way, I don't believe that is my job. Nevertheless here in lies the next issue. I knew by my own lack of "fruit" lack of peace, lack of love, lack of care, my desire for everything that was destructive that I did not know the Christ. I knew this very thing because of others, because of friends, because of those that actually lived out their relationship to Christ. They didn't live it perfectly, they didn't live it always right. They just lived it consistently and I knew way back then that I couldn't. It's not that I didn't want to, I did, but I couldn't, it wasn't part of my heart, my passion, my life period.

When I started youth ministry way back, I approached every with this ideal; that every student was not a christian even though they went to church. I viewed (and I still do) every student as a student that most likely knew very much but had not made the heart connection to the Lord. You see, when I saw them go south it wasn't a surprise. When I heard of what happened in their life as a result of bad choices, I wasn't startled. Interesting thought that many, many parents that are surprised about their student, never took the time to ask hard questions or never took the time to go beyond "Hey, how cool my student came to Christ now the church can raise them and teach them and ground them. Have you seen this? I have seen it often.

Look now, I must make clear that I know full well that I didn't know Christ. My life style as a 20 something and beyond proved something that many don't want to take on. I came to a place that I was honestly broken enough, sick of, hurt, dark, destroying myself, that the only thing I knew was that I needed Jesus Christ to forgive me and there is the rub. When I talk to many churched students today, many have a real problem with understanding depravity, sinfulness, conviction, selfishness and all the rest. So when they don't come to "youth ministry" or hate going to church, or spend not one minute with God, or seem to despise anything spiritual, or actually do whatever it takes to avoid "Christians" or church stuff the question shouldn't be "what is wrong with the youth ministry, the youth pastor, the church?" The real question is "where is this student spiritually that they don't care about spiritual things?" Isn't that the right question?

Some could say well Don, you had Jesus in you and He guided you back. Or some could say well once a Christian always a Christian. Right? Or some could say, well.... whatever they could say is not what happened to me. Here in lies the existential part... I knew, I know that I didn't know Him and my lifestyle proved it. I wasn't honest with people or friends, to the church, to my mentors, to anyone at all and when it was time to be honest, I went exactly where my heart took me. I went exactly where who I was on the inside led me. I went straight to all the stuff that my dark heart desired. Interesting that at some point a few years later, I knew deep down inside that a "Follower of Christ" did not live like I did. I knew deep down that someone "saved" was transformed and I was not. I knew that I was lost period and in truth I know many students right now that are exactly that-- lost.

Now, if you read any of my blogs or know me personally you will know that I do understand grace. I also understand that I came to the place where honest introspection sent me directly to Jesus Christ. You see, I came to the conclusion through brokenness that I needed the Savior. Yes, I did at least know the story of God's love for me and yes I did know that Jesus died on a cross for me, but now it was time to believe it. I accepted it by faith because I desperately needed Jesus Christ. You see, I do know Grace and believe me, I so offer this grace to all the students today that treat Jesus like a bad friend, like a jerk, like a pain, like nothing more than a trip to heaven. Grace is waiting and pursuing them if they would just come to the honest truth-- you know, that they just may not know Him at all.

Now, some could say, be thankful for growing up in church, and all those that had a part in my life. Well of course I am thankful, but I also know many students that didn't have my back ground that have come to the same conclusion-- that is that they also needed the Savior.

Maybe this will help--
The Parable of the Sower Matt. 13

1 That same day Jesus went out of the house and sat by the lake. 2 Such large crowds gathered around him that he got into a boat and sat in it, while all the people stood on the shore. 3 Then he told them many things in parables, saying: "A farmer went out to sow his seed. 4 As he was scattering the seed, some fell along the path, and the birds came and ate it up. 5 Some fell on rocky places, where it did not have much soil. It sprang up quickly, because the soil was shallow. 6 But when the sun came up, the plants were scorched, and they withered because they had no root. 7 Other seed fell among thorns, which grew up and choked the plants. 8 Still other seed fell on good soil, where it produced a crop—a hundred, sixty or thirty times what was sown. 9 Whoever has ears, let them hear."

10 The disciples came to him and asked, "Why do you speak to the people in parables?" 11 He replied, "Because the knowledge of the secrets of the kingdom of heaven has been given to you, but not to them. 12 Whoever has will be given more, and they will have an abundance. Whoever does not have, even what they have will be taken from them. 13 This is why I speak to them in parables:

"Though seeing, they do not see; though hearing, they do not hear or understand.

14 In them is fulfilled the prophecy of Isaiah: "You will be ever hearing but never understanding;
you will be ever seeing but never perceiving.
15 For this people's heart has become calloused;
they hardly hear with their ears,
and they have closed their eyes.

Otherwise they might see with their eyes,
hear with their ears,
understand with their hearts
and turn, and I would heal them.

16 But blessed are your eyes because they see, and your ears
because they hear. 17 For truly I tell you, many prophets and
righteous people longed to see what you see but did not see it, and to
hear what you hear but did not hear it.

18 "Listen then to what the parable of the sower means: 19 When
anyone hears the message about the kingdom and does not
understand it, the evil one comes and snatches away what was sown
in their heart. This is the seed sown along the path. 20 The seed
falling on rocky ground refers to someone who hears the word and
at once receives it with joy. 21 But since they have no root, they last
only a short time. When trouble or persecution comes because of the
word, they quickly fall away. 22 The seed falling among the thorns
refers to someone who hears the word, but the worries of this life
and the deceitfulness of wealth choke the word, making it unfruitful.
23 But the seed falling on good soil refers to someone who hears the
word and understands it. This is the one who produces a crop,
yielding a hundred, sixty or thirty times what was sown."

Easy question? Which seed was I?
Not so easy question? What in the world is Youth Ministry?

It's like the Power of the Wind

Leading is not always fun. Leading is not glamorous. Leading is not easy. Leading is not from a manual, or a how to book, or about how someone else did it. Leading is waiting on God. Leading is asking for wisdom. Leading means more times than not, crying out to God, seeking God, trusting in God and at the same time a reverence, an understanding if you will, that this thing called leading is an honor, a privilege, a gift from God that I sometimes forget.

Something happened last night at Uprising. Uprising is the Sr. Ministry that I get to lead, manage and care for. Oh I have an incredible staff of servants, of caregivers, of people that love God and love students no doubt about it. We all care about the Sr. Ministry. Every person on the NextGen team cares about each ministry the same, Middle School, Sr. High and College Young adult. All of the team has been praying, seeking God, asking Him to break through in the lives of our students and as the leader of the NextGen team I have felt totally responsible to cast that vision to my staff, to feel the total dependence on God, to feel the utter need for God to break through and to with much continued crying out to the Lord the trust and sense that only He will and can move students.

Of course if you are a reader of my little blog, you would know that I love the song "Love Broke Through" by Keith Green done by Phil Keaggy. Maybe it's the fact, the truth that only God could break through my heart. Maybe it's the truth that in my lowest times, my days of "waiting patiently" (Psalm 40) that in my own life I have seen what God can do as I trusted Him. Even when I was at the end of myself, even when I wondered where in the world my life was headed, even when I couldn't see to the next day, God broke through. It wasn't as though I had to "straighten up" or do something, or be somebody, I just began to know and to know again that unless God broke through, changed the direction, changed my heart, a break through if you will, I was to continue the path I was on, continue to seek Him, wait patiently, cry out to Him and ultimately like the words from the "Love broke through" – "It's like the power of the wind." And when that wind blows through, it is obvious that it is from God. I saw that happen back when I gave my life to Christ. I saw it happen when I was working at my sales job, which I actually began to enjoy, but I kept praying, waiting, praying, crying out for God to break through, to move, to do something absolutely that only He could do and He did. "It's like the power of the wind."

Well, well, well... I have felt for 2 years that God needed to break through in the Sr. High ministry. That God needed to show up into the lives of students. That God needed to break through and show Himself and He did last night at Uprising. I heard it in the lives of students as they shared their tough, difficult times they are living through. They shared how God had been sustaining them. They shared how God was using friends in their lives to hold them accountable. They shared how God had helped them through sickness, and hard times, and that they were learning how to trust Him, and love Him. They shared their stories, they shared honestly, they shared their needs, they shared and God was there. "It's like the power of the wind."

Last night was a reminder to me and to all of us that serve the NextGen ministry that we wait, we cry out, we let our hearts be known to our God that we serve and worship that it is through Him, by Him that lives will get touched. That is is only by the Power of God that Love breaks through and last night was I believe a foreshadowing of what is to come. I am praying for God to continue to break through, for God to continue to do amazing things.

Remember how I started this blog? Leadership. Leadership is what I get to do, leadership means that I can absolutely take not one bit of credit when God breaks through. That I get to lead a team of servants to understand over and over and over that God love us waiting on Him, trusting Him, waiting on Him, crying out to Him for what He and He alone can do-- to break through. "It's like the power of the wind." What I'm trying to say about leading this team is simply this: There is always a rub to try for the new things, to do it more this or that, to try and try and try harder, look for effective "new" things. Yes, as a leader I do believe in working hard, but, and that is the rub isn't it? That God breaking through is based on a "new" gimmick? Or because the leader is so Godly? Or because all of our P's and Q's are just right? No, after years of ministry, years in the trenches, years trying to overcome my shortcomings, I have learned, I am continuing to learn, to trust God, to seek God, to wait on God, to cry out to God for Him to "break through". I know that this NextGen ministry is His ministry. That the students that come here and will come here are His. That this ministry is not about me or anyone else.

I go back to the days not long ago when God broke through as I continued to fret, to ache, to ask, to cry out for God to break through. Oh He did, and I sometimes forget the stories of Joseph, and Peter, and Paul of course most if not all the Biblical characters and my own life how God so desired to break through that He took them, me, through the days of only trust, only crying out, only waiting, only believing that He would break through, and I get the sense that has been happening for quite sometime now-- and He is breaking through.

Tonight was an answer to prayer and a reminder that prayer, waiting, trusting, seeking, asking is exactly what the Father so desires because my little faith, your little faith pleases Him. Hebrews 11. 6 says-- "And without faith it is impossible to please God, because anyone who comes to him must believe that he exists and that he rewards those who earnestly seek him."

I'm praying for more of God, more of the Christ, more of the Spirit to "Break Through"

"It's like the power of the wind."

Thanksgiving   "It's not what you have, but who you know."

Ever get the feeling that there is not a lot to be thankful for?
Honestly--
Market is down
Problems at home
Relationships are difficult
Kids are going loco
The job is a hassle
Car broke down
Feeling a little sick

Well you get the picture

Thanksgiving time is here and for what or is it for who will you give thanks?
What brings you joy, in order to give thanks?

Joy—Excitement or pleasurable feeling caused by the acquisition or expectation of good; gladness; pleasure; delight; exultation; the cause of satisfaction and happiness.

Is there joy only when things are good?
Is there joy only when the feeling is there?

Habakkuk 3.17-19
[17] Though the fig tree does not bud
and there are no grapes on the vines,
though the olive crop fails
and the fields produce no food,
though there are no sheep in the pen
and no cattle in the stalls,
[18] yet I will rejoice in the LORD,
I will be joyful in God my Savior.

[19] The Sovereign LORD is my strength;
he makes my feet like the feet of a deer,
he enables me to tread on the heights.

A little background on Habakkuk—
The book is the authors dialogue with God and himself about the

people
Habakkuk was a prophet from God to the people.
Habakkuk would complain and God would answer
The key issue for Habakkuk is that while his world seemed to
running free, out of control from all the garbage from the
Babylonians. You see it was the Babylonians that were running the
government, the show if you will, the culture. To Habakkuk his
people, the people of God were well, just like everybody else.
(sound familiar?)

And Habakkuk struggles out loud
Sometimes I admit—I struggle out loud and yet--

[18] yet I will rejoice in the LORD,
I will be joyful in God my Savior.

[19] The Sovereign LORD is my strength;
he makes my feet like the feet of a deer,
he enables me to tread on the heights.

Take Joy in the God of Salvation

Joy is thus available to everyone—not in things, but in the person of
God
I am thankful for Salvation!

He will make my feet like deer's feet

He will give me the ability to bound through life's difficulties

He will make me walk on high hills

The mountain tops of victory and triumph!

Trust matters

"The more trust in a relationship, the fewer rules needed. Trust is built on truth." ~Rick Warren (tweet)

Isn't it true?

Way back when I was a kid, I had a paper route. The route was 2 full blocks with around 150 papers. Everyday, every weekend, rain, snow delivered by 7:30 a.m. The papers arrived at my house at 5 a.m. I had to be up to roll the papers, load my bike and the wagon I fashioned for pulling the big Sunday paper on Sunday's. On rainy days I wrapped them in plastic bags. I worked hard at delivery on time. I was trusted by the newspaper company and my people to deliver on time and the newspaper in the right shape for reading of course. Being on time mattered, and it built trust with to those whom I was responsible. Thus when it was Christmas time I received some big tips.

When I started working for a large grocery chain as a bagger I was expected to be at work on time. I punched a clock like everyone and of course my manager when it was time for review always checked my time cards to see if I was prompt. Why? Because being on time said I could be trusted. Being trusted brought raises and promotions. When a manager trusts, good things happen.

When I was a kid, I didn't have a curfew, until I stayed out one time till 2 a.m. With a bunch of friends. When I got home, I got in trouble. Trouble? I had no curfew, how could I be in trouble? From that day on as long as I lived with my parents, I had a curfew and as I continued to be home on time, trust was built and the curfew ultimately disappeared.

I have worked for many bosses over the years. I figured out early that trust mattered most. Not my smile, not my looks, not my words. My boss would say "this needs to get done" and I would do it. If I didn't do it, my boss could rightfully say "Don is not trustworthy" Right?

Students today need to learn quickly that trust is a high value that they earn.

As a parent, I have often given a chore, made a time, made an order yes an order to see if my sons were trust worthy. If they were not trustworthy on the little things, the big things were not given. Is that fair? Please. Fairness is not at all the issue in building trust. Now, was I a good son? Not always for sure. But, sometimes I lost trust with my parents, sometimes I had to get a "do over" sometimes I had to take the consequences of broken trust. Trust is earned.

"The more trust in a relationship, the fewer rules needed. Trust is built on truth." ~Rick Warren

In Luke chapter 19 Jesus tells the parable of the 10 minas. The parable is about trust.

"A man of noble birth went to a distant country to have himself appointed king and then to return. So he called ten of his servants and gave them ten minas. 'Put this money to work,' he said, 'until I come back.'

14 "But his subjects hated him and sent a delegation after him to say, 'We don't want this man to be our king.'

15 "He was made king, however, and returned home. Then he sent for the servants to whom he had given the money, in order to find out what they had gained with it.

16 "The first one came and said, 'Sir, your mina has earned ten more.'

17 "'Well done, my good servant!' his master replied. 'Because you have been trustworthy in a very small matter, take charge of ten cities.'

As a parent, as a leader I admit it. I sometimes give little "orders" to my sons, to my staff to build trust.

Trust matters.

Being on time matters. Fulfilling a chore matters. Going the extra mile matters. Is it any wonder that so many today want to be trusted, but refuse to be on time, push back at every order given and then become angry because they just aren't trusted? I believe that we parents must help our students on this matter. Leaders must help those we lead to understand that fulfilling the little things means big things will come.

another New Year

"New Year, same goal."
~Joe King

Another year done. Cliché right? Cliché for every human walking the earth I guess. Another year has flown bye. I can't even remember 2011. Is that good or bad? I don't know, it seems like yesterday I was thinking about 2010 ending, and that year flew bye. Sheeeeesh!

Will I make some resolutions? I don't know about resolutions, but I do know I have made some goals for 2012. Just like I made goals for 2011. I write a work plan every 3 months and that is valuable. I know that I have some personal issues I am continually working on new year or old year. I know that I am in process in my relationship with Christ and that process never stops. I know that I have work to do, people to love, relationships to build, truth to tell, fights to fight all sorts of stuff ahead. I guess the truth is, that a New Year doesn't change the day in day out work, movement, getting up, getting at it, being, loving, changing, growing, wrestling, praying, seeking and all that goes on in my life.

So, bring on the New Year with all that is ahead. Bring on the ups and downs, bring on the good the bad, bring on the "what in the world happened?" Bring on the hurts, the joys, the fun, the boring, the regular, the irregular, the goof ups, the screw ups, the knuckheads, the old pains, the new pains, getting older, the gray hair, the loss of hair-- just bring it.

Isn't that life? Life beats like a drum. Life ticks like a clock. Life just goes on. I may not even be here during this year. Who knows? I just know, life goes on.

The longer I live, the more I realize I have been given a new day to live, the more I do know, the less I do know. There are things that have stayed true, there are things that people say aren't true that still are true, there are people that will never like me, there are people that I may never fully appreciate. There are people that make me crazy, there are people I make crazy. There are things I get, there are things I don't get. Life rocks on.

So? I'm gonna start this "New Year" with these words.

33 But seek first his kingdom and his righteousness, and all these things will be given to you as well. 34 Therefore do not worry about tomorrow, for tomorrow will worry about itself. Each day has enough trouble of its own. ~Matt. 6.33,34

I'll admit that I have heard these words hundreds of times. Hundreds. But... as my life continues to tick off the years, I am beginning to understand them a little more. Not quite sure I understand all the implications of the "Kingdom" not really sure I understand what "things will be given, but that doesn't matter as much. I just know how much I desire to seek after the things that matter. Looking forward to a "New Year"!

Happy New Year

thinking about leadership? Be the first in

Leadership and learning are indispensable to each other.
John F. Kennedy

I love leading. I didn't say being in charge. I didn't say being a boss. I didn't say being the big cheese. I said, I love leading, I love leadership, I love it. I love to watch those leading and see what it is they do. I love seeing others lead by example on the field, on the ice, in the board room, in the church, in the sales department, I am always checking out leadership. I love leading.

Leading to me is not a title, it is not entitled, it is not about who is smarter, or who has more education, or who has more credentials. In my humble opinion, leading is first about saying "I'll do it." I'll be the first in, I'll be the first to take the shot, I'll be the first to try, I'll do it.

The second issue is that leading has much to do about understanding the role. I didn't say knowing all about the role. I have read books, heard from great leaders, read manuals. Just like I have studied many subjects over the years that did not mean I understood it. No, I am the kind of person that understands while in the process. So, when it comes to leading I don't have a degree in leading. I haven't taught a class on leading. I know I am not the best, not the most eloquent, not the most efficient, but I am willing to go out and do it and I was asked to go and do it and so I am.

What do I understand about the role? That others that are capable, that are unknown quantities, that are ready to go, can watch a person like me that doesn't have it all, that isn't the smartest, that only has a degree, that doesn't do it like everyone else, is typical of most people. Leaders aren't that special nor am I. That I understand. I understand that if someone is never given the chance to fail, to try, to have the pain of learning, to jump into the fire, they may never take the shot at moving beyond the mundane, pursue their dream, make a difference, do something they so want to do but live in fear. That I understand, and leading means dreaming the dream, pursuing and bringing people with me.

When I was a kid I was a leader. I led at things I did and I always had older leaders around me that always encouraged me. They may not have used words like "you are a leader" but they did encourage me to be the first in, to do the task, the job no matter what people thought and Oh, I wasn't confident, I wasn't even in tune with who was following, or anything of that matter, I just jumped in and did what I thought I "understood" what I was to do. Out of that comes this little truth, that being in first or going after it caused others around me to think, "If Don can do it, so can I" as simple as that sounds, that is leading.

These next few blogs are going to be about leading. The lessons over the years I have learned about leading. For those that are interested that is cool. For those that may feel that this about a pat on my back, believe me it is not. It may have helped me over the years to have read from a youth pastor in the trenches. It may have helped me to have heard from others some of the "not good" things to say or do. I learned in the trenches. I learned and I am continuing to learn from those that are successful, those that failed, those that tried, those that gave up, those that want to lead, those that think they lead, from those that are in the fray and just plain doing it.

I had a dream way back in the year 2000 to build a team of people to develop and build a student ministry that would do, be an incredible ministry. 10 years later I am in the midst of building a team to do just that. I am excited to lead a team with an incredible middle school pastor, a college young adult pastor, a director/administrator, and some great volunteers. So these next couple of blogs will be about some of the many lessons good and bad that I am learning while leading.

"Life is a place of service. Joy can be real only if people look upon their life as a service and have a definite object in life outside themselves and their personal happiness." ~Leo Tolstoy

I know some could say "Hey Don, isn't this little blog about puffing you up?" The answer is simply-- While it is about me, it's not about puffing me up. Not at all. I just want to share these experiences in my life. Maybe there is someone that is in leadership that often wonders "Am I doing it right?" Or may be thinking "Am I on the right track?" There may be a student that is feeling the Lord say, "Go for it" anyway I just offer this little blog as an encouragement to those in the trenches. I do believe like Tolstoy that life is a place of service and that I do get much joy serving others. One of those ways is to share some of the things I'm learning while leading.

Leading comes out of following

Action springs not from thought, but from a readiness for
responsibility.
~Dietrich Bonhoeffer

A long time ago. A very long time ago, I aspired to be a leader. I will
admit it. I saw leadership as something that I wanted to do someday.
You lead and many will follow. Lead and many will love you. Lead
and many will think you are the bomb. Lead and all will be well. Lead
and you will have the world by the tail. Yes, I wanted to lead for all
the wrong reasons.

Then one day in the middle of leading I realized how hard leading
really is. Leading means that many will not appreciate where you are
heading. Many found me to be somebody I was not. Many said "No"
to where I want to go. Yes, leading does not have anything glittery
about it. At least close up. Maybe from afar leading seems to many a
walk in the park. No, leading is not glamorous, it is not always fun, it
is not always well received. There are many critics. There are many
doubters. There are many that just don't believe. Well, that is A O.K.

At first it wasn't always o.k. After all, leaders are well liked. Leaders
are understood. Leaders always do it right. Right? Wrong. I have
learned over the years of leading that being liked or loved is not the
reason to lead. Actually, the reason to lead is not for anything other
than to get where I believe I am supposed to go. Leading is seldom if
ever about "what people want". I would be a terrible parent if I gave
everything to my children they wanted. The leadership trench has
been a tough teacher. There were many times and there will be many
more that I have to go and lead where I believe I am supposed to go
and not everyone will get it. Not everyone will believe, not everyone
will understand, but I must go.

Let me get a little more direct in this little blog. I have always felt that
leading a Student Ministry meant that I should care equally for those
that don't know Christ and those that do know Christ. I believe that
leading a student ministry means that students that love Christ and
those that don't know Christ are equally loved by God, therefore I
must build and lead a ministry that reflects love toward every
student present and not present. That a student ministry is not a

fortress to those that only know Christ. That a student ministry will incorporate opportunities for those that love Christ to grow and part of growing means living out their faith in the sick and twisted world. The student ministry I lead will be open to every student in the community and that may not be what some people want, but I will go there because it is where I believe I have been asked to go.

Over the years I have been blasted, overly criticized for leading the student ministry with both types of students in mind and in my heart. Many have said, "I'm about #'s. Many have said, "I don't care about discipleship." Many have pulled their students out, many have said some pretty awful things. Yes, there was a day when that really, really bothered me. Oh my, my job was on the line and sometimes it really was on the line. But, leading means that I had to follow a greater leader. I had to follow the Christ on this. After all, if He cared about people that didn't know Him, and equally cares for those that do know Him, how could I ever neglect one for the other. Besides, I believe that a student that knows and loves the Christ will care about, love, build relationships with those that don't know Him at all. Isn't that Biblical? Isn't that part of following Christ?

Leading isn't about the accolades. There are none whatsoever. Leading is not about "look at me". No leading to me is simply following the One that asked me to follow and go where He so desires. Interesting that the Tebow thing brings so much attention. Just a knee and a prayer has so many people jacked up. Well, Daniel did the same thing and Daniel took a lot of heat. (Get it) There are plenty of Biblical men and women that led by example. They didn't do it the way others did it. They didn't listen to all the criticism, they did what they believed they were supposed to do and that becomes leading.

One last little thing about leading. Leading means that I am the first in line to get hammered by the enemy. After all a leader is the first in, and the leader is the first attack of the enemy. The NextGen ministry, the ministry I lead is undertaking the most aggressive ministry plan I have ever experienced. The ministry plan is called the "Pandemic" a Pandemic to infect students with the Jesus Christ. All students. For those of us that have been in student ministry we are witnessing an apathy within "Christian" students we have not seen before. I am concerned for those students that once followed Christ that now just don't seem to care. How will they care? I could take the easy route. You know make a youth ministry that caters to the apathy. Entertain, never talk about the Biblical "hard things" of following Christ. Talk about transformation. Talk about, talk talk talk. That is the easy stuff. Leading means I along with my team have got to jump into the fray and because of just that-- an aggressive student ministry plan the enemy is hard at it right now. His attack will confuse, get some people crazed, and get those that love to be critical motivated. The enemy is coming and I feel it and that is part of leading.

Yes, I love leading because I love following.

There is not a place to which the Christian can withdraw from the world, whether it be outwardly or in the sphere of the inner life. Any attempt to escape from the world must sooner or later be paid for with a sinful surrender to the world. ~Dietrich Bonhoeffer

"When we trust, we have learned to put our very lives in the hands of others...we now know that only such confidence, which is always a venture, though a glad and positive venture, enables us really to live and work..."
~D. Bonhoeffer from Letters and Papers from Prison

Trust and Leading

Every day I go to work. Every day I lead. Every day I FEEL it. I feel what a leaders feels. I feel responsible for caring about right things because that is what leaders do. Right? I feel responsible for being the person that others are watching. I feel responsible for being a Youth Pastor, a team leader and ministry builder. I feel responsible for all of the NextGen team. I feel responsible for walking with God. I feel responsible for being a good father. I feel responsible for being a good husband. I feel responsible to students and their parents. Leading means I care. Leading means I must be on top of my "game". Leading means that there are many things in which I feel responsible.

Which leads to this truth. There is no way that I can take on all that responsibility without totally blowing it, getting frustrated with myself, feeling many times inadequate, feeling sometimes overwhelmed. Leading means from my years of experience that I will be honest about my inadequacies, I will be honest about my shortcomings I will be honest about sometimes being overwhelmed. My team will see me sweat. My team will see me cry. My team will know that as the leader I am a man, I am a sinner, I am not that special but I feel responsible for the right things cause that is what leaders do. I own my responsibilities. I own the health of my team, the ministry. I must lead the best that I know how and more.

All that to say that is why I need a team around me. I need a team that I can trust and they need a leader they can trust. Trust is not a given. Trust doesn't come by desire. Trust doesn't come by verbage only. Trust comes through the difficulties. Trust comes through the give and take of relationships. Trust comes through strain, through hardship, through honest discussion, honest interaction and just plain daily interaction with the team.

There is no way that I can do everything that needs to be done in 3 ministries. That is why I brought on personnel. The needs of the ministry far outweigh what one person can do, let alone what 1 person should do. I know full well my shortcomings and my responsibilities and so building a team is a must for me. Trust then is vital to being and having an effective ministry. As I lead, I must trust those on my team. I must trust them to walk with God. I must trust them to feel responsible for all of their area of ministry. I must trust them to do what is right, to care about what is right and to just plain ole work everyday at doing ministry.

Interesting to me is the word trust. The action of trust. In truth I don't always trust. In truth there are mechanisms by which trust can be built. Trust is not assumable. Trust is not a given. 1 of the mechanisms of trust for me is leading the team and looking behind me to see who is following. Right? I mean if no one is following, just maybe they don't trust me. If I ask my team to do something and it doesn't get done, then I may not trust them. Right? Trust takes time to develop. Trust means that as a bridge gets built it goes through many tests as each new piece gets put in place. A bridge just can't be built and then 1 day just open without being tested. The same goes for trust on a team. I must be tested for my team to be trusted and they must be tested in order for me to trust them. That process happens all the time with parents and students. That process happens everyday in relationships. That process is brutally important for the next step, for growth, for building a ministry. Trust is not a given. Trust is earned.

I am learning, especially this past week how important trust becomes when leading. Trust is a 2 way street. As I lead I want to put many aspects of ministry into the hands, and hearts of my team. As a leader it's not always easy at first to give away parts of the ministry. But I must. I cannot do it all. So, as I disseminate aspects of the ministry it is to lighten the load no doubt but the bottom line is for me to build trust with my team. After all, I believe that those on a team given more and more responsibility says I trust you, I believe in you, I have faith in you and what God is going to do in you.

Lastly, I'm learning a little more these days as a leader how easy it for my team, for others looking in to give up on trust before really working at listening, or maybe making a real try to understand what is being said, what is being asked, what is needed. It seems to me that the trust that has been built over a period of time is easily thrown away with a misunderstanding, a possible difference of opinion, a purposeful bad attitude, or even a difference in the methodology.

Trust takes a long time to build, but it is easily broken that is for sure. So, I am continually trying to show my team and those around me that I will fail, I will blow it, I will not do everything correct 24/7. Why? Because the team must know that I know the same thing about them. That is that they will blow it, they will fail, they might not always come through. But I will continue to go farther with trust, I will trust them more, I will be long suffering. I know I will blow it. Should that automatically take apart the trust that has been built? No way. I know that there is no one perfect therefore, I want my team and those around me to know that they have the freedom to fail, the freedom to try, the freedom to be themselves so that when it is time to as Bonhoeffer wrote in his book from prison – "When we trust, we have learned to put our very lives in the hands of others...we now know that only such confidence, which is always a venture, though a glad and positive venture, enables us really to live and work..."

Trust builds confidence through the venture. Not without the venture. Leading is a venture. Leading is daily. Leading is 24/7 and the same can be said of trust. Trust helps what I do become a glad and positive venture regardless of how hard my job, the ministry, life can be because trust builds, trust grows, trust is something I hang onto longer, stronger, harder because it's my responsibility and I feel it. I know the value of trusting even when those around me are trying to find reasons not to trust, to throw in the towel to give up.

Lastly. Here is the bottom line for me as I am learning to lead from the one I follow. I have learned to Trust in the Lord through some very tough times in my life. When I was hurting not to long ago, I was upset, I lost trust in the Lord. I blamed Him for everything to the point that I no longer trusted Him. I was angry, I found ways to blame Him for everything that went wrong. In truth, that dark time was a teaching time to me of His faithfulness. He proved over and over that even though not much went my way, He was trustworthy. Because I learned that lesson pretty firmly, I learned out of that dark time and experience that human nature, my human nature lost trust very fast. It was only His long suffering, His steadfastness, His ability to take my lashing out, my anger, my hurt on. He wasn't saying to me "Hey when you say it right, do it right, be right, I'll prove myself to you." No, He, the Lord allowed me to wrestle with His leadership in my life.

It wasn't always easy, I had to look deep down inside myself, my heart, my darkness. Moreover, I had to hear from Him, from His Word, from time in the pit to believe, to trust that He wasn't finished with me. And that lesson rings true to me as a leader. I know that it is really easy to point fingers, to lose trust, to wonder where I am being led. Therefore I also know that to those I am leading (and I'm not perfect) that they like me can find certain things (right or wrong) to find fault, to not trust, to give up.

As a leader learning from my leader that sometimes I will be the issue, I will be under the micro scope, I will be a reason not to trust. But I will trust. I will continue to put my very life in the hands of those on my team even if they may falter. Why? Because the team I lead needs to know I trust them. The team I lead needs to hear from me that they are valued, that I will not give up. That I will be steadfast. That I will be long suffering. That I will go the distance. I am learning that principle more and more from the one I follow.

Hand in Hand Leadership

Empower: v. to give or delegate power or authority to; authorize

Lead. That is what I am expected to do. Lead.
I know, I know, to some that may sound arrogant. I certainly don't think I am a "great" leader. I certainly don't think I do it perfect and I certainly don't think I am all that good at doing it. Therefore, I have learned over the years to do what is best when leading. Empower. That is why I believe in TEAM. I believe in my team. I believe that as I empower my team to take ownership of the NextGen Ministry much more can be accomplished, many tasks completed, much ministry can be furthered.

I have found over the years of ministry that there are plenty of great youth workers, youth pastors, volunteers, parents, students that can do many many things as well if not better than I. So, the best thing for me to do is empower the people involved in the ministry to get it done with me.

I found out a long long time ago that I am not a lone ranger. Not even close. I need people around me. What kind of people you may ask? Perfect? No. Smart? Yes. Smarter? Yes Diligent? Yes. Hard working? Yes. All together? No. #1 person I need around me are those that enjoy following, those that enjoy serving, those that want to go, those that want to fulfill God's purposes, those that just plain ole want to be part of the ministry. That's right. Those that want to be part of the ministry and want to fulfill God's purposes in their life make for great team players.

Empower: to give or delegate power or authority to; authorize

The fact that I am part of a staff means that I have been empowered to fulfill the mission of the church. I have been empowered to carry out, to move forward, to do what 1 man cannot do alone. So as I learn more about empowerment, I in turn continue to empower my team. It has to be that way.

Isn't it interesting that Jesus the Christ actually empowered His vagabond 11 to fulfill His ministry and now I am part of that ministry. Yes. To empower is extremely important. Empowerment may well be the most important part of leadership.

Teach a bility

Lessons in Leadership from the trenches. (My 20+ years in the ministry trench)

"You can never learn less; you can only learn more. The reason I know so much is because I have made so many mistakes."
— Buckminster Fuller

I had lunch with a former student that goes all the way back to 1988. He is now married with a daughter (I had the privilege of "doing" the wedding.) I remember when he was a student, not coming to the student ministry, not involved, just sitting at home. One day I went over to his house and asked him to come to the Wednesday night thing. When he graduated from CCU the school I graduated from, he came to my second church to intern for me. What a newbie, but what a teachable young man. To this day, he is a teachable man.

I like newbies. I like working with fresh. I like leading those that are ready to go indeed. My hope for the millennial's is huge. I enjoy their new enthusiasm, the fresh ideas, the ability to go go go. I like that. I remember when the "I have a social life" kind of attitude "so I can't work all these nights" was part of my mantra. I know, I was once not married, not worried about paying bills, thinking that this job is just a stepping stone, or an "I will move on, so I have to pace myself" kind a thing. I was there along time ago, and I can relate.

In my opinion it really comes down to teachability and being teachable is what I notice and enjoy. The lack of teachability in my experience is sometimes about arrogance, sometimes about not being vulnerable, sometimes not willing to let their guard down because they may think that a leader is really looking for something better than the best effort. In truth, because I lead I'm not looking for perfection, I'm not looking for even above an honest effort. I'm looking for teachability. Being teachable means that there is openness. There is a view of oneself that they have not arrived. I'm 52 and I know I haven't arrived.

Which leads me to the matter of working with newbies. The journey of 20+ years of ministry has been a very sobering 20 years. Just when I thought I had arrived I would be busted. Just when I thought I got it, I got raddled. Just when I though I was more than adequate, I found myself inadequate. Is it my job as I lead to "speak into their lives"? Yes, I think it is. Here comes the rub. When the green horn is not teachable it makes it things a little sketchy.

Yes, I know, I may not speak grammatically correct. I may not do things the way they do things. I may not be their image of what a leader is or isn't, but is that the issue? I know full well that I didn't get to the place of leading because of a degree, or because I say it right or do it right. I got to the place of leadership through years of hard knocks, through years of tough experiences, through the daily grind of ministry, through experience and by the Grace of God. Through some tough years of marriage, through some tough days of raising kids, through being a Sr. Pastor of a hurting church plant, through pain, through much angst, through all sorts of stuff. I'm not a leader because I graduated. I'm a leader because of my record in student ministry and the trust from those that called me to lead. No matter how I look at it, I have not even come close to all there is to learn. I hope I'm still learning.

I may be a little tired after a couple of years of restarting. I may be a little tired because of some home struggles with 2 late teenage sons, I may be a little frustrated with having to redo much of the ministry. But 20+ years of ministry means I have a little bit more knowledge, understanding, work ethic, sense, than a fresh student out of college. Teachability will take them a long long way. Give me 1 teachable green horn and much can get accomplished in their life. Teachable stands out more than G.P.A., or a degree. Teachability means much to a leader.

"In a humble state, you learn better. I can't find anything else very exciting about humility, but at least there's that."
— John Dooner

Note: I like the word Dubious; adj. wavering or hesitating in opinion; inclined to doubt.

Leadership and Trust pt. 2

Leadership from the Trenches #6
Trust: n. reliance on the integrity, strength, ability, surety, etc., of a person or thing; confidence.

There is so much about trust and leadership that I have added another entry on the subject. From the trenches of course.

Trust. Trust is a huge, huge, big, big, issue in leadership. Indeed, if I am not trusted then I know where I would like to go with a team, with students, with parents will most likely take much more time, energy and extended time or may just be utter failure. Trust. What have I learned about trust?

Of course, I'm not the corner on leadership by any means, and I'm not the best at defining the word trust as I have been leading student ministry over the past 20+ years. I have learned some things though. Hopefully for readers of my blog you understand that I get it a little bit.

Let me start by saying I have blown trust and I am sorry for the way I have blown trust. As I deal with trust on a daily basis I often refer to my early years of ministry when I actually believed that saying what people wanted me to say, or agreeing with what I was told to do (even though I didn't believe it was right) or the many times I showed up late or missed an appointment or said something that wasn't quiet the complete truth or the many times I just plain old failed, I believe has made me a better leader, has made me a better coach, has made me a better person and a better Christ follower.

For you see, I believe that many, many students, many parents, my team, my friends, my family want someone to trust and want to believe with their whole heart. In truth, outside of Jesus Christ, His Word, God's promises everything else falls short. That being said, as a leader I still have to work hard and being trust worthy, for my team to trust, for parents to trust, for my comrades to trust, for my wife to trust, for my sons to trust and so on. There are many that want to trust me. You see?

So, here is an important truth. I admit that when I started being a youth pastor back in the late 80's I was in it for a little of myself. You know the being a big deal to students, the being the "pro", the being the "guy" and all that supposed leadership stuff. In truth things changed when I failed miserably at being a youth pastor, when I failed with the peoples trust, when I learned head on how untrustworthy I really was. Then, I had children and realized the importance of being who I said I was. On being looked upon by my to sons as the "man" not because I earned it but because I was their dad. I wanted to be a great dad, not a dad that they couldn't trust. Here are a few lessons.

1. That when I told my sons things, it wasn't for me, it was for them.
2. That being truthful doesn't feel good most of the time. For both party's For the sake of Trust
3. That being a father means that how I live is being watched 24/7
4. That I better believe in what I am talking about
5. That I better explain consequence and follow through with all consequences for the sake of trust.
6. That I do many things for the benefit of others, not just myself. (Principle of first in)
7. That in order for others to trust me, I sometimes have to wait for a silent "I told you so."
8. That in order for others to trust me, my past (which has been forgiven) is actually a good teaching tool. (for those that are teachable)

Just a few things about a few of the above points.

Today when I speak to students, or my team, or parents, or whomever it is not for me. I'm speaking to them about a certain thing, or something to do it's for them-- I don't need accolades, I don't need to be the man, I don't need to feel good-- I'm saying it for their benefit period. I am speaking on a subject, or about something because I want them to try it, to do it, to believe it, but not for me, but for their growth, for their process, for them to get it.

Compared to when I first started before children and getting a little older and wiser it may have been so that someone could say, "man, is he smart, or is he cool, or is he...whatever" Those days are long gone. I do ministry, I lead for the benefit of students, my team, my church.

Which leads to the statement about a silent "I told you so." In truth, I can't make people trust me. I can't work their volition to trust me, I can't and I don't try. Sometimes, the greatest thing I can do is explain what I have learned (honestly) tell the truth, give the possible outcomes and let the people or persons learn on their own that I was telling them the truth. 99 time out of 100 the same people come back and say, "you were right, I should have listened to you. That builds trust.

Finally, trust is a tough thing. Really? Shouldn't that be a given? Well, there was a day when constituted authority, authority was given. Trust was part of what we did for teachers, for pastors, for police, for presidents, for many in authority. Thanks to those that have blown it (myself included) trust is no longer a given. As a matter of my experience, trust is actually a large mountain to climb with many set backs, many things that can come up unintentionally or by mistakes, or by things out of my control. Hopefully at those times trust has been built enough to where those time bring even more trust.

Yes, trust is a vital thing. Trust is not a given. Trust is not about a title anymore. Trust is not about a position.

Last thing. I'm now 52 years old. I'm not the corner on trust. I have failed many times. I'm not special or exceptional. This I know. During all of my lowest times in my life. Some brought on by me. Some because of wrong choices, some because I failed at looking farther than my nose. This I know. That through my life I have found the Word of God, through the Scriptures that God is trustworthy. How? Because in those times I learned to trust Him. To trust Him completely. To throw my circumstance, my life into His arms. As I have learned to trust Him, I am learning to be someone that others hopefully can trust.
"Some trust in chariots and some in horses, but we trust in the name of the LORD our God.
~Psalm 20.7

"He trusts in the LORD," they say, "let the LORD rescue him. Let him deliver him, since he delights in him." ~Psalm 22.8

Styles of Leadership

There really are so many STYLES to leadership. Isn't that true? Autocratic, heavy handed, free and easy, all over the map, visionary and so on.

Interesting that as a leader I know my style at least on a normal day I do. In the tough times I question myself and all that goes into questioning. "Should I do it this way? Is this the right way? Am I doing it like this person? How would they do it? How would my dad do it?

Then I look at those that have been leaders in my life. Pastors, bosses, fathers, coaches, mentors and so on. I basically have had to learn on my own. Really. My gifting does fit to a degree, but occasionally being a visionary means that I see it, but those around me may not. I see it before it happens. I feel it, I want it, and then lots of things can happen.

1. I have to trust where the vision is coming from
2. I have to look deep inside to make sure it's not about me
3. I have to work with others
4. I have to explain it Lucy
5. I have to reshape it sometimes
6. I have to trust others around me to jump in even if they don't see it like I do

Which leads to Leadership. Leadership then becomes a little dicey. Leading becomes, looks like many things.

I often think about the strong leaders in my life. Those that said what to do and I just did it because that was my role. I think of the leaders in my life that gave more directives than I thought were needed, so sometimes I cut out some directives and the mission was accomplished. I had leaders in my life that wanted things done exactly like they wanted them done. I had leaders in my life that left it up to me to accomplish what they thought I was capable of doing and that probably has been a little more of how I lead. After all, I'm a pro and the people around me are pro's and we are all in it together, so what is our objective and lets go get it.

I'm not a very good administrator I know that full well. So I get people around me that are highly administratively skilled. I may not always be able to give directives because I think there others are much more creative so the how to isn't that important to me, but the outcome is. Which sometimes leads to people wondering what I specifically want. One step at a time.

Well, here I lies the real issue and it goes back to trust. Am I trusted with leading? Trust is a high value for me. Indeed, trust means that those I need and want around me to accomplish the the vision I am casting. I may have to rethink this, I may have to do some tweaking. Nevertheless I have watched some dreams come to reality over the past few weeks and I saw it way before it happened.

I don't know, I may actually have the style of leadership that is either obsolete, old school, too new school, too much of me not doing the things I didn't like done to me. I don't know, but as I'm sitting here just blogging and listening to some great worship songs and thinking about how my God leads me. His style is certainly not always easy for me to understand, but I think I know more about where He is leading me today, than oh lets say... a few years ago or even yesterday as I become more and more dependent on Him to lead me.

I know I'm 52 I should know all this stuff. I should be a leader like Spurgeon, or like the seminary profs say it should be done, or like the leaders of great churches, or like the leaders of great corporations. Well? I'm in the trenches everyday like those around me and I'm finding out more and more that there really are many ways to do this thing called leadership and I'm still trying to find my sweet spot.

"From the ends of the earth I call to you, I call as my heart grows faint; lead me to the rock that is higher than I." ~Psalm 61.1-3

"if it is to encourage, then give encouragement; if it is giving, then give generously; if it is to lead, do it diligently; if it is to show mercy, do it cheerfully." ~Romans 12.7-9

Messy Leadership

"Individual commitment to a group effort - that is what makes a team work, a company work, a society work, a civilization work." ~Vince Lombardi

"Just as a body, though one, has many parts, but all its many parts form one body, so it is with Christ." 1 Corinthians 12.11-13

The longer I live, the longer I do ministry, the longer I lead, I see the value of team. I see the high value of each member of the team. That being said, as the leader of a team I am beginning to understand that each member of the team is completely different therefore each member is to be treated differently and that can sometimes get a little messy.

Leadership is a weird animal for sure. Leadership means that there aren't many days that look and feel the same. There are many variations to leading a team. No kidding. Right? Right. Many would love to be called a leader. Many would love the title, or the notoriety or the "accolades. What I am continuing to learn about leadership is that there really aren't many accolades, there aren't many gathered around for the desire to be led, there aren't many that want leadership for just plain leadership. It is always easy to just plain want to do one's own thing and stay relatively safe and secure.

Whenever I think I get it, it seems that I have so much more to learn about leadership. Leadership gets messy from my point of view when my passion is misunderstood. It gets messy when I wear too much of my heart on my sleeve. Leadership is messy when I fail to explain, or give clear directives, or when I think that what I say is easily understood. Yes, I as the leader can create a mess if I'm not checking my emotions, if I'm not clear, if I'm not on top of my game in all areas of team work. You know, that is not easy for me to be on top of my "leading" thing 24/7. Sometimes I want to take a break, and that can create a mess.

I'm learning more about myself in this role called leadership than I previously wanted to know. I'm learning more about how much I need to grow, how much I need other leaders to teach me leadership.

When I first started student ministry years ago, I used to live by the ups and downs of events and successes. There was a time that God showed me that the ups and downs were not the issue. That so called "success" was not about the moment or the win, or the circumstance. Student ministry by the fact that events, moments, things in general ebb and flow. Numbers go up and down. Parents complaining come and go and life goes on and getting caught up in the success is not good because tomorrow comes quick.

Yes, leadership is messy and I need to continue to work on my leadership skills so that I can minimize messes that I make. I'm not afraid of messes, I'm not afraid to fail, I'm not afraid to lead. But I do need to work smarter at my own issues in order for the team to move forward, to continue to do great things for God, to build the Kingdom.

"The ultimate measure of a man is not where he stands in moments of comfort, but where he stands at times of challenge and controversy." ~M.L.K. Jr.

I love that quote by Martin Luther King Jr. He is right. There really aren't many moments of comfort and I don't want to be the reason. Doing ministry, leading and doing the right things is a daily challenge for sure. Moreover the essence of ministry in and of itself in this day and age brings controversy. That is the greater responsibility I have in front of me. Minimize the mess by doing the things that count.

It's about the Process

"These have come so that your faith--of greater worth than gold, which perishes even though refined by fire--may be proved genuine and may result in praise, glory and honor when Jesus Christ is revealed." 1 Peter 1.7

Student Ministry has many facets. There are so many nuances, so many angles, so many different ideals, philosophies, views and on and on. There are Christian students, there are growing Christian students, there are apathetic students, there are students from broken homes, there are students using, there are students engaging in sex, pornography, hurt, insecure, neglected, living for Christ, not interested, disenfranchised with the church, good families, broken families, in trouble, in serious trouble, doubters, some even under the direct influence of demons.

So the question is simply can the student ministry handle all of it? Can a ministry do it all? As a leader of student ministry I have learned over the years that building a place for all is the starting place. Exclusion is never an option period.

I believe that every student, every family is in process. Therefore, my goal week per week, month by month is to help in the process. The student ministry is not about a consistent mountain top. That is not reality. That is not Biblical. The drive for student ministry is the understanding Biblically that every person whether they know Christ, know of Christ, or are being sought after by Christ is in process.

There are problems with the above. Right? After all, wouldn't it be easier to just have a student ministry of "good" students? Wouldn't it be safer? Wouldn't it be nicer? Wouldn't it be more comfortable? One problem: Who decides who is really worthy of being part of safe or good? Is that decided by parents? I know parents that have been bamboozled by their so called "good" student. Safe? What is the determining factor of safe? Don't talk about sex. Don't deal with the culture? Don't deal with anything that someone deems unsafe? Avoidance and knowledge to many is considered safe.

I have chosen over the past 20 + years to build a student ministry that is open to every student no matter where they are in their spiritual life and I believe with my heart that this is what God wants me to do.

Not long ago there was a student coming to the H.S. Weekly event I do called Uprising. For a year this student was coming. Good student, good family, good everything. He knew much about Christ, He most likely asked Jesus to enter into his life a few years back. But through many let downs by people, in life, through circumstance he didn't understand, he began to fade away, he began to let go of the things that were once thought to him to be a high value, at least they were taught to him as a high value. Nevertheless, he began to walk a different walk, a walk toward darkness.

I prayed for this student, every time I saw this student I always let him know that I missed him, I cared about him and the ministry was here for him. One day he came back. I believe he came back because he knew he would be accepted period. Ultimately he responded to the voice of God during a talk and decided to make a choice to pursue Jesus Christ. Interesting that over these many years of ministry I get to witness the "process". I get to build a ministry that is about the process, and the process is life as a high school student. The process is not easy, the process is not safe, the process is difficult.

You see, we are all in process. I am way different than I was way back when because during this life I have had days of doubt, days of hurt, days of pain. Honesty matters when dealing with the subject of sin. Honesty matters when dealing with normal every day life. I believe that leading the student ministry means that I must be honest about the process, that I must help in the process, and that ultimately, the process goes far beyond the years I have with a student. Student Ministry is about embracing the "process" no matter where the student is in the "process."

"Has now become my souls desire
Purged and cleansed and purified
That the Lord be glorified
He is consuming my soul
Refining me, making me whole
No matter what I may lose
I choose the Refiner's fire

I'm learning now to trust His touch
To crave the fire's embrace
For though my past with sin was etched
His mercies did erase
Each time His purging cleanses deeper
I'm not sure that I'll survive
Yet the strength in growing weaker
Keeps my hungry soul alive"

~Steve Greene The Refiner's fire

Yes, students are in process. Just like adults. No one arrives, no one is perfect, the H.S. culture is tough, parents don't always model it right (they should also be in process and understand this) life is a process period. Ultimately who leads through the process? Answer that question and the reason for student ministry becomes pretty easy to understand.

Leadership and Emotional Intelligence

"Great leaders move us. They ignite our passion and inspire the best in us. When we try to explain why they are so effective, we speak of strategy, vision, or powerful ideas. But the reality is much more primal: Great leadership works through the emotions." ~Daniel Goleman

There are so many views, ideas, philosophy's, attitudes, experiences, situations that cause a leader to have to answer this question-- What kind of leadership model will I choose?

My take has been over the years to use some, what I call "from the street of experience" and to apply what some of my mentors have taught me, some wisdom watching others, a little of this and that and then this: Emotional Intelligence.

I have read the book Primal Leadership by Goleman, Boyatzis and McKee. I have chosen over a year ago to institute in my leadership development of first myself, and then to my team a high value in Emotional Intelligence. Allow me to explain from an online article from Business Listening.com

"Primal Leadership authors Goleman, Boyatzis and McKee identify four emotional intelligence "domains" which bridge 18 leadership "competencies," the majority of which depend upon skills in listening to one's self and to others.

Domain 1, Self Awareness includes the competencies of emotional self-awareness, accurate self-assessment, and self-confidence.

Domain 2, Self-Management includes the competencies of emotional self-control, transparency, adaptability, achievement, initiative, and optimism.

Mastery of domains one and two, which the authors describe as personal competence, depends heavily upon listening to one's self, becoming aware of one's emotional state, values, standards, and impact upon others. Self-examination and gathering feedback about oneself through coaching and 360 reviews assist with the development of personal competence.

Domain 3, Social Awareness includes empathy, organizational awareness, and service.

Domain 4, Relationship Management includes inspirational leadership, influence, developing others, being a catalyst for change, conflict management, and teamwork/collaboration."

These 4 domains make so much sense in leadership. I can also say that these 4 domains apply to even parenting or for any person that is leading in any circumstance. Over the years I will admit that I have let circumstances determine how I would react and often times I blew it. Even today as I have begun to put into personal practice these 4 important domains if Emotional Intelligence I still blow it. It really is hard to be in touch with my emotions.

It may sound really simple but because I believe in ministry, I believe in God's calling, I believe that God has me where I am supposed to be, there is work for me to do personally and with my team and I don't take that lightly. Therefore for me I have embraced emotional intelligence as a grid, a construct by which I operate.

This past month has been a real eye opener for me about leadership and I have much work to do. These 4 little domains hang on my wall, sit on my desk to remind me to listen to myself, listen to individuals, to remind me to have healthy handles on my emotions and so on.

20+ years of leadership in Church ministry and parenting I recommend this book for all leaders. The Apostle Paul said it like this in Romans 12.3 "For by the grace given me I say to every one of you: Do not think of yourself more highly than you ought, but rather think of yourself with sober judgment, in accordance with the faith God has distributed to each of you."

Notice the Apostle Paul's view of himself in 1 Timothy 1. 15, 16 "Here is a trustworthy saying that deserves full acceptance: Christ Jesus came into the world to save sinners—of whom I am the worst. But for that very reason I was shown mercy so that in me, the worst of sinners, Christ Jesus might display his immense patience as an example for those who would believe in him and receive eternal life."

I have searched and read much about Paul as a leader. As I have read from the scriptures of the Apostle Paul, I have found him to be honest about who he was and who he is. It seems to me that as a leader the Apostle Paul was pretty good at practicing some principles called "emotional intelligence".

I know, it could be said that Leadership is not rocket science. True. For me, leadership is what I'm called to do and I better do it to the best of my ability. I need to lead by example, I need to lead like Jesus (another great book) I need to stay in touch with Christ daily and I better know myself.

The Heart of the Matter

For where your treasure is, there your heart will be also.

Matt. 6.28-34 "And why do you worry about clothes? See how the lilies of the field grow. They do not labor or spin. Yet I tell you that not even Solomon in all his splendor was dressed like one of these. If that is how God clothes the grass of the field, which is here today and tomorrow is thrown into the fire, will he not much more clothe you, O you of little faith? So do not worry, saying, 'What shall we eat?' or 'What shall we drink?' or 'What shall we wear?' For the pagans run after all these things, and your heavenly Father knows that you need them. But seek first his kingdom and his righteousness, and all these things will be given to you as well. Therefore do not worry about tomorrow, for tomorrow will worry about itself. Each day has enough trouble of its own.

Today was a day for me to consider the continued struggle with what I would call along with many—the externals. You know? The stuff that we all are concerned about—

Clothes, looks, passions all the stuff on the outside—all the stuff that we consumers feel we must consume to be somebody. On the other hand—I actually believe that many look the other way when considering the above mentioned and pass it off as—I'm o.k., I don't do the big outside stuff—I don't cheat and steal and whatever else on the outside is big—so I can seek after money and nice clothes with labels and I can pursue whatever I want as long as I'm not committing the big ticket items.

Here is my personal deal for the day as I read Matt. Chapter 6. First, I did not read it with other people in mind—I heard from the Lord today as I wrestled with "my treasures". Yes, I considered my treasures, my heart, my passions, my stuff on the inside that is lived out the way I pursue my life.

I do very much want to build a ministry built on the "right" things. I thought about my passions, my heart and came away moving past ministry and into my ego. Is my student ministry working toward reaching campuses, students, moving from group to ministry about my ego? Is it about big? Is it about large for me? I came away from this day of contemplating Matt. 6 evaluating the reason why reaching students is my passion and my heart and dealt with this: That I am about reaching students because it is right. That reaching students and building a ministry that is focused outward is right—why? Because reaching students is not about big—although big will be the result—it is about all the students that are unreached because in truth not many have thought beyond themselves. I want students to see and learn first hand that where their treasure is-- will show itself-- in the how and what they pursue-- 24/7 and hopefully they will be more like the one they call Lord and Savior. That is my passion, that is my heart, that is where my treasures are located.

Selfishness is actually a very large part of Matt. 6 People, myself included that only think about themselves think and move toward the externals as the fix—the clothes, the stuff all the trimmings somehow make us happy. The Words of the Christ prove the sadness of selfish living. Selfishness is based from a heart that is all about the person. People that struggle with the stuff have not yet trusted Christ for all of their needs and wants. In truth, my treasure is where my heart is—and reaching students is my heart. Why? I think I know the truth to this—its because, I have seen first hand what selfishness does to families, to churches, to people that love Christ but think its all about them. A youth group is developed for safety, for protection, for fun, for personal gain.

I have learned over many years of personal stuff with the Christ that I matter as much as others that don't even know Him personally-- And that keeps me on track. Yes, I understand my fallen heart, I also understand my redeemed heart—and my redeemed heart says to pursue the stuff that matters—others, building ministries that make a difference for all.

My selfish fallen heart continues to say it is all about me. I believe that is a battle for every honest follower of Christ. The handles for dealing with the above mentioned struggle-- denial. I believe the most fulfilled people, students and parents are those that have learned to make thier passion---others.

To allow the passion of Christ to rule their hearts and their lives.

Jesus showed His disciples about passion from within lived out—by emptying Himself, becoming nothing, taking on the form of a servant and going to the cross— His passion? His heart? The world that needed Him more!

"But seek first his kingdom and his righteousness, and all these things will be given to you as well."

Surrender

Surrender: v. to yield (something) to the possession or power of another.

What does it take to surrender? How long does it take? What does it mean to surrender to God? Is it possible? Does it only happen once, twice, three times? Does surrendering to God ever stop?   Is there fear in surrender?

Well, being a parent, being a leader, being a student ministry pastor means that I daily see students, parents, people wrestling with self, with things, and with God. We are taught to grab the bull by the horns. We are continually told that our life, our destiny is ours to control. We live in fear, we live in striving, we live with addictions, with issues, with trials, with the constant bombardment of all sorts of stuff, ideas, philosophies, theories, desires, the flesh, our hearts desires, our dreams, our wants, our everything. What to do with all of that? Am I in control? Is it really my life? Isn't my life, mine to cling, to manage, to hold on, to do with what I want?   Don't I do that the best?

I have met many over the years myself included that seem to never overcome. It took years to deal with my constant pain of self doubt, inner hurt, addictive behavior, substances, ways to cope with this constant feeling that I would never ever be the person that I wanted to become. In truth I still deal with that issue on occasion.

The other day I visited a young man going through a difficult time in his life. Substances hurt him, inner angst was driving him to do things he by himself cannot deal with, along with wanting to be approved by others and his inability to say no. After all, to all of us that struggle with wanting to be liked – how do you overcome this stuff? How do you get to the point where all that is driving us nutty, hurting us inside, not being able to control our lives ends? Does it? Or is that exactly where our Father in heaven wants us? To stop trusting in ourselves and the lie that says we have enough to do something of value and surrender to Him our total inability to fix ourselves because we are hopelessly broken without Him period.

I believe I know the answer. I believe I have experienced the answer. I believe that on a good day surrendering is possible and on a bad day surrender is the only option we have. Surrender. Surrendering to what? To whom? To ourselves? To our desires? To our perceived needs, our goals, our wants, us? Surrendering to that stuff has failed us all. Surrendering to our stuff causes nothing but pain, more excesses, more eating, more drinking, more spending, more self medicating more inner hatred, more hatred toward others, more and more of the stuff that ultimately is destroying us.

Surrender do what? To whom? How?

"Do not be anxious about anything, but in every situation, by prayer and petition, with thanksgiving, present your requests to God. And the peace of God, which transcends all understanding, will guard your hearts and your minds in Christ Jesus." ~Phil. 4.6,7

Way back when I started sobriety. (Check out the first 3 steps of AA) I admitted I was powerless over my addiction - that my life had become unmanageable
Came to believe that a Power greater than myself could restore me to sanity
Made a decision to turn my will and my life over to the care of God as I understood God
(and by the way, I only understood God through some pretty screwed up ideals even though I grew up going to church, had great parents, I even went to Bible School.) I know I'm not alone.

Of course many have put down the twelve step program. Many don't really understand the power of surrendering to "a high power". I do? Obviously the "high power" is God Almighty Himself. I know Him personally by faith through a relationship with the Living Son of God Jesus Christ. I once yielded, surrendered to Him. I once gave Him my life and thought that was it. Right? After all, once you give Him your life, now it's yours to control, to live, to do.

That is not true though. Surrender is daily. Surrender is a constant thing. You know what? I don't do a good job of surrender. I'm not always the first to give my life to God. Sometimes giving Him my life is the last thing I do. I should know better. But, I'm like everyone else. Surrender is not easy. I was taught to do it myself. To work myself out of the situation, the heart ache. I should know better by now. Right? (I know I'm not alone)

How bout you?

Surrender comes down to trusting in the Lord with my life. Do I trust Him with my life? My future? The day? Others? Do I trust in Him? Sometimes I'll admit it trusting, surrendering to Him is not my first choice. I'm gonna take the time today to surrender to Him my life and trust in Him today.

"Trust in the Lord forever, for the Lord, the Lord himself, is the Rock eternal." ~Is. 26.4

How bout singing this Hymn today, tomorrow?
By Judson W. Van DeVenter 1896

All to Jesus, I surrender;
All to Him I freely give;
I will ever love and trust Him,
In His presence daily live.

I surrender all, I surrender all,
All to Thee, my blessèd Savior,
I surrender all.

All to Jesus I surrender;
Humbly at His feet I bow,
Worldly pleasures all forsaken;
Take me, Jesus, take me now.

Surrendering to God, giving our life back to Him is a daily opportunity for faith to take action in trusting in the Living God for every detail of the day. I believe that a life surrendered to Christ can take, can do, can be absolutely without a doubt, not without crisis, not without trials, not without problems but with much hope, joy, peace and Love.

"He cannot bless us unless He has us."
~C.S. Lewis

Building on a Rock

"Therefore everyone who hears these words of mine and puts them into practice is like a wise man who built his house on the rock. The rain came down, the streams rose, and the winds blew and beat against that house; yet it did not fall, because it had its foundation on the rock. But everyone who hears these words of mine and does not put them into practice is like a foolish man who built his house on sand. The rain came down, the streams rose, and the winds blew and beat against that house, and it fell with a great crash."
~ Matt.7.24-27

Interesting—"Anyone who hears these words of mine and puts them into practice…"

I think that statement is life changing. The words of Jesus are life changing when put into practice. Words are words—yes. The words of Jesus—still words unless, unless one puts them into practice. What words? What did He say? What is He talking about?

The context—
17Likewise every good tree bears good fruit, but a bad tree bears bad fruit. 18A good tree cannot bear bad fruit, and a bad tree cannot bear good fruit. 19Every tree that does not bear good fruit is cut down and thrown into the fire. 20Thus, by their fruit you will recognize them.

21"Not everyone who says to me, 'Lord, Lord,' will enter the kingdom of heaven, but only he who does the will of my Father who is in heaven. 22Many will say to me on that day, 'Lord, Lord, did we not prophesy in your name, and in your name drive out demons and perform many miracles?' 23Then I will tell them plainly, 'I never knew you. Away from me, you evildoers!" ~Matt. 7.17-23

Jesus speaks of good trees bearing good fruit. Jesus speaks about the issue of checking ones "influence" or what is being produced, or what is coming from a relationship with Christ—if there is one— there is good fruit…. Right? Maybe He is saying—good fruit is impossible outside of a relationship with Christ for— "Every tree that does not bear good fruit is cut down and thrown into the fire."

I remember when I tried desperately to bear good fruit. Yes, obeying my parents, going to church, doing all the right stuff. In truth—that could only go on for a while—then one day—I came to this conclusion—I didn't know Him period. I knew all about Him, but it was only He that could create good fruit from a changed heart.

Notice verse 21-23 "Not everyone who says to me, 'Lord, Lord,' will enter the kingdom of heaven, but only he who does the will of my Father who is in heaven. 22Many will say to me on that day, 'Lord, Lord, did we not prophesy in your name, and in your name drive out demons and perform many miracles?' 23Then I will tell them plainly, 'I never knew you. Away from me, you evildoers!'

Hmmm—Think about His words-- "Therefore everyone who hears these words of mine and puts them into practice is like a wise man who built his house on the rock."

why does this stuff still get to me?

"Accept who you are; and revel in it."
~Mitch Albom

Easier said then done right? I mean really? Is there anyone out there that struggles with who you are? Anybody feel the stare from others that you are not what they want, expect? Ever get that feeling that you are looked down on for just being you? Does that ever bother you? Well it does me. Sometimes I just don't get it. I do embrace who I am-- I thought I was actually pretty good at being able to accept me, my shortcomings, my issues, me just being me. But, sometimes-- maybe its that I'm a youth pastor or maybe because I am 52 or maybe because others have an expectation of what I should be or not be, but sometimes it really does bring me down. You know? Anybody feel that? It really does drive me crazy. Sometimes it really saddens me. Sometimes it makes me angry. Angry that I let others opinions get to me, and angry that someone is so arrogant that they think I should be what they want. It's crazy right?

How bout this? Sometimes in youth ministry when numbers are down, when students don't come to the weekly ministry events, when a night is flat, I feel responsible. Is that fair? Is that right? I actually don't think it is right for me to make the above about me or about the team around me. If something isn't perfect does that mean I shouldn't like it? If someone isn't perfect does that mean that I don't have to love them? If a message or a sermon falls flat, is that on the communicator? Obviously winging stuff, doing things half hearted, not putting time and effort into something is a problem. But, if all is done, if 100% is given (not quite sure who's foolin who, after all since when does fallen humanity give 100% 100% of the time?) Never the less, I'll admit that when things don't go right, when students bail, when it seems that my effort is being judged, when my heart is being examined, when someone or others just don't care-- well that bothers me.

I know after years in the trenches of ministry that I shouldn't let this stuff get to me. But it does and that bothers me. I should know that growth, that ministry is a process and the process isn't up to me to rush, to manipulate, to make happen. I should know by now that critics are always going to be here. I should know by now that I will not be liked by everyone. In truth, I know I'm not the most lovable person. I know I have lots of shortcomings. I know that I don't give 100% 100% of the time. I know that I tend to view myself poorly, I just don't need help in that. I know that I am not the smartest, the brightest, the best. I get that.

I needed the Savior back then, I need the Savior now. When I fail (daily) I ask for forgiveness. I don't play games, I don't pretend, I don't lie, I do revel in who God made me, the environment I grew up in, I do know that I fall short often. So why does ministry get to me sometimes to the point of exhaustion? To the point of feeling utterly worthless? To the point of just not being good enough?

No question that the devil loves to jack with all of us. "You are no good" he says. "You are incomplet, and you need others approval." Who says that? I think many people say that, believe that, live it and I get caught up in it sometimes. Sometimes its the culture of achievement. Some times its the half baked idea that people should be perfect. Sometimes its even Christians that have bought into the notion that if its not perfection than I don't have to love it, embrace it, be part of it. Sometimes its the christian culture that says be who we expect you to be, be loveable and we then will love you.

I certainly don't treat my wife like that. I certainly don't treat my friends like that. I certainly don't treat students like that. I certainly don't treat fallen imperfect parents like that. (I am one of those parents) So why does this stuff get to me?

I'm a fallen, broken person that's why.

I'm reminded today of God's Unconditional love for me. The proof being Jesus His Son. I'm reminded again of God's forgiveness that is as far as the east is from the west. I am reminded today of God's grace that surpasses any effort I could ever possibly make towards Him. I am reminded again how significant I am because He created me just like He created me. I am reminded again how much I matter to Him through His adoption for I am called His child. I revel in being His.

I accept this truth that to the many I will never be what they want me to be, that I can only do so much, that perfection won't happen while

I'm on this earth. I will continue to do all I can do to allow God to work on my rough, jagged edges. I will continue to listen to those that actually do care about me and not some weirded out agenda, I will continue to trust God for all that I need. I often wonder why Jesus commanded us to love others like we love ourselves. I do find it interesting that when I listen to all the negative stuff about me, I can easily start hating me and others. "Why aren't they perfect?" "Why are they not...or why are they....?" But when I embrace what God is doing with me, admitting my shortcomings, embracing His unconditional love for me, I can accept me, I can love me and in turn actually love the imperfect people around me.

"I know the one in whom I have put my trust, and I am sure that he is able to guard until that day what I have entrusted to him."
~2 Timothy 1.12b

Curly's Law ? the Rule of One

Have you ever heard of The Rule of One or Curly's Law?

Curly: Do you know what the secret to life is?
Curly: This. (Holds up 1 finger)
Mitch: Your finger?
Curly: One thing. Just one thing. You stick to that and the rest don't mean S*#$.
Mitch: But what is the "one thing"?
Curly: (He smiles) That's what you have to find out.

Remember that scene from the movie City Slickers? I do. Remember this scene?

"She had a sister called Mary, who sat at the Lord's feet listening to what he said. But Martha was distracted by all the preparations that had to be made. She came to him and asked, "Lord, don't you care that my sister has left me to do the work by myself? Tell her to help me!" "Martha, Martha," the Lord answered, "you are worried and upset about many things, but few things are needed—or indeed only one. Mary has chosen what is better, and it will not be taken away from her." ~10.39-42

Priorities. Martha and Mary. One working, one sitting at the feet of Jesus. One distracted, the other engaged. Ah yes, the life of following Christ. Right? The life of ministry? Right? I mean there is so much to do. There is so much planning, so much implementing, so much work to do.

Some could argue that Martha was doing the right thing. After all, there is a time to "get things done" there is a time to do, go go go, there is a time to just put your nose to the grindstone and work work work. True. Except-- Jesus was pointing out Martha's "worrying about many things." The worry of the work? The worry of not getting it done? The worry of it not being right? Martha as Jesus points out is also upset. "Worried and upset about many things." Ever been there? You know worried and upset about "many things"? I know I have. I know there have been times that the work of ministry actually can drive me to the worry of many things and actually being upset about things not getting done. I feel for Martha.

On the other hand, Jesus calms, Jesus cares, Jesus loves Martha enough to point her to the "most important thing. Himself. Remember Mary was sitting at the Lord's feet listening to what he said. Jesus points out to the worried and upset Martha that Mary was at the place that was most important-- that is at the feet of Jesus taking in all He had to say. Wow! Right? How simple is that? How cool is that Jesus said often as He spoke "for those that have ears to hear." For those that are postured toward his voice. To those that get it. To those that want what Jesus has to say. To those that are ready, they will put aside all the stuff (it really can wait right?) their worry, their being upset-- and get back to what is most important. That is hearing from Jesus.

I find ministry to be an interesting life vocation. Often times there is so much to do. There really is. There is always calendering, always relationships, always planning to do, always details to take care of, always things that most of the time bring worry, times of being upset, times of wondering how do catch up? Jesus points us all back to the most important thing-- Himself.

I have actually come to love these words over the past few weeks-- "you are worried and upset about many things, but few things are needed—or indeed only one." Indeed the only one-- finding time with Jesus to hear His voice, to hear from Him and all the other stuff matters much less.

"But seek first his kingdom and his righteousness, and all these things will be given to you as well."
~Matt. 6.33

Yes the rule of One-- Sitting at the Feet of Jesus is a great place.

"Only servants"

"Only servants, through whom you came to believe—as the Lord has assigned to each his task."

I have some favorite sports people-- Stan Mikita is my all time favorite Chicago Blackhawk. I have always worn his #21 ever since I was a kid playing floor hockey, street hockey and ice hockey. I had dreams of being like Stan. I loved #51 of my beloved Chicago Bears. #51 Dick Butkus brought fear to the opposite team he played against. Butkus feared nothing. I always wanted to be like Dick Butkus.

There are so many other people in my life that I have looked up to, I emulated, I wanted to be. I saw their effort, I saw their hard work, I cared about what they had to say, I thoroughly enjoyed looking up to great people. Well, I thought they were great people.

I live and breath ministry. It's my life, it's how I make a living. It's what I do. I have had great mentors in my life. Some have been very close to me. Some have been from far away. I always admired Billy Graham and I know why. It was at a crusade where my father came to know Christ. For that I have always appreciated his ministry. I have seen so many great people doing Kingdom work. I have seen, heard, been around so many great, great people doing Kingdom work.

This I know for sure. That none of the people in ministry I think about, remember, that I have emulated, that have helped me, have loved me, have taught me-- ever believed that they were all that. They didn't believe that it was their hard work, their wise sayings, their teaching method, their anything that made the difference-- at least they never said that, or did anything that made me think that they believed their work was all about them and that without them the Kingdom would suffer.

Every once in awhile I find myself struggling with me. Am I doing all I can? Am I doing everything right? Am I reaching students? Am I effective? Am I teaching enough? Am I doing it right? I mean really right? Is it enough? Students aren't coming to Christ, it must be me?

Right? Students aren't walking with Christ. It must be me? The ministry is just not growing. It must be me. Right?

None of my above mentioned battle is right.

"Brothers and sisters, I could not address you as people who live by the Spirit but as people who are still worldly—mere infants in Christ. I gave you milk, not solid food, for you were not yet ready for it. Indeed, you are still not ready. You are still worldly. For since there is jealousy and quarreling among you, are you not worldly? Are you not acting like mere humans? For when one says, "I follow Paul," and another, "I follow Apollos," are you not mere human beings? What, after all, is Apollos? And what is Paul? Only servants, through whom you came to believe—as the Lord has assigned to each his task. I planted the seed, Apollos watered it, but God has been making it grow. So neither the one who plants nor the one who waters is anything, but only God, who makes things grow. The one who plants and the one who waters have one purpose, and they will each be rewarded according to their own labor. For we are co-workers in God's service; you are God's field, God's building. By the grace God has given me, I laid a foundation as a wise builder, and someone else is building on it. But each one should build with care. For no one can lay any foundation other than the one already laid, which is Jesus Christ." ~1 Corinthians 3.1-12

I find it interesting that the Apostle Paul says "I planted the seed, Apollos watered it, but God has been making it grow. So neither the one who plants nor the one who waters is anything" isn't that the way it really is? Is it? I know the people in my life believed it. I also know that there are many that don't. But the longer I do this life of ministry the more I can't help understand how little I really am. How unimportant I really am, and how big, how important the God's work must be.

I don't know how I have gotten caught up in it being about me. Maybe it's my insecurities. Maybe it's my self esteem. Maybe its my flesh. Maybe its just my plain ole fallenness that messes with me. I don't know. This I do know-- this the ministry I do, the ministry I live is all about God's work in students, in families, in His Church, in this world.

"So neither the one who plants nor the one who waters is anything, but only God, who makes things grow. The one who plants and the one who waters have one purpose, and they will each be rewarded according to their own labor. For we are co-workers in God's service; you are God's field, God's building." ~1 Cor. 3.7-9

Finally. I do believe that hard work, that doing all that I can to be the vessel God can use is a high value. I do believe that I must be about doing the right things. Most of all, in truth it ain't about me and that is a great great thing.

"Only servants, through whom you came to believe—as the Lord has assigned to each his task."

Drugs kill. Period.

Life is short. Tomorrow is guaranteed to no one. Right? Well, I received sad news this week. Another death due to drugs. I hate drugs. I hate what it does to people. I hate that addiction is a reality. I hate that a "good" man is dead due to the addiction of drugs. I hate it.

I worked at a motorcycle shop on Saturday's in Dayton back in the mid 90's because I wanted to be around motorcycles and the people that rode. I love motorcycles, the lifestyle, the freedom, everything about motorcycles. One of the owners of the Bike shop was Phil "Flipper" Alderton. I liked being around Flipper. Flipper had a way of calling me "pastor" Don. Flipper was always fair and kind to me. Sometimes he liked to say things to maybe "shake" me up, to get a rise out of me. But I never let it bother me. I enjoyed working at the shop. I enjoyed the race team, the open houses, the sales, the vibe of the shop. I enjoyed Flipper. He was a trip.

One day Flipper asked me to perform his wedding that was going to take place in L.A. CA. I told him that I would only if he and his wife to be would meet with me a couple of times so they could prepare for marriage. Flipper said yes and we met a few times. I still chuckle a little as I think about Flipper asking me to perform the wedding, the few days in L.A., and the wedding. I always liked Flipper. I actually found him to be a breath of fresh air.

I had a few lunches and dinners with Phil. He gave me an Oakley hat (I still have it) just because I liked it. One time we were at a race in Indy and his mom was there, and he asked me to drive her home with my 2 sons, so of course I did. Flipper was a one of a kind type of person. I had reconnected with Flipper over Facebook about a year ago. It was fun to chat back and forth a few times. I had no idea he was heading back to Dayton. I wish I would have known. I wish I would have reconnected in person with him.

Sadly, I found out that Phil "Flipper" died this week from a heroin overdose. Sadly, I have known over the years many "users" of drugs and many abusers of alcohol and I have not seen very many doing well after years of use and abuse. Yes, Flipper had a problem. It's called addiction. Yes, Flipper was a fun loving motorcycle man. No, drugs could never solve his problems. No, drugs would never treat him as good as a friend. No, drugs could never do "right" by him.

I blog about my life as a youth pastor, a father, a friend, just a regular human being. This 100th blog is kind weird. Kinda weird because its about the death of a man that I barely knew, I barely understood. Kinda weird because in truth I have never known anyone that died of a heroine overdose. Kinda weird because this kind of stuff is a part of my my life. Oh I could've chosen to avoid people, avoid the ugly, the sick, the down trodden, the users, the messed up people, those like me that aren't perfect. For some odd reason God called me to ministry and ministry means people and people are messy and life is weird and life is tough and life is sometimes very sad and tough to understand.

I am reminded again this week of my own addiction. I am reminded again of the friends that spoke truth into my life. I am reminded again of how people, loving people, not perfect people, but people that made a choice to come close enough to love me even when I pushed back. Oh, I am saddened by the death of Flipper, at the same time I am hopeful that his death may save a life. That a friend that knows someone with a substance addiction may just have the courage to say something, do something for their friend. Yes, I am reminded today how much I actually love life and the people in my life. I am also reminded why I wanted to work at the motorcycle shop-- to connect with people-- people like Flipper. I wish I could've helped him.

Maybe some people don't like the word hate, but I hate drugs. I hate substances that brings about such devastation. I hate this stuff. I hate it that Flipper couldn't overcome. I hate this kinda stuff with a passion.

"There is value in life...even if it is misspent. Phil Alderton achieved so much in life that the circumstances of his death can't reduce my respect for him. In truth, his fall from grace carries within it a powerful message—not about drugs or life on the edge—but about friendships that see through the fog of addiction. It is bittersweet that a path so inevitable and painful could not be altered by well-meaning friends and family—or by a man who wanted so much to do the right thing." ~ Jody Weisel

Compare and Contrast-- you make the call.

Leviticus 19.1-37

1 The LORD said to Moses, 2 "Speak to the entire assembly of Israel and say to them: 'Be holy because I, the LORD your God, am holy.

3 "'Each of you must respect your mother and father, and you must observe my Sabbaths. I am the LORD your God.

4 "'Do not turn to idols or make metal gods for yourselves. I am the LORD your God.

5 "'When you sacrifice a fellowship offering to the LORD, sacrifice it in such a way that it will be accepted on your behalf. 6 It shall be eaten on the day you sacrifice it or on the next day; anything left over until the third day must be burned up. 7 If any of it is eaten on the third day, it is impure and will not be accepted. 8 Whoever eats it will be held responsible because they have desecrated what is holy to the LORD; they must be cut off from their people.

9"'When you reap the harvest of your land, do not reap to the very edges of your field or gather the gleanings of your harvest. 10 Do not go over your vineyard a second time or pick up the grapes that have fallen. Leave them for the poor and the foreigner. I am the LORD your God.

11 "'Do not steal.

"'Do not lie.

"'Do not deceive one another.

12 "'Do not swear falsely by my name and so profane the name of your God. I am the LORD.

13 "'Do not defraud or rob your neighbor.

"'Do not hold back the wages of a hired worker overnight.

14 "'Do not curse the deaf or put a stumbling block in front of the blind, but fear your God. I am the LORD.

15 "'Do not pervert justice; do not show partiality to the poor or favoritism to the great, but judge your neighbor fairly.

16 "'Do not go about spreading slander among your people.

"'Do not do anything that endangers your neighbor's life. I am the LORD.

17 "'Do not hate a fellow Israelite in your heart. Rebuke your neighbor frankly so you will not share in their guilt.

18 "'Do not seek revenge or bear a grudge against anyone among your people, but love your neighbor as yourself. I am the LORD.

19 "'Keep my decrees.

"'Do not mate different kinds of animals.

"'Do not plant your field with two kinds of seed.

"'Do not wear clothing woven of two kinds of material.

20 "'If a man sleeps with a female slave who is promised to another man but who has not been ransomed or given her freedom, there must be due punishment. Yet they are not to be put to death, because she had not been freed. 21 The man, however, must bring a ram to the entrance to the tent of meeting for a guilt offering to the LORD. 22 With the ram of the guilt offering the priest is to make atonement for him before the LORD for the sin he has committed, and his sin will be forgiven.

23 "'When you enter the land and plant any kind of fruit tree, regard its fruit as forbidden. For three years you are to consider it forbidden; it must not be eaten. 24 In the fourth year all its fruit will be holy, an offering of praise to the LORD. 25 But in the fifth year you may eat its fruit. In this way your harvest will be increased. I am the LORD your God.

26 "'Do not eat any meat with the blood still in it.

"'Do not practice divination or seek omens.

27 "'Do not cut the hair at the sides of your head or clip off the edges of your beard.

28 "'Do not cut your bodies for the dead or put tattoo marks on yourselves. I am the LORD.

29 "'Do not degrade your daughter by making her a prostitute, or the land will turn to prostitution and be filled with wickedness.

30 "'Observe my Sabbaths and have reverence for my sanctuary. I am the LORD.

31 "'Do not turn to mediums or seek out spiritists, for you will be defiled by them. I am the LORD your God.

32 "'Stand up in the presence of the aged, show respect for the elderly and revere your God. I am the LORD.

33 "'When a foreigner resides among you in your land, do not mistreat them. 34 The foreigner residing among you must be treated as your native-born. Love them as yourself, for you were foreigners in Egypt. I am the LORD your God.

35 "'Do not use dishonest standards when measuring length, weight or quantity. 36 Use honest scales and honest weights, an honest ephah and an honest hin. I am the LORD your God, who brought you out of Egypt.

37 "'Keep all my decrees and all my laws and follow them. I am the LORD.'"

Compare and Contrast--

2 Corinthians 3.7-18
7 Now if the ministry that brought death, which was engraved in letters on stone, came with glory, so that the Israelites could not look

steadily at the face of Moses because of its glory, transitory though it was, 8 will not the ministry of the Spirit be even more glorious? 9 If the ministry that brought condemnation was glorious, how much more glorious is the ministry that brings righteousness! 10 For what was glorious has no glory now in comparison with the surpassing glory. 11 And if what was transitory came with glory, how much greater is the glory of that which lasts!

12 Therefore, since we have such a hope, we are very bold. 13 We are not like Moses, who would put a veil over his face to prevent the Israelites from seeing the end of what was passing away. 14 But their minds were made dull, for to this day the same veil remains when the old covenant is read. It has not been removed, because only in Christ is it taken away. 15 Even to this day when Moses is read, a veil covers their hearts. 16 But whenever anyone turns to the Lord, the veil is taken away. 17 Now the Lord is the Spirit, and where the Spirit of the Lord is, there is freedom. 18 And we all, who with unveiled faces contemplate the Lord's glory, are being transformed into his image with ever-increasing glory, which comes from the Lord, who is the Spirit.

Interesting right? When I read the Leviticus passage, I recognize with an open an honest heart that I don't practice all of the "rules". Right?

When I read the Corinthians passage I realize that even Moses recognized that His meeting with God caused His face to radiate-- and also fade. Why? Why compare and contrast these 2 passages?

If you are a pharisee, or legalistic you probably still believe that your obedience to the "list" still brings merit, still brings righteousness, and gives you an attitude of being better than others. If you live by the Spirit you find much joy in the realization that you can't fake it (covering up the fading radiance) you are free, your righteousness comes by faith.

I grew up with the whole "what are people gonna think" mantra. I grew up with the "worry" about this or that because of other peoples views and such. I grew up never measuring up to everyone's wishes. I never did anything right according to 10 or50 different people. There has always been those that love to judge the externals, love to put things up against the Leviticus passage, the 10 commandments--

the truth is that no one practices any of it 100% of the time. In truth, the failure to comply actually points to the cross, points to the freedom to fail, points the inability for any person to gain access to God through any and all of our efforts.

When I read the Leviticus passage-- I do have tattoos. I on occasion have enjoyed a metal idol (my motorcycles and cars) I have never planted fruit trees when I moved into a new house. I do wear clothes with different fabrics (reread Leviticus) I have friends that are farmers that do plant different crops together. I do trim my beard. I try not to slander, but I know people that slander big time, but they don't have tats. Hmmm

I have never eaten anything I have sacrificed, because I have never ever made a fellowship offering to the Lord. He made the sacrifice for my by sending His Son. To me the whole idea that someone could actually read the Leviticus passage and hold themselves up as accomplished and then judge others over such things as tattoos blows my mind. There is something more to their judgment.

Compare and contrast-- where do you stand?

This may help.

Matthew 12.1-14
1 At that time Jesus went through the grainfields on the Sabbath. His disciples were hungry and began to pick some heads of grain and eat them. 2 When the Pharisees saw this, they said to him, "Look! Your disciples are doing what is unlawful on the Sabbath."

3 He answered, "Haven't you read what David did when he and his companions were hungry? 4 He entered the house of God, and he and his companions ate the consecrated bread—which was not lawful for them to do, but only for the priests. 5 Or haven't you read in the Law that the priests on Sabbath duty in the temple desecrate the Sabbath and yet are innocent? 6 I tell you that something greater than the temple is here. 7 If you had known what these words mean, 'I desire mercy, not sacrifice,' you would not have condemned the innocent. 8 For the Son of Man is Lord of the Sabbath."

9 Going on from that place, he went into their synagogue, 10 and a man with a shriveled hand was there. Looking for a reason to bring charges against Jesus, they asked him, "Is it lawful to heal on the Sabbath?"

11 He said to them, "If any of you has a sheep and it falls into a pit on the Sabbath, will you not take hold of it and lift it out? 12 How much more valuable is a person than a sheep! Therefore it is lawful to do good on the Sabbath."

13 Then he said to the man, "Stretch out your hand." So he stretched it out and it was completely restored, just as sound as the other. 14 But the Pharisees went out and plotted how they might kill Jesus.

The Pharisees were NEVER right then, they are NEVER right to now. They love the law over the Lord of the Sabbath. Their idol may just be the rules they believe make them better, worthy, safe and self deceived. Doesn't it say in the Leviticus passage "Do not lie"? A lack of honesty about ones inability to "do it" 100% of the time is called what?

I wonder what they think about the cross and the resurrection?

The Performance Religion is deadly

How bout it? Is it o.k. to judge a book by its cover? Is it o.k. to judge people by the way the look? Ever? Really? What is your standard by which you believe someone is spiritual or righteous? When I was a kid that answer was based on hair length or maybe the kind of clothes a person chose to wear or even tattoo's. In truth that hasn't exactly changed. People love to judge people by the way others look. It is easy to judge someone by the outside stuff.

There is something more sinister at play in the judging of people by the externals (the outside). For those that are trapped in their judgment of the externals, could it be because they themselves are stuck believing that God cares about the outside stuff? That God wrings His hands 24/7 about such things as looks, who isn't dressed right, who isn't clean cut, who isn't wearing all the right threads? Does God really get vexed over such things? The scriptures say "But the LORD said to Samuel, "Do not consider his appearance or his height, for I have rejected him. The LORD does not look at the things people look at. People look at the outward appearance, but the LORD looks at the heart." ~1 Samuel 16.7

So how did that get screwed up? It sure seems obvious to me that God is not one bit concerned about the outward appearance. The truth-- broken people love to puff themselves up, even when they are merely looking down on others, which is who they are exactly like-- that is indeed, humanity is completely depraved always looking for a way to somehow prove that we are good, we are getting better, that we really don't need a Savior, that if we can clean up the outside, the inside will end up at least o.k.

The real issue in my mind is not so much about appearance, but about performance. You see, I know many, many people (myself included) that have spent many days, nights, wondering-- "Am I good enough? Am I doing enough? Am I doing it right? Am I o.k.? Does God love me?" Its true, right? Maybe even you?

So you come to Christ as the one that goes to the cross to take all of our sin on Him. Jesus suffers a brutal 40 lashes, He is mocked, He is crucified on a cross to take all of the sin past, present and future on Him, He says it is finished, and that was not enough? Right? After all there has to be more to do. There has to be a way to earn His favor. There has to be a way to show Him you and I are worthy? Right? Wrong. Totally wrong, sick, false and actually a lie from Hell itself.

Well? I know I am not always together. I don't walk with God every minute. I know plenty of people that don't do it 100%, 100% of the time. There are little lies, there is bad tudes, there are bad thoughts, there are many things that no one sees. Then there is the list that others love to place on others-- do this and this and this and life will be perfect. That is another false statement. (Beware of the new list)

Performance is not the standard for God. Righteousness is the standard. The Scripture says "there are none righteous, not one" So where does righteousness come from? How does one get to be righteous? There are those that love to pretend they are righteous by what they do or don't do. That is called self deception, pride, even self righteousness. "All our works are filthy rags" So how is one righteous?

"Clearly no one is justified before God by the law, because, "The righteous will live by faith." ~Galatians 3.11

"Clearly"? Really? Not to those that love to perform their "righteous acts and righteous judgments". That is not clear at all. They have been muddied by their own desire to somehow out perform Jesus on the Cross and His rising from the dead. Somehow they actually believe regardless of what the scriptures teach that they can become righteous and even Holy by their performance.

If a person really is sick of the performance religion they find themselves living, they just need to look at the Scriptures for the truth-- (and the truth will set you free) The truth is demonstrated by "Abraham believed God, and it was credited to him as righteousness." I wonder if Abraham continually asked -- am I good enough, what else must I do, I keep sinning (it doesn't stop) I keep messing up, God must not love me because of this or that-- If Abraham did have angst over his "performance or lack there of" he must have gone back to the gift of righteousness that comes by faith.

Remember asking Christ to "save" you? Did He? Or was something missing? Righteousness comes by faith period. Righteousness has no human additions to it, then it would not be holy and righteous. No one can add to God's righteous. "All our works are as filthy rags." All the time. Righteousness comes by faith.

1 What then shall we say that Abraham, our forefather according to the flesh, discovered in this matter? 2 If, in fact, Abraham was justified by works, he had something to boast about—but not before God. 3 What does Scripture say? "Abraham believed God, and it was credited to him as righteousness." 4 Now to the one who works, wages are not credited as a gift but as an obligation. 5 However, to the one who does not work but trusts God who justifies the ungodly, their faith is credited as righteousness. 6 David says the same thing when he speaks of the blessedness of the one to whom God credits righteousness apart from works:
7 "Blessed are those
whose transgressions are forgiven,
whose sins are covered.
8 Blessed is the one
whose sin the Lord will never count against them." ~Romans 4.1-8

Not enough?

Then please, please read this from Romans Chapter 4 and let the Scriptures speak into your heart and get off the performance disaster. Get free. Get back to the truth.

13 It was not through the law that Abraham and his offspring received the promise that he would be heir of the world, but through the righteousness that comes by faith. 14 For if those who depend on the law are heirs, faith means nothing and the promise is worthless, 15 because the law brings wrath. And where there is no law there is no transgression.

16 Therefore, the promise comes by faith, so that it may be by grace and may be guaranteed to all Abraham's offspring—not only to those who are of the law but also to those who have the faith of Abraham. He is the father of us all. 17 As it is written: "I have made you a father of many nations."[c] He is our father in the sight of God, in whom he believed—the God who gives life to the dead and calls into being things that were not.

18 Against all hope, Abraham in hope believed and so became the father of many nations, just as it had been said to him, "So shall your offspring be." 19 Without weakening in his faith, he faced the fact that his body was as good as dead—since he was about a hundred years old—and that Sarah's womb was also dead. 20 Yet he did not waver through unbelief regarding the promise of God, but was strengthened in his faith and gave glory to God, 21 being fully persuaded that God had power to do what he had promised. 22 This is why "it was credited to him as righteousness." 23 The words "it was credited to him" were written not for him alone, 24 but also for us, to whom God will credit righteousness—for us who believe in him who raised Jesus our Lord from the dead. 25 He was delivered over to death for our sins and was raised to life for our justification.

Re read it--The words "it was credited to him" were written not for him alone, 24 but also for us, to whom God will credit righteousness—for us who believe in him who raised Jesus our Lord from the dead. 25 He was delivered over to death for our sins and was raised to life for our justification.

I believe in Him who raised Jesus our Lord from the dead. Do you? Is that enough? Not according to the performance people. Re look at Easter. If it's not about the complete work on the cross, then we are all in trouble.

Paradise

"Truly I tell you, today you will be with me in paradise."

I was thinking through the whole Easter happening over the past few days. I was reading the historical week account in the book of Luke and came to the scene of the 2 criminals hanging on their crosses next to Jesus. Remember the scene?

39 One of the criminals who hung there hurled insults at him: "Aren't you the Messiah? Save yourself and us!" 40 But the other criminal rebuked him. "Don't you fear God," he said, "since you are under the same sentence? 41 We are punished justly, for we are getting what our deeds deserve. But this man has done nothing wrong." 42 Then he said, "Jesus, remember me when you come into your kingdom." 43 Jesus answered him, "Truly I tell you, today you will be with me in paradise." Luke 23

I started thinking, and thinking, and wondering and then I began to imagine paradise, heaven, the place where this criminal went after his death on the cross next to the Savior of the world. Imagine for a minute the people there with Jesus and the criminal in paradise. Well, for starters there would be criminals for sure-- like murderers, like all the addictions that are known to mankind will be represented, there will be people that over indulged in every way. There will be winners and losers, successful people and not so successful people. There will be those that smoked till their last breath and those that died from cancer due to smoking. There will be liars and cheats and every kind of scoundrel. There will be rich and poor, ugly and gorgeous. There will be divorced people, married people, adulterers, those that had sex before marriage. People with tattoos and people without, there will be those that did everything right to the best of their abilities and people that broke every commandment. There will be those there that lived evil despicable lives. Really?

That is the question isn't it? After all, don't we still tend to believe that only the good, the successful, the people without too many blemishes get to paradise? Don't we? Well I know first hand what it is like to be in ministry and have a not so good track record and have people-- fellow "Christians" treat me like somehow I shouldn't be doing the "Lord's" work because I have said it before and for the sake of this little blog I'll say it again... I'm an addict, I have a long list of sins that I'm sure goes way beyond most. I'm not proud of it one bit. On the other hand I happen to know that I'll fit right in paradise.

Really? Well, I just celebrated Easter. I took the past 3 days to look deep into the historical account of Easter. As I soaked in the triumphal entry, His mock trial, his brutal death and the resurrection I was drawn in, I was moved to tears, I was moved to amazement, I was moved to thankfulness, I was moved to prayer, to joy, to astonishment in grace, in forgiveness. I heard deep down in my heart, in my gut, in my mind a quiet voice, a soft voice that reminded me of the complete nonsense of the belief that only certain people get to partake in paradise. The nonsense that during this short life of some poor choices, some evil choices, some sinful choices with evil all around and inside, that being "all that" that being smarter, and brighter, and being better somehow causes God to smile. The nonsense that somehow our works are greater than filthy rags, the nonsense that those that in their hearts know they are not perfect believe that if they look perfect, perform to perfection that somehow God loves them more and to those that don't-- they don't go. "They" to many can just go to hell. They don't deserve paradise. They aren't as good, they have bigger issues, they didn't give it the best college church try.

Isn't that the way it is?

Interesting that most of the people we see on Sunday have all the above issues. Right? Really? Of course we don't know, or do we? Over the past 20 years or so of ministry I have had hundreds of counseling conversations, hundreds of broken lives in my office, hundreds of broken people asking for help. Think about it. I know many many many many people over the years and not one is perfect. Not one deserves paradise, not one has done life completely right and that's just talking about the outside stuff. What about our thoughts, what about the things we say and do that nobody sees? Right?

C'mon who deserves paradise?

19 Now we know that whatever the law says, it says to those who are under the law, so that every mouth may be silenced and the

whole world held accountable to God. 20 Therefore no one will be declared righteous in God's sight by the works of the law; rather, through the law we become conscious of our sin. 21 But now apart from the law the righteousness of God has been made known, to which the Law and the Prophets testify. 22 This righteousness is given through faith in Jesus Christ to all who believe. There is no difference between Jew and Gentile, 23 for all have sinned and fall short of the glory of God, 24 and all are justified freely by his grace through the redemption that came by Christ Jesus. 25 God presented Christ as a sacrifice of atonement, through the shedding of his blood—to be received by faith. He did this to demonstrate his righteousness, because in his forbearance he had left the sins committed beforehand unpunished— 26 he did it to demonstrate his righteousness at the present time, so as to be just and the one who justifies those who have faith in Jesus. 27 Where, then, is boasting? It is excluded. Because of what law? The law that requires works? No, because of the law that requires faith. 28 For we maintain that a person is justified by faith apart from the works of the law. 29 Or is God the God of Jews only? Is he not the God of Gentiles too? Yes, of Gentiles too, 30 since there is only one God, who will justify the circumcised by faith and the uncircumcised through that same faith. 31 Do we, then, nullify the law by this faith? Not at all! Rather, we uphold the law. Romans 3.19-31

This Easter is a reminder to me once again-- "all have sinned and fall short of the glory of God, and all (everyone with every issue) and all are justified freely by His grace through (here it is) the redemption that came by Christ Jesus. God presented Christ as a sacrifice of atonement, through the shedding of his blood—to be received by faith..."

The thief next to Jesus to most didn't deserve paradise. To most, myself included I don't deserve paradise. How bout you? Is this "Christian" life deal still all about you? Are you still looking down your nose at people that you think don't deserve paradise, which means somehow you think you do?

One more lil Biblical reminder
"For it is by grace you have been saved, through faith—and this is not from yourselves, it is the gift of God— 9 not by works, so that no one can boast." ~Ephesians 2.8,9

Yep, there will every kind of sinful broken people in paradise even those that thought while they were walking this earth they weren't "that bad, they weren't like those people". But before their life was over they finally came to the conclusion that while they tried and tried and tried it just wasn't enough and they finally realized their need of the Savior.

Conditional Love?

Conditional love? Really?
I see it all the time. Especially amongst people that ought to know better.
"Do it my way and I'll love you."
"Obey and I'll love you."
"Be this or that, look like this, do everything right, and you get the prize. My Love."
I know so many that have said, "If I have to earn it, no thank you." or "I'm tired of trying to earn your conditional love."

When my 2 young men were little boys there were many rules to protect them and of course us as parents. Rules to protect the boys from hurting themselves, pain, and possible death. The same rules protected their mom and me from angst, worry, and our possible pain of going through watching and being with one or both of them getting hurt. Their mom and me did not make rules for the boys to follow so that if they followed the rules they would get the idea that their obedience caused us to love them more. Because of my background I was and I am dead set against making obedience or lack thereof a condition for love or withholding love. Consequences natural or calculated have meaning. Indeed, discipline, honest disapproval is all part of screwing up. In truth, sometimes natural consequences are a great teacher.

I hope my two now young men have never felt from me that their obedience moved me closer to them. On the flip side I hope my boys never felt that when the disobeyed I moved away. A long time ago one of my boys picked up a rock and through the rock through the neighbors car window and then denied it. What would I do? Would I yell at him? Make him feel more shame? I had to deal with him, and I know that I thought first its time to move toward him. I didn't want him to think that because he did wrong I would love him less. As a matter of truth, there were many times I failed and there were times I felt I had to earn my parents love back. There is a difference between trust and love.

Of course I lead a student ministry. I work with many students which means there are many parents. Interesting that most of the parents I don't know very well. On the flip side they don't know me very well.

One of things they most likely don't understand is why I can't stand the whole idea that following rules makes someone more lovable, better and even spiritual. It doesn't. That is not Biblical, that is not how God loves people. That is not how Jesus interacted with the pharisees (they were great at following the rules) or His disciples that most likely had chucked the law years prior to Jesus asking them to just plain ole follow. On the flip side, many students know that I don't appreciate their bad attitudes toward "righteousness" because they are only hurting themselves in the long run. Hard hearts, hard shells are part of the misunderstanding of spiritual matters. Indeed. Many times a hard heart is due to the belief, the idea that God has turned away, therefore the student says "because I can't do this thing 100% I will give up, go inward thus a harden my heart. After all, I messed up, I blew it, God isn't happy with me, God must not love me the same, so to get past letting myself down, letting God down, I'll just get tough, be tough, hate the stuff that I know brings me peace and joy and move on with my life without what I know I really want and desperately need-- a relationship with God that goes beyond the list that I keep failing-- and the more I fail, the harder I will allow my heart to get."

What's this all about?

Biblical truth. The fundamentals. People are not justified by works. People are not better or more lovable because they do it all. The fundamentals matter. Its the base, the foundation. If students don't get the basics they are bound to become either pharisees, arrogant, God haters, apathetic, indifferent and so on.

Check out this basic Biblical principle:

Romans 4.18-25
Against all hope, Abraham in hope believed and so became the father of many nations, just as it had been said to him, "So shall your offspring be."19 Without weakening in his faith, he faced the fact that his body was as good as dead—since he was about a hundred years old—and that Sarah's womb was also dead. 20 Yet he did not waver through unbelief regarding the promise of God, but was strengthened in his faith and gave glory to God, 21 being fully persuaded that God had power to do what he had promised. 22 This is why "it was credited to him as righteousness." 23 The words "it

was credited to him" were written not for him alone, 24 but also for us, to whom God will credit righteousness—for us who believe in him who raised Jesus our Lord from the dead. 25 He was delivered over to death for our sins and was raised to life for our justification.

Basic principle? God will credit to us, make us righteous who believe in Him who raised Jesus our Lord from the dead. We are justified by the work Jesus Christ by His death for our sins and being raised to life. We that by faith believe that Jesus is the Christ are considered righteous and therefore justified not by our works, not by our not breaking the rules, not by anything more or less than by our faith. Basic right? Not. But every one that has been around "Christians" should know this right? Not really. I know so many students and parents that are confused. Some still practice the idea that doing right things makes a person lovable for God. Some still live in shame because they can't seem to get past porn, being loved by the opposite sex, using, being used, drugs, or some other thing that is afflicting them. Where does righteousness come from? Is it in obedience? Or is obedience due to an understanding of God's provision called Grace? Does faith produce righteousness or does behavior produce righteousness? It's one or the other. It really is. The scriptures do answer the question.

Basic principle #2

Notice Romans 5.1-8
Therefore, since we have been justified through faith, we have peace with God through our Lord Jesus Christ, 2 through whom we have gained access by faith into this grace in which we now stand. And we boast in the hope of the glory of God. 3 Not only so, but we also glory in our sufferings, because we know that suffering produces perseverance; 4 perseverance, character; and character, hope. 5 And hope does not put us to shame, because God's love has been poured out into our hearts through the Holy Spirit, who has been given to us. 6 You see, at just the right time, when we were still powerless, Christ died for the ungodly. 7 Very rarely will anyone die for a righteous person, though for a good person someone might possibly dare to die. 8 But God demonstrates his own love for us in this: While we were still sinners, Christ died for us.

Paul starts in verse in verse 1 saying because you received justification by faith-- here's what happens. Peace with God. Really? Isn't that important? After all, isn't that why most people go nuts pursuing the law, pursing "righteousness" through works and such? Peace. Inner peace. Peace with God. Isn't that true? We somehow have believed that peace with God comes because He loves us so much because we are so awesome in obedience... but there is no peace. We keep trying, and teaching our students to do this, don't do that, be this, wear this, don't listen to, do do do, but look at our lives-- there is no peace, we haven't found peace because we just aren't ever going to be good enough period. I see so many students hurt by the idea that they just can't do it. So many parents that want others (pastors, leaders) to do it for their student-- give the list, make them obey, make them understand--thus parents then are filled with angst and hurt as they watch their student not "do it" like they are "supposed" to do it. You know live for Christ, walk with Christ.

Notice basic principle #3 in Romans 5 "Not only so, but we also glory in our sufferings, because we know that suffering produces perseverance; perseverance, character; and character, hope. 5 And hope does not put us to shame, because God's love has been poured out into our hearts through the Holy Spirit, who has been given to us. 6 You see, at just the right time, when we were still powerless, Christ died for the ungodly."

Suffering matters-- it produces perseverance, character and hope. Suffering is part of being a follower of Christ. Suffering does not produce shame but because His love has been poured into our hearts-- notice given to us-- poured into our hearts. Interesting. Right? Dig the last basic principle: In His time, while we were powerless to do it for and by ourselves, Christ died for who? The powerless. the ungodly. Who is the that? All of us. I believe because of my own experience, and the support of Biblical truth that once a person understands their utter, complete depravity, their total need for God's unconditional love and kindness they can then embrace their life of ups, downs, failings, moving forward, lover for God, love for others, compassion and just a plain ole movement through life with a settled heart fixed on Jesus the Christ. Suffering may not just be about the obvious, it may be that as we go through life we suffer our depravity until we wear the robe of righteousness supplied us by His unconditional love and GRACE!

If God's love for us is really unconditional. If that is true. What does it look like? How does that truth get lived out? Hmmmmmmmm

It's Impossible period.

To many, many "Christians" this scripture verse is something to strive after...
"Be holy because I, the LORD your God, am holy." ~Leviticus 19.2
For the record... this is an impossibility period.

Really?

So many things are running around my mind these days. Hurting students. Students that find church to be irrelevant. Parents that are struggling. People that want "good" things and only "good" things and fear the daily grind of living in a fallen broken world with broken people. Students that refuse to engage God. Students that were once excited about God and now won't have anything to do with Him. Why? What happened?
Could it be that a person is aware enough to understand that the total scriptures teach that mankind is hopelessly lost. He cannot work himself out of his depravity? That a person finally understands the impossibility of the verse from Leviticus? Could it be that a person works to the point of trying to please everyone, even God to the point of utter emotional and spiritual exhaustion?

Compare and contrast Leviticus 9.2 to Romans 3.10-12
"There is no one righteous, not even one;
there is no one who understands; there is no one who seeks God.
All have turned away, they have together become worthless;
there is no one who does good, not even one."
Is it true? You know that there is no one righteous? No one who seeks God?
All have turned away? No one that does good? Is it true? Some will say not true. I do many good things. I feed the poor. I don't love everyone especially those that are not good, but I try. I go to church. I take care of my family. I'm good. I can live holy, I can.
Really?

Impossible. No one can ever muster anything even close to the holiness of God. It's impossible. For starters there are motives.
What if the motive to "look" good is part of why a person strives for holiness? What is that called? What about judging others? What about speaking badly about people? What about the lack of love for

brothers and sisters and even just plain ole people in general? Really? No one is holy and will never be holy in and of themselves period.

Maybe that's why students have had enough? Maybe that's why so many are done with "going" to church or getting involved with anything "spiritual? Think about it. How can we demand in our hearts and in our heads that people live holy when we know they can't, we can't, we don't.
Isn't it true? No? Now what's that called?

The truth is this:
Scripture teaches that God pursues us first.
Scripture teaches that righteousness comes by faith.
Scripture teaches that anything that is not of faith is sin.
Scripture teaches that faith Justifies
Scripture teaches that there are none righteous
Scripture teaches that all our works are what? Filthy
So how does one get holy?

Not by works. Not by doing. Not by playing a game. Not by wearing our Sunday clothes. Not by this or that or omissions of this or that. Then how does one get into right standing with God. How in the world?
Isn't that the problem? I know so many that have bailed. (I did and I know why I did) because the contradiction is not in Scripture. It's in the "code" that most are smart enough, deep enough to understand. The code that says, "be a clone of all of us that do all this stuff that makes us so much better than everyone else." That's the code that most people see through now.
The answer is the the Scriptures. No one can become holy by themselves period. Nobody. Never. It's impossible period. People that think they can are obviously not holy period. People that love to think they are all that are not being holy period.

Romans 3.22-28
22 This righteousness is given through faith in Jesus Christ to all who believe. There is no difference between Jew and Gentile, 23 for all have sinned and fall short of the glory of God, 24 and all are justified freely by his grace through the redemption that came by Christ Jesus. God presented Christ as a sacrifice of atonement, through the

shedding of his blood—to be received by faith. He did this to demonstrate his righteousness, because in his forbearance he had left the sins committed beforehand unpunished— he did it to demonstrate his righteousness at the present time, so as to be just and the one who justifies those who have faith in Jesus.
"Where, then, is boasting? It is excluded. Because of what law? The law that requires works? No, because of the law that requires faith. For we maintain that a person is justified by faith apart from the works of the law."

By faith one receives righteousness. It is a gift from God-- all of it is from God.
Maybe that's the stuff that drives all of us crazy. Those that mandate a false spirituality through works. Yea that's right. Works. Not the works that are a product of ones relationship with Christ. Not the works that come out of faith. Not the works that come from a broken and contrite heart. Not the works that are because a heart has been transformed by the holy spirit. Not the works that have come because a person has trusted in Christ Jesus for their salvation (I still believe in salvation) not because of the works that come from the Great mystery "Christ in you."   The works that say, "I can be holy by what I do." I can be holy because I dress like people did in the 50's and 60's and they did it right." The works that say, "I am so good because I'm not like them." The works that say, "I haven't sinned at least not as bad as "those" people." The works that say, "Man, I am so good."
Stop striving. It's impossible period.

1 Therefore, since we have been justified through faith, we have peace with God through our Lord Jesus Christ, 2 through whom we have gained access by faith into this grace in which we now stand. And we boast in the hope of the glory of God. 3 Not only so, but we also glory in our sufferings, because we know that suffering produces perseverance; 4 perseverance, character; and character, hope. 5 And hope does not put us to shame, because God's love has been poured out into our hearts through the Holy Spirit, who has been given to us. 6 You see, at just the right time, when we were still powerless, Christ died for the ungodly. 7 Very rarely will anyone die for a righteous person, though for a good person someone might possibly dare to die. 8 But God demonstrates his own love for us in this: While we were still sinners, Christ died for us. Romans 5.1-8

Now where is the boasting? Tell me, can you do it really? The only thing we can do is to live by faith. Not faith in our "works" to do it. Faith in Christ period. I would love for students and many adults to finally get this. I would change everything. By the way, trying doing student ministry knowing the above stuff. I have watched over the years many that refuse to by faith trust for their salvation and when life, bad choices, sin shows its head (like every day) they give up. Wonder why?

One of the hardest things about doing ministry? This truth that so many don't want to admit -- that all the "holiness" that is believed to be "holy" is short lived at best and falls short. Really. I can't imagine, nor fathom how anyone thinks that even for a minute a holy act (if there is such a thing) does one bit outside of what God has had to do in order for a person to be in right standing with God. Without Jesus Christ, our faith placed in Him, nothing else gets even close. The judges of others and "what they perceive as "holy or not holy" is an impossibility. They are stuck in a belief system that is faulty and actually sinful as they judge others and yet believe somehow that they are holy. Its Crazy. So then,where does this lead? Think about it. The contradiction is not in the Scriptures but in the way the truth is lived out. If one could be holy, who needs the Savior? If there is anything to add to Salvation, then the Savior was not enough? If all are works are as filthy rags, which ones aren't? The Scriptures tell the truth period. No one will ever be enough, that is why the Savior came, died and rose again. Then anything less than faith is sin. So then, how we live proves the transforming power of the great mystery "Christ in you.

You gotta read Romans 5 which leads to Romans 6.

Not done next blog on Romans 6

Oh by the way: Did you know that there are "Christians that actually have picket shrimpers with signs that read "God hates shrimp" and then quotes Leviticus? True. Interesting due to the fact that God created shrimp. Again when people determine what is holy the whole issue becomes nonsense. Maybe this generation has finally seen through the nonsense.

not by faith = confusion leads to indifference

I wrote this article for Youth Worker Journal a few months ago. As a youth pastor and parent I often wonder about the issue of indifference in the hearts/lives -- how a student becomes-- I'm beginning to understand this: That any person, most people, myself included all have to deal with the belief that somehow following rules for first the idea that "being and doing" good somehow brings something i.e., God's love, righteousness, "better", consistently becomes impossible and thus indifference becomes a reality at some point. Why? Because a person, a student finally ends up with the conclusion-- I can't do it, I keep failing, I don't get it, I don't want it, this relationship with God is too hard, therefore, it is easier for me to just not care. = indifference. True? Think about it before you react. Second, there is a false theology being taught. Oh, I get it as a parent and youth pastor that keeping one's nose clean benefits the person, but it does not guarantee a good life, an easy life without trials, and mostly it does not bring righteousness period. Students become confused and the way out of confusion? = indifference.

The article

We as youth pastors/workers and parents live in some crazy times. Everything seems to up for grabs. From right things to do to things that at one time were taboo to being perfectly OK instead of a gray area, from being taught about what Scripture says to the Bible being guide book. Follow the people who do righteous things, but don't worry about what they believe.

Have you ever asked a student either or all three questions: What will it take for God to love you? What kind of things can you do so God will love you? If you read the Bible, why? Do you believe any of the above? If you do, maybe you are confused, too.

We live in a day when confusion is all around us. Government is a disaster, people in leadership are struggling as much as anyone...Who do you trust? The local church is all over the place— people want this, want that, want music a certain way, this church, that church, my denomination, this theology, this opinion, this you can do, this you can't do, God loves this, God hates that...What is a student to believe?

Here is what is missing. What brings *righteousness* to humans? Works? Never. Really? Yes—never. So where does righteousness come from? From placing one's faith in what Christ did on the cross and rising again three days later. It is by faith that a person is saved. Works? None—faith and faith alone.Ephesians 2.8,9   Works come out of one's faith and love for God. Works do not produce righteousness period. Ever.

When you ask a student why he or she does this or that (Do they talk about faith?)—it's always about being better by doing this or because in truth he or she may just be living externally, going through the motions; and when life gets tough...look out. I believe living by faith is not just trusting in Jesus for eternal life. That is only the start. From there, we must give our students the foundation on which when life turns, so when difficult things happen, they can trust in God, His Word, His character.

Read the Bible. That's the place to start. Other peoples control, behavior issues, opinions, "the way" I do it, "what I believe"-- that stuff is not where to start.

Abraham *believed*, and it was credited to him as righteousness. He acted on what he believed (faith), and that is what brought righteousness. How about you? How are you righteous? By your works? By church attendance? By reading your Bible? Never. Those are by bi-products of one's faith. The acts do not bring righteousness. Never. Now, try to teach it correctly to students. Really? Yes! That is our world of student ministry.

Don't mix getting good grades with being righteous. Don't mix remaining a virgin as super righteousness. It's not. Remaining a virgin is great for one's future, knowing Christ or not; but abstinence does not bring righteousness. Faith in Christ brings the righteous robe we will wear someday. Don't confuse a commitment not to smoke with righteousness when it's simply a choice to stay away from a harmful substance and protecting the temples of our bodies.

If you tell students something because you believe it is right, fine; but why should they make it their belief? If you tell them a rule is for safety, great; at least you are honest. If you tell them because you know firsthand the damage something will do by doing the sick stuff of the world...now you are being transparent, and that is even better; but never tell students that behavior is about righteousness.

This is our world and our job. I believe that now more than ever students who say they follow Christ, have grown up in Christian homes, hang out at church or are part of a youth group must put their faith in Him and Him alone and live life as a testimony of that faith. Living a life of doing the hard things is a bi-product of one's righteousness.

How do you help your students? Some try lots of guilt trips. Some try lots of shame. Some are so honest that it actually backfires. In truth, you and I know followers of Christ by the fruit they bear. If students are not bearing fruit, what does that say?

Our God is not a God of confusion, but somehow this living by faith is awfully confusing. Hmm...
What becomes tougher and tougher as a youth pastor, and a parent (from my 20 year plus years of student ministry and parenting) is the many students I am connected with that just don't get it. Sadly, fear is not what keeps parents and others from telling the truth. It may very well be that parents and others involved in student ministry are also living "the list", the "performance", "the other stuff" that keeps themselves and then students from understanding a basic, fundamental truth-- Faith in Christ is the only thing one can do and ultimately righteousness is provided by... God. Never, ever by what someone does or doesn't do.

We all must check our stuff. We all must check or actions. We all must check our conscious choices and decisions. Living by faith is the key. Our faith brings righteousness, and the way we live proves it. "Therefore being justified by faith, we have peace with God through our Lord Jesus Christ"
~ Romans 5.1

Nothing but the Truth

(Transcript from sermon "Nothing But the Truth")

Have you ever heard these words?
"Then you will know the truth and the truth will set you Free."
I can't count the times I have heard, seen it twittered, a quote on Facebook....
What is it about this statement that makes it so powerful?

Is it because Jesus the Christ said it? I doubt many see it that way or even know who said it.
Maybe because of the word Truth? Maybe because of the word Free?
Maybe because who isn't looking for truth? Not just any old truth—but nothing but the truth.

What is Truth? What does it mean to be Free?
What does it mean to "know the truth and thus be Free?
These 2 words Truth and Free have meaning—

But notice these words again by Jesus the Christ...

John 8.32 "Then you will know the Truth and the Truth will set you free."
First question that comes to my mind when I read this verse? When is Then?

No one asks that question do they—Jesus said—Then you will know the Truth...

Notice verse 31—John writes— "To the Jews who had believed Him, Jesus said, If you hold to my teaching you are really my disciples. – Then, You will know the truth...

The phrase "If you hold to my teaching" in its original form is actually—
If you abide in me—Jesus isn't saying—Hey folks just pick and choose the teachings you like... or the teachings you agree with, or the teachings that are the easiest, or my teachings that are now Politically correct.

John 8. 1,2 says
8 ¹ but Jesus went to the Mount of Olives. At dawn he appeared again in the temple courts, where all the people gathered around him, and he sat down to teach them.
Verse 12—When Jesus spoke again to the People
Verse 30—even as He spoke many put their faith in Him
and finally
Verse 31—"To the Jews who had believed Him, Jesus said—

Jesus is speaking to people of course we can surmise
Many Kinds of People—
Curious
Those seeking to find the Messiah
the Religious
the Pharisees
Scholars—teachers of the law
some of His Disciples
Followers

People and of course—to the Jews that had believed Him

Jesus says—"If you abide in me then you will know the truth and the truth will set you free."

Think about it for a minute—

Jesus is speaking to an audience of

Followers—people wanting to hear, some religious, some scholars
His Disciples
the Pharisees
the religious
all sorts of people

and John distinguishes – "to the Jews that believed Him."

You see my friends, Jesus points out to the Jews that believed Him—
believing in Him is not the end... the next step is to Abide in me—

It's one thing to believe, its another thing to Abide in me—

Jesus is speaking to people just like you and me—you know— like right here now— by the way – Notice how Jesus treated all these people—You know all the people gathered together all coming from many different places, backgrounds, ideals, and even belief's

Followers
Disciples
Religious
some out of routine,
Some seeking
Who knows—lots of people

He wasn't trying to force anyone into anything—
Maybe way back when we said Yes to Jesus—we said yes to His promise of eternal life. We said yes to His forgiveness. We said we believe in that He is the Son of God—

Every Sunday or Saturday night across the globe there are those that believe—that follow, Jesus is saying—to all of us in these 2 verses— it's one thing to believe—it's quite another thing to abide in me—

Which leads us to the word Truth—

You see, unless someone understands the truth—then abiding in Jesus, or as the NIV says it "If you hold to my teaching" you know abide in me—is merely phrase, a form of knowledge a possible set of rules or a list to maintain, or a Sunday activity—or some form of holding to His teaching—but what is the Truth?

I want to remind you that at the center our Faith—the center our Christianity – well it's not the Bible—

We may love the (Spell it) B I B L E—but its on Christ the Solid Rock we stand—

You see, Jesus says it this way—"I you abide in me, you are really my disciples. Then you will know the Truth and the truth will set you free,"

The Truth?

John 1.1-5

1 In the beginning was the Word, and the Word was with God, and the Word was God. 2 He was with God in the beginning. 3 Through him all things were made; without him nothing was made that has been made. 4 In him was life, and that life was the light of all mankind. 5 The light shines in the darkness, and the darkness has not over come it.

The Truth?
John 8.12 I am the Light of the World
John 8.18 I am the one who testifies for myself; my other witness is the one who sent me—the Father.
Jesus said it this way in John chapter 8
"If you knew me, you would know my father also"
Jesus is the person that said—"I am the way THE TRUTH and the Life.

How bout this statement in this day and age of relativism and political correctness nonsense--
"I told you that you would die in your sins; if you do not believe that I am he, you will indeed die in your sins."

So Jesus said, "When you have lifted up the Son of Man, then you will know that I am he and that I do nothing on my own but speak just what the Father has taught me. 29 The one who sent me is with me; he has not left me alone, for I always do what pleases him." 30 Even as he spoke, many believed in him.

It's one thing to believe, it's another to abide in Him—

What's the Truth? The word Truth in its original form denotes— Faithfulness

Jesus is Faithful to who He is...

He Jesus is faithful to what He said and did.
He is the complete opposite of those that say one thing and do another

He is always true to His word
He is always faithful to everything he said and did
He is always period.

That first time you came to Jesus with all your sin stained heart and asked for forgiveness—did He forgive you?

When life doesn't turn out the way you planned—Does Jesus still love you?

When you totally fall apart, when you are angry, when you totally just implode is Jesus there for you? Are you sure?

I watch a show the other night and during this show there were stories of people the are jobless, beat up, hurting, out of work, they feel abandoned—

I remember the day when I was searching for work—

I remember feeling all that I could feel – I was whipped.

I was hurting, I was falling apart—I cried out to the Lord day after day

Until I just stopped—I began to pray—I believe in you—
Only you can help me--
I'm lost—please help me find the way through this

And then it moved to something else—

I began to TRUST Him, to abide in Him—

I didn't know the answers—I didn't know the timeline, I didn't know anything really—I just trusted Him—and that changed everything—

I didn't trust in my resume, I didn't let my failures run through my head,

After all -- He forgave me. Completely He Loves me completely
He is after all the Son of God. He Is after all the Bread of Life, He is

after all the Living Water, the Good Shepherd, the Friend of sinners, the King of Kings...

He didn't have a list of past failures that was keeping me from living Even when being jobless. All I could do was Abide in the Truth—He is faithful to who He said He is... that He loved me, cared about me, He forgave me, had a plan for me, would not let me sink to the bottom of the pit--- I trusted in the Truth—that He Jesus is faithful to Who he says He is.

—He is faithful to Who he said he is period and that is the Truth—

"If you hold to my teaching (Abide in Me), you are really my disciples. 32 Then you will know the truth, and the truth will set you free."

You see, Abiding in Jesus is Trusting in His Faithfulness to Who He is, what He says and does and that Truth will set you Free—

Free? What is Free? What does He mean—to be Free?

First lets talk about what being Free is not—Being a disciple—is what Jesus is saying—a disciple is not free to live like they want if one is Abiding or holding to His Teaching. Being Free is not knowing the Truth and living like you and I want—then we might as well admit that we are like those that just believe—

Jesus addresses that group of people when He goes beyond that idea and moves into abiding— What does it mean to "Know the truth and be set free?"

To be set Free is in essence to being a slave and being set free...

Notice beginning in John 8.33
They answered him, "We are Abraham's descendants and have never been slaves of anyone. How can you say that we shall be set free?" Jesus replied, "Very truly I tell you, everyone who sins is a slave to sin. 35 Now a slave has no permanent place in the family, but a son belongs to it forever. 36 So if the Son sets you free, you will be free indeed.
In other words—

Ummm Jesus—I don't think you understand—we are deeply religious, God fearing people—by blood of course—we are Abraham's descendants—we are good to go.

Ummmm Jesus—we are free because we have never been slaves to anyone?

Jesus is pointing the Scholars, the Pharisees back to the issue—that without a relationship with Him—with out knowing Him, abiding in Him, there sinful hearts remain—sinful

— Very truly I tell you, everyone who sins is a slave to sin.

And we all know right—that being set free is having the chains of sin broken—and that brings Freedom—

As the Apostle Paul said it like this in Romans chapter 6

6 For we know that our old self was crucified with him so that the body ruled by sin might be done away with that we should no longer be slaves to sin — 7 because anyone who has died has been set free from sin.

8 Now if we died with Christ, we believe that we will also live with him. 9 For we know that since Christ was raised from the dead, he cannot die again; death no longer has mastery over him. 10 The death he died, he died to sin once for all; but the life he lives, he lives to God.

11 In the same way, count yourselves dead to sin but alive to God in Christ Jesus. 12 Therefore do not let sin reign in your mortal body so that you obey its evil desires.

One last thing about being set free—

I know and you know that sin is not something we don't deal with—what's dealing with sin like for you?

Once a week?
No really?
Once a day? Something you deny?

I mean I know me—I am a sinful man—

I also am like a doctor that sees patient's everyday that have the disease—
I'm watching students struggle with sin
I'm watching adults struggle with sin

If it's not anger, its substance abuse. If its not lying its just plain gossip
If its not apathy it's the idea that one can fix themselves
If it's not total freedom then its legalism completely trusting in the list to clean you up, and in truth you and I both know that doing and doing is about:
Looking good, being better, arrogance, self righteousness—it's not about abiding in Him, its about you doing it yourself and that is killing you inside. Sin is still running your life.

You see the truth about the statement being set free—

Check this out
The original meaning of being set free is: the chains of the slave are broken

And thus...

the chains of the slave to sin are broken—Interesting that through out the Scriptures often more times than not the word FREE or being set free

This gift of freedom connects the one set Free to thus being bound to the giver of Freedom. When the chains of sin are broken—when you have been set Free

And thus bound to the giver of Freedom
Paul calls himself a bond servant of Christ Jesus
he states also as Being United with Christ
Sharing His Spirit

Its as you are set Free, you then are bound to the one that set you free—

In the original setting, milieu of this phrase Set free
The gift of Freedom is bound to the giver of freedom—

Again the words of Paul
"Don't you know that when you offer yourselves to someone as obedient slaves, you are slaves of the one you obey —whether you are slaves to sin, which leads to death, or to obedience, which leads to righteousness? [17] But thanks be to God that, though you used to be slaves to sin, you have come to obey from your heart the pattern of teaching that has now claimed your allegiance. [18] You have been set free from sin and have become slaves to righteousness.

John 8.47 Jesus says it like this
Whoever belongs to God hears what God says. The reason you do not hear is that you do not belong to God."

Maybe Jesus is actually saying
You don't abide in me, you don't trust my Word, that is my unfailing faithfulness to who I am, you really aren't my disciple because you are still in bondage to sin…

You see my friends—

You can today read John 8.31, 32 like this

To those that believed him—to those attending church today, being part of a community—to those that believe in Him…

"If you abide in me, trust me to be faithful to all I am, all I did and will do you are really my disciples. Then you will know of my faithfulness to my Word, that I am the Christ and that truth will break the bonds of sin in your life."

I want to go back to one very important—Phrase from our 2 verses – this phrase "If you hold to my teaching" which again means " to Abide"

This is not a word we use much… Abide? What is to abide?

Is it about knowledge? The fact that you know all about someone—does that make their friend? No. The fact that you work next to someone daily, talk everyday, share stories—you do things that people next to each other-- would that be an example of abiding together? Probably not…

The Example of Martha and Mary—

Jesus is coming to visit some family and friends—Martha goes wild with baking and taking care of the details, while Mary sits at the feet of Jesus and washes them with her tears—Martha knows Jesus—Mary is abiding with Jesus… Mary wants to be close, to love, to touch Jesus, to worship Jesus.

Maybe well all shy away from the word intimate—too bad for most of us that we connect intimacy with a sexual connotation—but abiding is intimate.

Abiding— is the same as Paul states—United—bonded—

Do you abide with Jesus—are you intimate with Him? Are you deeply connected?

Maybe the issue is really that the followers know an awful lot about Jesus-

That followers, the audience Jesus is speaking to are amazed, wishing, hoping, wanting, to know more—and in their heads they just can't come to grips with this..

Jesus wants to be intimate with them. Jesus wants to abide in their souls. Jesus wants more then their brains, their minds, He wants the essence of people—their Soul.

Isn't it true—many of us here even tonight/Today came to a place, came to a time, when knowing Jesus became much more than knowledge—but we entered into an intimate relationship with Him because we actually found Him to be faithful to who He is… that is the Son of God, the lover of our souls, the only one that could completely forgive us, love us and heal us.

"If you hold to my teaching, you are really my disciples. Then you will know the truth and the truth will set you free."

Think of these verses like this:
If you and I are intimately united together, you are really my disciples. You will know and Trust me for who I am, and that will break the chains of sin in you.

The question then is—Are you a disciple? Or are you one that just believes?
Do you have an intimate, abiding relationship with Christ?
Do you want this intimacy? Do you want to abide with Christ?

You see—this is not about who is better? Jesus didn't rip into those that just believed—He was taking them to the next step—being disciples—

Right Now—you are a prayer away from moving from following--to becoming intimate with Jesus the Christ--

Thank you so much for taking the time to read my thoughts "As I Go"

Twitter: dsolin
Webstite: www.donsolin.com